MW00329991

High Price for Freedom

by

Maria Regina Imre

WingSpan Press

Published in the United States and the United Kingdom

ISBN 978-1-63683-010-0 (pbk.)
ISBN 978-1-63683-027-8 (hardcover.)
ISBN 978-1-63683-990-5 (ebk.)

First edition 2020

Library of Congress Control Number 2021907714

Printed in the United States of America

1 2 3 4 5 6 7 8 9 10

PROLOGUE

Lying on the lawn one starry summer night, we watched the shooting stars. It was at this time that my husband was diagnosed with brain cancer.

"Please do me a favor," he said.

"When I leave this world, write a memoir about our life's journey. Our sons and grandchildren deserve to know the real story about their family background. I want them to be proud of us and their Hungarian heritage. We came to this country from far away, for freedom which we never had. We and our ancestors lived in oppression in Czechoslovakia. That is why we left behind our country, family, friends, and all of our belongings for which we worked for twenty years. We started a new life in America, the best country in the world. I believe that book will be the nicest gift from us to our future family members. Promise me you will write down our story." He squeezed my hand and kissed it.

"I promise." It has been two decades since that day. Year after year, I have kept journals of my memories. The book is based on our true story. The first part offers a glimpse into the life of the "Felvidék" Hungarians in Slovakia between the years 1965 and 1985. The second part covers the years between 1985 and 2001, during our life in America.

My husband, father of my children, was a remarkable man with highly inventive skills. All his life he worked very hard to reach his dreams, but unfortunately, his life was cut short.

On one occasion he told me, "I know that one day I will discover something that thousands of people will need. I can

i

feel it; it is sitting in my brain. I have a knowledge that will solve the unsolvable, and then I will fulfill my destiny. I was born for that."

We enjoyed life and the journey to reach the destination of which we had always dreamed. We lived by the words of the famous Hungarian writer, Madách Imre: MAN MUST STRIVE AND BELIEVE.

I dedicate this book to my sons, Attila and Csaba, as well as to my granddaughters, Nicole and Michelle. I hope our family's story will be a strong foundation for their lives.

PART ONE

THE WEDDING

It's been insanely hot for days, a classic Californian summer. The air conditioner is on night and day. The temperature in my room is pleasant, as I sit reading in my comfortable armchair. I close the book. I'm just not interested. Somehow, nothing amuses me. Maybe the heat... or old age? God, it's been so long since I was young.

My phone rings. I pick it up, but it's a wrong number. The blinds are completely shut; the darkness irritates me. I can't breathe. I open the curtains. Within seconds, light brightens the room. My Czechoslovakian lead crystal collection sparkles. *Life needs light*, I say to myself.

From my wedding photo, Dezső smiles at me. I close my eyes, and I am able to feel his embrace, his breath. I exhale. My God, I wish he could be here with me.

I've been thinking about him a lot lately. Our life through the years was happy and unforgettable, in spite of the bitter beginning.

It was a cold, sunny afternoon when my father walked me down the aisle of the Catholic church of Loons (Lučenec) with tears in his eyes. I was twenty, very in love, eager to say "I do". My groom had been courting me for years. He was an honest, smart man who loved me very much.

Dad said, "My little Marika is all grown up. The funny years are gone, but this is life."

I was holding on to him tightly, as my high heels kept

slipping on the snowy sidewalk. I loved my father very much. I knew I was the light of his life. It was hard for me to see him tearing up. I had to do something to bring a smile to his face. When we reached the church gate, I gave my bridal bouquet to my friend who was standing there. I wrapped my arms around my father's neck, like I used to do when I was a little girl. I kissed his face all over, which made us both burst into laughter.

"You are never going to lose me; I will always be your little girl who will always love you."

"Be happy, my big girl. Dezső loves you".

The heavy, carved wood door of the church opened before us, and the church organ played Ave Maria. I recognized the delightful voice of my piano teacher who sang the song. What a lovely surprise it was from her. The church was packed with people. I blushed as they all turned to face me. Dad squeezed my hand and we slowly walked down the aisle. My wedding dress was made by my Aunt Magda, from a beautiful, snow white lace. She had a famous salon in Hungary. The guests looked at me with admiration as they whispered, "You look beautiful."

Dezső stood at the altar wearing a black tuxedo and white bowtie. White calla lily was on his lapel. I looked at him and saw not only a handsome man, but a man with integrity. His big, blue eyes were sparkling as he smiled at me.

I noticed how no one was sitting in the left front row. That was reserved for Dezső's family. I was shocked, wondering where they could be. My godmother, a slightly fat, but very agile woman, who loved giving orders to others, as my father used to say, stepped out from the church. The fact that the wedding ceremony would start without the groom's family had her beside herself. Right when the altar boys started heading towards the altar, my godmother barged into the sacristy, begging the Father to hold off on beginning the ceremony until Dezső's family arrived. What I found out after the wedding was that my godmother stood in front of the church when an old car pulled up next to her. Dezső's eldest brother nearly flopped out from behind the wheel, clearly in a visibly drunk state. Cow manure hung from his shoes, which he tried to scrape off on the edge of the sidewalk. Dezső's mother slowly climbed out of the car. She always complained about her back pain. Her wrinkled face reflected sadness. Dezső's twin and his middle brother merely stood on the sidewalk. The sight of each other made them burst into loud laughter, of which their clouded minds were unable to get hold. They were clumsily picking the hay off of each other's shoulders and hair, and shining their shoes against the backs of their pants.

Then, one of the brothers shouted at my godmother, "What are you looking at? Mind your own business! We are working men, not mushy city boys."

The twin brother spat on the sidewalk and smeared it with the sole of his shoe. My godmother opened the church door. Led by my soon to be mother-in-law, they all came in. A few minutes prior, I had been walking lightly by my father's side, radiating with joy. The train of my dress softly rustled behind me as I was basking in the loving smiles of the guests and in the mesmerizing light of the colorful mosaic windows of the church. Dezső's squeeze of my hand promised lifetime happiness.

Now I was scared. I felt something wasn't right. The waiting seemed endless. All I could do was stare at my white calla lily bouquet. Calla lily is a beautiful flower. A pure, innocent, white, fragile flower on a sturdy stem, created by our Lord for brides. This flower is like me. I smiled at my own thought, as it was innocent, pure, and fragile.

A soft murmur from behind us broke the silence. I can recall my mother sighing, "Dear Lord!" After that, I only caught fragments of words. "Sit there…no, I'm leaving… leave me alone. I will drag him out." Then someone shushed the latecomers, and it was finally quiet. I don't quite remember the service. I wondered at the time if Dezső knew what was happening. Can it be that he kept from me the fact that his family didn't like me? I felt chills. Dezső's voice came to me from a distance: "I do". Then I returned the words and said, "I do". Dezső kissed me gently. His mother started sobbing inconsolably, as if she was at a funeral. Soon after, she left the church with her sons.

"Marika, I swear to God, I don't know what's going on," Dezső told me.

The priest gave us his blessing and walked us out of the church. Family, friends and acquaintances followed us. In front of the church, a long line waited to congratulate us. Dezső's family stood and waited with defiant grimness. Mom and Dad were chatting with their acquaintances, but kept their eyes on us. Dezső turned pale. His expression reminded me of the crucified Christ. I could feel the storm in the air as Dezső's family stepped closer to us. My father came behind us as my mother-in-law embraced her son, then firmly shook him by the shoulders.

"My son, we are now going to the sacristy and you take back your word. You cannot marry such a spoiled, city girl. I won't let you ruin your life. A good mother must save her son from the consequences of his recklessness."

Dezső escaped from her embrace, but she continued, "Look around, my son, these aristocrats will use you, squeeze you like a lemon, then throw you away. They got you all dressed up like a clown. Look at us. You are just like us. We are your family. You belong with us."

The three brothers then came to Dezső. They wanted to fight, but my father stepped before us. His sharp, strict voice put an end to the lamentation and sniffling of the crowd.

"Now I ask our guests to get into your cars. We shall see you at the dinner table. Dezső, you must decide now if you are joining us or staying here."

Dezső loved and respected his mother. He used to talk to

me about her self-sacrificing life and her endless love for her sons. Now he turned away from her. He looked at his brothers with scorn and moved to my father's side. Shoulders hunched, as if carrying a heavy load, he stared at the ground. He looked paralyzed by sorrow and anger. The tense silence lasted for what seemed like forever. I couldn't think of anything that would help solve this tragic situation. Eventually, he started speaking in a soul-wrenching voice.

"I don't like to speak in public, especially not about my feelings, but now I am forced to do just that. I've been courting Marika for many years. A man could not love a girl more than I love her. This day could have been the happiest day of my life. I don't know why my family, whom I love dearly, has chosen to cause me such pain and humiliation. I know my apologies do not change what happened here. I have no excuse for my family. I never thought my mother would cause me such sorrow. That my brothers would come here drunk and dirty. I will never forget. Our hearts have been deeply wounded, but time and love will eventually heal us."

"But, son, we love you so much."

Dezső turned to me and kissed my hand. "I love you, I always will. No matter how long I live, I'll protect you from all harm," he said.

My heart was racing. His words erased all of the bitterness. He took me in his arms and walked to the car.

The dinner was delicious. Many childhood stories surfaced, especially funny ones. Despite my family's best efforts, Dad, Mom, and Dezső could not conceal how much they were waiting to end the celebration. Mom was going to have a hard time in the hair salon (she was a hairstylist) where the women loved to gossip. Before our wedding, a few families subtly commented that it was not right for an upper-class girl to marry a peasant boy. Now this was the scandal, and the whole city would be talking about it, but there was nothing to be done about it.

The bridal dance was at midnight. I stepped on the dance floor flushed, in my red and white polka dot dress. I danced with the older guests to the beautiful melody of Hungarian country songs. The animated Csárdás was for my younger guests. Then, I danced with my father. His asthma was bad late at night. We moved slowly to an old song, "The girl blossoms into woman, the bud into rose". Dezső asked for the last dance. We moved slowly to our favorite song, "How can I tell you how much I love you." Then, he whisked me up and ran from the room.

Our suitcases were ready, waiting for us. We got on the bus to Budapest at dawn. I collapsed, exhausted, on Dezső's shoulder and fell asleep instantly. The bus often stopped, picking up commuters. I was half asleep as I kept hearing good morning greetings. Eventually, the morning sun rays woke me up. I squinted, which got me a kiss on both eyelids. I rewarded my new husband with a big smile.

"Good morning."

He kissed me on the forehead and rubbed his nose against mine. It made me laugh; this soon became a habit of ours, whenever we were really excited about something.

"This is our first morning, first day, the first everything. Do you know how long I've been waiting for this day?" he said.

"Long?" I asked, giggling.

He radiated joy through every pore of his body.

"Four years, six months. God, you don't know how much I've waited for this day."

"It is a very long time, we shall see if it was worth it," I said. He kissed me.

An old man sitting behind us patted Dezső's shoulder. "Love is in the air. I can feel it."

"It is, we got married yesterday," Dezső responded.

"Honeymooners on the bus!" shouted the man.

The passengers applauded and wished us well.

The bus had a fifteen-minute stop in the city of Vác. Many got off to have a smoke or a cup of coffee. Dezső stood up and stretched.

"Come, let's move around a bit. We can go into the bistro for a coffee."

"It's cold. Get me a hot tea."

He winked and glanced back at me as he was leaving. The bus started filling up again. Dezső returned with the hot tea. Its pleasant smell reminded me of something, but I couldn't quite put my finger on it. I was watching the people, huddled in warm scarves, rushing on the street. We slowly left the city and the Danube appeared, glittering amidst the snowy mountains. It was a beautiful sight as the enormous, gracious river flowed through the valley.

"Look at the Danube. It looks like a silver ribbon in this blinding sunlight."

Dezső leaned over and looked out the window.

"It is really beautiful and so are you."

His voice, his smile, and the smell of tea – I finally knew what it reminded me of.

* * *

We met in the very famous Hungarian Industrial School for Machine Designing (Magyar tannyelvű gépészeti ipariskola Kassa). When I first saw Dezső, I thought he was a teacher at the school. He stepped into the classroom where we students had a tea afternoon and remembered the Hungarian composer Erkel Ferenc's life and the wonderful operas he wrote. Teachers often attended these monthly events. I was the organizer and presenter. A couple of classmates helped me put the program together. I chose famous Hungarian writers, poets, composers, painters, all who had birthdays in that particular month. We commemorated their work, life, and the political situation of that time. What I liked best about it was that it gave us the chance

7

to express our patriotic sentiments and to show our Hungarian pride in our Slovakian homeland. I filled a cup with tea then, and now the smell of tea brings back such beautiful memories.

I walked across the room. The teacher was sitting at the last table. I could feel him watching me attentively.

"Professor, may I offer you a cup of tea?"

"Certainly, thank you."

"You are welcome." I went to the podium and began the presentation. I announced the next performers, who interpreted the composer's creations on violin, while there was also singing and poetry recitations. The highlight of the afternoon was the "Motherland, motherland, you are my all" aria of Bánk Bán opera, to which we all sang along. The building of the school was echoing, "I'd gladly die for you, my Hungarian motherland."

We enjoyed these afternoons. Many teachers had tears in their eyes as they praised us for them. After the official program, we served tea, with folklore music accompanying our conversations. We sang, laughed, and enjoyed being together. Our school was our home away from home. Eight in the evening was closing time. We cleaned the room, the boys rearranged the desks and chairs in the classroom, and we walked in groups to the dormitories. At that time, it was mostly a boys' school, so there were only a few of us girls. I can still recall the deep respect and true brotherly love with which they treated us. We took up the whole sidewalk, still telling our stories to each other, when the rain started pouring.

"Run girls, you'll get soaked!"

Like in St. Peter's Umbrella, a Hungarian old movie, an invisible hand opened an umbrella above my head. Everyone ran around me as I stopped and turned and find Dezső standing behind me.

"Allow me to introduce myself. I'm Imre Dezső, from third A class." I couldn't conceal my surprise. I blushed.

"You are not a teacher?" I asked, incredulous.

"No, I am a student, just like you, only slightly older. Probably about four years."

I started laughing.

"Do I have the honor of being in the presence of a serial failure?"

He laughed. Never before had I seen such bright blue eyes. The rain from the umbrella was dripping on my hair and shoulders, so he drew me closer to him.

"No, I am not. I graduated from the toolmaking and locksmith apprentice school. The factory referred me for further education because I am smart...very smart."

He was cute and I admired how he played the smart guy role.

"That's how I got here at this school."

I liked him from the first moment I saw him. I felt as though I had met him before, maybe in another lifetime.

"You can close your umbrella. The rain has stopped," I said.

He stuck his arm out from under the umbrella. "You're right."

He shook the rain drops off. He didn't seem to know how to continue the conversation.

"I'll go catch up with the others. Thanks for the umbrella."

He took my hand.

"You are very welcome. Please let me walk with you to your dormitory."

"Sure. You live that way, too?"

"Yes, in the boy's dormitory."

That's how our relationship started. Sometimes we met in the school corridors; we would wave at each other, but nothing more. I started observing him, to see if he had a girlfriend. On rare occasions, I saw him on breaks. I found out that he was the president of the school's CSISZ (Czechoslovakian Communist Youth Association). He was in close connection with Schulz György, the principal of our school, whom he often assisted with official affairs.

* * *

One day, I received a package from home, full of goodies.

Whenever this happened, my friends and I shared the food. We laid a big towel in the middle of the room, took everything out of the box, and everyone found their favorite food. We sat on the bed and the conversation went on about all-time favorite topics. Boys and love. At sixteen, there was nothing more exciting.

"Guess what? I heard at breakfast that Eva got kicked out of nursing school."

"Why?"

"They say she's pregnant."

"I'm not surprised," said Erzsi. "She had her fair share of boys. She deserves it!"

My best friend, Barbara, stopped nibbling on her breaded chicken thigh and looked at us with graveness.

"Girls, you won't believe what I saw yesterday evening when I got off the train."

"What?"

"Our CSISZ king, Dezső, was unloading sacks of cement from the cars in the station. Józsi, Dezső's classmate who lives in my village, told me that Dezső often works there at night, especially on Saturdays and Sundays. He comes from a poor family so if he wants to visit them, he needs to earn money for the trip. Józsi said he is also supporting his mother."

Toncsi took a bite out of a pork roast and sighed.

"You can tell he's sad."

"What makes you say that? I responded. When I spoke to him, he was cheerful. He has a good sense of humor. There is no shame in working. My father says hard work is the only way to get ahead."

"I guess that's true," said Kati. "He will make a good husband, at least according to my mother. She always says: a man should not be handsome because he will become a womanizer, he should not go out drinking to the bar because

10

he will turn into an alcoholic. He should know hard work and love his family. That's what matters the most."

Toncsi made a face.

"Well, I can't be with an ugly man. Dezső is handsome. Did you see those eyes? Blue like the sky!"

We all had a good laugh watching Toncsi stare at the ceiling.

That night I was tossing and turning in my bed. I had always had everything I needed. I never knew whether my parents were poor or wealthy. Money was never discussed. Mom always ran our household efficiently and there was no wasting of things. My clothes were cheap and simple because I'd grow out of them anyway. From the age of fourteen, I had ten Korona spending money, which I used to save for family birthday presents. My mother taught me that giving is a sublime feeling which is good for the heart.

Dad doesn't like money. I'm sure of it. He is an interesting, special person. He grew up as an orphan. His father died before he was born. At the age of fourteen, he found his mother dead in her bedroom. She was from Transylvania and his father was the son of Italian painters who traveled from one city to the next, restoring frescoes in churches. He had no family in Losonc, and the city took care of his mother's burial. After the funeral, my father went back to the church, but it was already closed. He sat down on the curb of the sidewalk; he cried and started praying to God for help, when a hand stroked his head.

"Come with me, son, I take you to my blacksmith's shop. I teach you the craft so, one day, you can make a living. In exchange, you will clean the shop, start the fire at five in the morning, so my workers have hot coal ready, waiting for them. I'll give you some spending money. My wife cooks every day for the apprentices. You will eat with them. I will set up a bed for you in the corner of the shop."

"Thank you, I will work very hard to repay you for your kindness."

Dad often mentioned this day during our many talks. He was a man of faith, though he rarely went to church. He said to me: "You don't have to be in the church to speak to God; he listens to you wherever you are." He never spoke of money or wealth, but he did speak about honor, perseverance, character, and especially, strong will. My father never gave orders, rather told stories from his life and said to observe people and learn from their mistakes. He was born in 1905 and could remember the First World War. He returned from the Second World War from Stalingrad the Don River in Russia, injured. On countless occasions, I found inspiration in his stories which helped me with my own predicaments. In my life, my parents were my role models.

Their love for each other was deep and unique. My mom highly respected my father, so they never argued. At eighteen, my dad opened his own blacksmith's shop where he created beautiful forged gates and fences. He learned the locksmith profession, bought machines, and the city gained a reputable, qualified professional. Even today, the shop windows and entrances created by the Regina Company are still standing on the main street of Losonc. The ironwork of Vinkler's house, the famous construction engineer, was also done by my father. In the graveyard, many forged iron fences are a testament to his work.

After the capitalist regime collapsed after the Second World War, the communists nationalized his factory and seized his finances. He never talked about that time. I imagine that the disgraceful and wrongful confiscation of the personal property for which he worked so hard, must have been so painful that he erased it entirely from his memory. He wasn't willing to waste any time pining or feeling hatred for the atrocities perpetrated by the communists. When my dad talked with his friends, sometimes he'd sarcastically state: "The success story of my life is that at the age of fifty-seven, I am a destitute, Hungarian, rotten, capitalist exploiter."

He'd say it in such a detached manner that I didn't even realize how terrible his conclusion was.

* * *

I came back to the present and found myself wondering about Dezső's family's story. Why were they poor? Essentially, there can be no poor people in socialism, as everyone is equal. At least that's what they taught us in school. I couldn't sleep. I rolled onto my stomach and leaned on my elbows, watching the main street of Kassa. A couple stopped under the tree across from the window. They hugged and talked. The girl laughed out loud and then they kissed for a long time. I rested my head on the pillow. I thought of Dezső, whom I hadn't seen in weeks. I wondered if he ever thought of me? Then I wondered why he would, as he had no reason to. There was something about him, an invisible force, something that was only in him, something very lovable. I looked down at the kissing couple, but they weren't there anymore. The street was empty, only a worker in boots hurrying home. It was Dezső.

Days later, we met in the paper store. I was paying when he walked in. He looked at me with a big smile.

"Hi, nice to see you."

He didn't let me speak. "Do you have some time? There is a very good ice cream shop nearby. Do you like ice cream?"

"I don't."

I was waiting for his reaction, but before he could say anything, I leaned closer to him.

"But I can have some for your sake," I added.

"Naughty." His blue eyes sparkled as he looked deep into my eyes. "I wouldn't have survived if you said no."

He held my hand and pulled me out of the store. His touch triggered an unfamiliar feeling in me. At sixteen, he was the first boy to have ever taken my hand.

The customers at the ice cream shop were sitting at small tables outside. There was one free table left.

"Sit here, before someone else takes it. I will get the ice cream. What's your favorite?"

"You won't believe me, but I don't have a favorite. I really don't like ice cream."

"Then I will take you for a cup of coffee in the cake shop across the street."

"Coffee sounds good."

Unexpected Event

A week later I got sick. I had a high temperature, but no pain. I was tired and wanted to sleep all the time. The doctor gave me antibiotics, but after two days, my temperature was still high. I decided to go home. I knew Dad would make me Agrimony tea, as he believed it was the best cure for everything, with lemon and honey. He would sit by my side, telling me stories about old days, and I would soon be as good as new. I finished the penicillin, but still had a temperature. The doctor wasn't able to find out what was causing it. He suspected a strong virus in my body that was clearly capable of resisting the medicine. He gave me a stronger version of antibiotic pills. A few days later, my temperature dropped. I rushed back to Kassa to make up for the ten days I had been absent. I had frequent headaches, often studying late into the night. The school's strictest teacher taught machine parts, where we learned about the calculations, functions, and designs of machines.

"This subject will be your livelihood. A good technician must know the formulas by heart," he said. I wrote them on my palm and arm, hoping that constantly seeing them might help me memorize them. I was scared of him. We girls had a hard time, because it was professor Rezsucha's personal belief that girls should be handling ladles, not calibers.

I ran out of medicine, and by the weekend, my temperature had gone up again. On my left shin, a red, inflamed, palm-sized spot appeared. Late at night, my friend Barbara had to take me to the hospital with a very high temperature. The doctor assumed it was some sort of bite. They kept me under observation. The nurse put Ichthyol ointment on the red surface and wrapped it tight. At night, I could feel my leg throbbing and everything aching in my body, even my hair. In the morning, the doctor looked at my leg in disbelief. The sight made the nurses turn away. I looked at it, too; there was a crater, as a big piece of flesh had fallen out of my leg, leaving my bone bare. I wanted to leave and go home. The doctor got upset with me.

"Give her a sedative. This is a serious infection. Let's inject the antibiotics; they will take effect faster."

He ordered the nurses to reapply Ichthyol in a thick layer on the open wound. I was devastated as I laid in bed, weak and helpless. I called my mother in tears for help, but after that I don't remember anything else until Barbara came to visit me in the early afternoon. She greeted me with great worry in her eyes.

"Barbara, please call my parents. Ask them to come and get me. I'm going to die here."

She hugged me.

"Don't be silly. You can't die. I'll call your dad."

After dinner, I had no temperature, but I still felt weak. My tears were flowing steadily. I wasn't crying, just feeling sorry for myself. The nurse stroked my cheek. Dezső was standing behind her, holding a bunch of red roses.

"You can only stay five minutes," she told him. "If someone sees you, it will be big trouble. I will close the door and let you know when the hall is clear. Then I will walk you out."

Dezső forced himself to smile as he sat on the edge of my bed. I tried to smile, too, but all I could manage was a twitch of a muscle in my cheek.

"My darling, you must gather your strength. We have our entire lives ahead of us. We didn't even begin yet. Be strong, don't give up. You must live for us. I have loved you since the moment you called me Professor."

My tears were streaming uncontrollably. He was speaking to me, but I couldn't hear him. I must have fallen asleep from all of the medications. When I opened my eyes, Dezső wasn't there. I could have imagined I dreamed it all, but the roses on the nightstand proved he was real. He loved me. I knew I couldn't die.

In the morning, I heard my mother sobbing in the hallway and the firm voice of my father. "Yes, I take responsibility for discharging my daughter. Wait for what? For her to die here? You don't even know what you are treating her for. A bite? What kind of bite?"

There was a long silence before the doctor said, "It is possible that she has leukemia."

"That's not true. You are speculating!" my father said angrily.

After we left, we drove in silence all the way to Losonc in our little "Trabant" car. I was mostly asleep. Mom held my hand, and whenever I opened my eyes, she asked immediately: "Are you hungry? Are you thirsty? Should we stop?"

"No, Mom. Let's hurry home."

The next week we went from one doctor to another. They tested me for everything possible. They found that the infection was in my blood. My leg wasn't worse, but the wound wasn't healing. By this point, I was constantly taking antibiotics. I heard my father on the phone asking how long I could live on the medication, as it was keeping me in the same condition. I couldn't hear the answer.

One day, Mom came home from the hair salon with the name of a professor, a doctor in Budapest. A friend of hers arranged for us to visit him the next day. People said the doctor had cured many hopeless patients.

I watched him as we were sitting in his office. We could see on his old, benevolent face that he was a serious specialist in the field of medicine. He spent a long time reading the previous test results. When he finished, he closed the thick file.

"Unfortunately, I can't help. My colleagues have already done all that is possible. Science still leaves us with many unanswered questions. Perhaps the combination of the young body and the antibiotics one day will prevail over this stubborn infection. He got up and extended his hand. I had to help Dad up from the armchair.

"Thank you," he mumbled, as he shook the doctor's hand.

The receptionist approached us and said discreetly, "The doctor can't help you, so he doesn't charge for the consultation."

Then the door opened behind us, and the doctor appeared. "Perhaps there is one thing you could try," he said. "In the files, there is no mention of any tonsil problems that your daughter might have had in the past. In my fifty years of practice, I read about one single case where the death of a twenty-year-old man was caused by a similar infection in the blood. During the biopsy, it was discovered that he had an internal undetectable tonsillitis which infected his entire body. I recommend removing the tonsils. It won't have any negative side effects, but it is possible that it will turn out to be the source of the infection."

The next morning, in Balassagyarmat, my mom's hometown, I had my tonsils removed. All I remember is that the doctor pressed my tongue down with a little silver tray and snipped my tonsils off with a clamp. It was done in an instant. The nurse stuffed cotton wads in my mouth. The doctor laughed. He believed we had gotten the culprit. A terrible smell filled the little operation room. My healthy-looking tonsils were rotten inside.

We had days filled with joy. I was recovering at incredible speed. A great dent was left on my shin, but nobody cared about that anymore. I was healthy again!

It was end of April, and the school year was to end in eight weeks. I had missed two months of school. The principal and my top-class teacher recommended that I repeat the year. It is impossible to make up for two months' worth of study material in one month, they told my parents. The brain is incapable of absorbing so much information, from calculations, to formulas, to technical procedures, in such a short time. Also, the rest of the class would keep moving ahead, which meant another month would soon be necessary to make up.

Dad listened to their arguments. Then, he expressed his.

"My daughter is smart, hardworking, and resilient. Please allow her to stay with her classmates. This illness took a lot out of her, and I can't imagine how it would affect her if she has to fall behind."

The principal nodded and said, "We can try. If she passes the test, I have nothing against her continuing with her class." Soon enough, I was back with my friends.

One of the most beautiful memories of my life is from this time. In the history of our school, there wasn't another class like ours. Teachers and schoolmates have been saying this for decades since we graduated. We were class B of 1962 to 1966. Words cannot describe the solidarity, relentless willingness to help, and the willpower that my classmates supported me with. We studied together until exhaustion. I will never forget Bolyky Pista, as he explained where and how the energy is converted in the Löffler plant. For four weeks, my smartest classmates, Pupala Pista, Szalai Sanyi, Horváth Pistike, and Krakovszky Istvan spent every moment of their time with me. Some evenings we'd study until eight o'clock. Everlasting friendships were forged in those weeks. I was able to pass the year, and I owe it all to them.

The most difficult subject matter was machine parts design. Professor Rezsucha told us that the knowledge of what he was passing on to us would earn us good money when we became professionals.

There were days when he had the boys bring in a big box of machine parts. We got different pieces: a piston from the engine, or a cogwheel, for example. In three hours, we had to make a drawing for production purposes. At the end of the third hour, he collected all sketches. During the next hour, he evaluated our work in front of us. We stood by his table with the machine part in our hand. He mercilessly criticized our work. His humorous remarks made us feel ashamed, but we learned a lot from it.

I was scared. It was to be my hardest test. We had long, wide tables in the classroom so our drawing boards would fit, and there were office chairs to sit on. My classmates were ready to prompt me. We had secret signs, too. A stroke of the forehead meant to continue, a nose rub to stop and that it was the wrong formula.

One day, Pupi, whom I had been in school with since I was six, patted my shoulder and said, "Relax, don't speak too much. You'll make fewer mistakes that way. Don't try to be smart. The important thing is to pass the class. Do you understand?"

"Yes," I responded.

The school bell marked the beginning of the class. We all took our seats. I was looking at the clean, dark green blackboard. It was wall to wall, sometimes still not long enough for a complete calculation. In the corner, a spider ran out from under the blackboard and stopped on the ceiling. It was looking at me when the door behind us opened and professor Rezsucha raced through the classroom.

"We are already five minutes behind. Turn your chairs around to face the back wall!"

We were perplexed.

"What's the matter? You don't speak Hungarian?" he continued.

Everyone turned their chairs around.

"There is nothing to see, so just listen. Maria, come to the blackboard."

I stepped to the podium, took a piece of chalk, and waited for the question. Looking at my classmates' backs, I begin to panic. I was alone; I had no one to help me. Then I felt like lightning struck me, giving me power. I knew I could do it on my own. My whole body straightened and I made eye contact with my professor. He stepped next to me.

"I know you are nervous."

"Yes, professor."

"You've been studying intensively, or, in other words, cramming. That's good for the brain, but in life, logic is what you need. I decided to use my method to explain in a nutshell the two-month study material you missed. This is the foundation that you can build on next year. Class, you can turn back. You don't need to prompt her. Knowledge is what she needs in life."

He got a piece of chalk in his right hand, and had the sponge in the left. He drew, explained, and calculated. As the blackboard filled up, he erased the unnecessary data with his left hand. For four straight hours, without a break, he went through two months of study material. At the sound of the school bell, he stepped away from the podium.

"I believe you now understand the main points necessary for the next grade. You still have the summer to perfect it. You passed."

There was complete silence in the class. I could see the victory smiles of my classmates. Professor Rezsucha opened his notebook and wrote the passing mark. I was still standing in front of the blackboard. I couldn't believe what had just happened.

"Professor, thank you. I am grateful. Today you not only helped me understand machine parts design, but you gave me a life lesson. Your dedication to teach and passionately transmit your knowledge not only gives me confidence, but lets me see how to care, how we can help those in need. Thank you, Professor, for this remarkable day which I'll always remember."

It was rare to see him smile, but that day, he did.

"I have been teaching for many years. I could have retired years ago, but I am doing this job with my heart and soul. I love to teach. I will be honest with you; your appreciation makes it worth staying on the job. I give my best so my students can thrive. Thank you for your recognition."

* * *

The summer was filled with wonderful experiences. We spent two weeks visiting galleries and museums in Budapest, sitting on the bank of the Danube while Dad talked to us about Hungarian history. Everywhere we looked, there were landmarks of the Hungarian nation's prominent culture. The Castle, Fisherman's Bastion, Parliament, Liberty Statue, and the bridges over the Danube were all breathtaking sights.

Dezső was in my thoughts. He congratulated me after my exams. He laughed as he praised me for being smart.

I remember when he laughed, I asked, "Is that funny to you?"

"No, you are smart and I'm happy to see you. School is over tomorrow. We won't see each other for two months."

He pretended to wipe imaginary tears. Then he got serious.

"I have big plans for the break. I got accepted to the welder's course and will work as a toolmaker for two months."

Much to my disappointment, he didn't even hug me, just wished me a nice summer. "Take care" was all he said.

On the first day of September, I was traveling back to school in Kassa. The train was late; I arrived after midnight. I had to rush through the crowd to catch the last tram.

Out of nowhere, Dezső stepped in front of me.

"May I carry your suitcase?" Then, without warning, he kissed me, just like I had seen in the movies. It was my first kiss ever. It felt so good. I hugged him and we kissed for a long time. I wanted the moment to last forever, but I gently pushed him away.

"People are looking at us."

I was ashamed to look him in the eyes. He kissed my forehead.

"You know, I love you. I love you with all my heart. I have been thinking about you all summer. My days started and ended with your name. I waited for you and now you are finally here.

22

Come, there's a small coffee place. Let's have tea." His words were echoing in my head: "I love you, I love you." His kindness, those blue eyes – my heart would jump with joy whenever he was close to me.

He put the cups on the table. I saw his hands.

"I worked a lot this summer. The emulsion dries the skin. That's why my fingers are cracked. They will recover now in school."

I wanted to put some nourishing cream on his wounds and kiss his fingers like we do for the children to make the pain go away. I took his hand and touched it lightly.

"You are sweet. Now they don't hurt anymore. Guess what? I finished my welder's dissertation. It's a well-paying profession. We never know what the future will bring."

"Mom says the same thing. She listed all the things a good wife and mother must know. I must admit, I am far from that."

"Well then, you better hurry up and meet the requirements."

The school year went by quickly. Dezső was preparing to graduate and for two years go to serve in the army what was mandatory in all socialist states. We spent lots of time together, but he never talked about the future.

When we were sitting side by side at his graduation party, his mother and his brothers were with us very quietly. They ate their food and no matter how hard we tried to make conversation, all we got in response was 'yes' and 'no'. We walked them to their hotel and returned to the party where we celebrated till dawn, dancing and having fun. The farewell was very hard. We hugged through tears. Nothing could compare to the life we had in the great, old industrial school where we were like a family. Our beloved school armed us not only with technical knowledge, but also with humanity, integrity, solidarity, and the importance of hard work, resilience, love, selflessness, and the list goes on. We got all that as a farewell present, so that we could make it in every aspect of life. We knew that the moment we stepped out into the big world as Hungarian individuals wanting to build a life in Slovakia, we would need to work twice as hard to achieve our goals. Professor Putanko said to us: "It is important in life not to look for excuses, but to find solutions. If you bear this in mind, you will have a successful life."

After saying goodbye, we dried our tears and each of us went on our own path across the country. Dezső and I stopped for a prayer in the Dome. Since I had miraculously regained my health, I felt immense gratitude to God. I was a tiny person under the Dome vault, but I knew He listened to my prayer:

"My Lord, please watch over Dezső in the army. Bring him home, safe and sound! Help us make our dreams come true, to be able to live in peace and love. Bless our everyday journey. Amen."

The sun was coming up. Hand in hand, we headed toward the dormitory. Then, with a brief embrace, we said goodbye.

REAL LIFE

A year later, I graduated. I found a job in the crane factory (Turcianské Strojárne Lučenec) in Losonc. I was a technical controller measuring parts made on lathe and mill machines. I worked in the production hall, walking from one machine to the other, inspecting all products. I loved my work. It was fun doing my job and talking with all of the workers. We always had a lot to share about TV programs, politicians, and later on, about our families and school years.

Time went by fast. I spent evenings reading Dezső's letters. He loved serving in the Air Force and became the fastest Morse code operator. Our letters were not love letters. We wrote six, sometimes eight, pages about our life experiences. I wrote to him that my boss openly hated Hungarians and former capitalist families. In his reply, he discussed this topic at length. He made me promise not to argue with anyone about politics and matters of nationalism.

"You never know what kind of snitch is lurking around."

At the end of our letters, we'd encourage each other with how many days until we could see each other again. Under his signature he always wrote, "I still love you."

I was rushing home from work on a cold March afternoon. There were lots of people on the street, but from a distance, I saw Dezső. He got five days leave for his accomplishment in the Morse tests. We stood on the sidewalk locked in embrace, without words. Then the rain came. We ran as fast as we could. My house was nearby, but we were soaked by the time we got home. My parents had already met Dezső at my graduation. After the warm welcome, Dad brought him sweatpants and a sweater because his clothes were dripping wet. Mom brought hot tea with honey and lemon and her homemade, delicious cookies.

That afternoon, I knew that the door was open for Dezső, if he decided to be part of our family. Mom invited him to stay for dinner. Dezső mentioned that he would like us to meet his brothers and mother. Dad liked the idea. He offered to visit them the next morning so that Dezső wouldn't have to take the bus home late night.

"My mother is going to be happy to meet you. She has a heart of gold."

My father turned to him and said, "That is very important. In life, the voice of the heart is the one that matters most. Living with love, respect, and not hurting people make life noble."

The next day, we were heading towards the small village of Darnya. The visit was tense. On the table was homemade strudel, as well as coffee and tea.

In the garden we saw many beehives, so Dad asked about the bees. All of the brothers complained how they had lost so much money because the weather was cold, so they had to feed them with sugar.

Dezső hugged his mom. "No one can make strudels like you," he said before my mother asked for the recipe.

"These are so crispy and delicious," she told Dezső's mom.

I mentioned what a great joy Dezső's visit had been.

The brothers looked unpleasantly at me.

"We need him here. There is a lot of work to be done around the house. He might not even be able to finish it."

Dad stood up, and we thanked them for their hospitality. Dezső walked us to the car.

"Only 178 days until I can be with you again."

He winked at me. I could see one of his brothers staring at us from the gate. Because they didn't have anything to say to me the whole time, I felt like doing something that would outrage them. I jumped into Dezső's arms and kissed him.

On the way home, Mom said with sadness, "I don't think they're going to love you."

"Don't be silly, Maria, these are simple people, just wait until they get to know Marika. They will praise the Lord that their son found her. They just need time to adjust to us. Look at Dezső. He has deep-rooted values and principles. He will love and protect our daughter until the day he dies. I have no doubt about it."

Around that time, I forced my Dad for longer walks around the park. He had been quiet because his asthma got worse. We sat on the park bench.

"Dad, can you tell me a story?"

"Do you think I will live to see your wedding day?"

"Dad, you told me, we never give up. If you try to walk more, you definitely will. You can walk in front of the house, too. You don't need to wait for me."

We didn't go for summer vacation. I saved my days off for the time when Dezső would return. I thought that maybe he would want to marry me. Mom knew that I loved him very much and planned to say yes.

"Marika, you will have a great deal of problems with your mother-in-law. I know your father says that Dezső is a nice man, but mothers have a huge influence over their sons. If she won't love you, it will cause a lot of pain to both of you. Think about it."

* * *

In early September, my boss called me into his office. I walked anxiously between the machines. I'd been working under him for over a year but he rarely spoke to me, only a good morning and goodbye. Twice he asked me to type a six-month evaluation of the technical controllers' work. Now he waited for me with a pile of documents in his hands.

"I am not asking for favor. These documents must be typed immediately for our Communist Party. This is the yearly activity report for the management. The president of the party assigned you to be his temporary secretary, which is a great honor."

He looked at me, waiting for my reaction.

"It's not a problem that I'm not a member of the party?"

"At this time, it is not, but you will become a part of it when you earn it. I'll divide your work between your coworkers."

By my fifth day typing, there was still about two days' worth of work remaining. I kept thinking about excuses to get myself out of this position that had been forced on me. I looked at the dusty clock on the wall. It was two o'clock. My coworkers came into the office with their daily reports and jokingly demanded a bottle of vodka for the favor of doing my work. Then, the door opened.

"Hello!"

"Oh my goodness, what a surprise! Dezső, let me introduce you to my coworkers. Guys, he is the one I told you about."

Mihaly, the senior colleague, pulled a flask from his pocket.

"Let's drink to the health of this beautiful couple. It is homemade. I brought it in for tasting," he said, holding the flask up again.

We all had a sip from the bottle. Mihály slipped the flask back in his pocket as my boss walked in. He didn't even say hello to us.

Dezső had been running around since morning. He got the job at the construction and technical development department and found a place to rent close to my home. He was beaming with joy when he turned his big blue eyes on me.

"There is one more thing I have to take care of, but for that I need your help. Come, let's go to the grill bar, we can talk there." We sat down in the dark corner, where nobody was around.

"Two coffees, two brandies, and a slice of Drum cake, please.

28

"What are we celebrating?"

"That I am sitting here, by your side."

I blushed, and he added,

"And there is one other reason."

He got on his knee, took my hand, and asked me, "Do you want to marry me?"

"Yes, I do," I said, without hesitation.

Tears of joy ran down my cheeks as he hugged me and whispered, "You will be the happiest woman on Earth. I will always love you and take care of you as long as I live, so help me God."

We chose to get married on November 11, 1967.

HONEYMOON IN BUDAPEST

After our wedding, we arrived in Budapest. In the Sport Hotel, a romantic, special honeymooner room was waiting for us. The drapes allowed only a thin, mysterious light into the room. Red, heart-shaped pillows decorated the crisp white bed. A trail of small, red paper hearts on the floor were leading to the bed. Salted almonds and pretzels sat on the smoking table. Next to it, two intertwined candles flickered in the company of a bottle of champagne.

The day that we had long been yearning for had finally arrived.

I wondered whether it would fulfill all of the dreams that we had been having for years. Just the two of us, in the romantic setting, selflessly giving our hearts, bodies, and souls to each other. I sat down while my husband was in the bathroom. I noticed a heart envelope on the table. It was a card from my parents, wishing us all the best. I felt enormous gratitude towards them. So many times I disagreed with them, but I obeyed out of respect and love. It was then that I realized how right they had been all along. It's true, if one wants to be happy, everything must happen in its own time. Celebrating life in a unique way was our goal from that point.

"Seek and find your own path," my mom said, "where you walk hand in hand with your partner in sunshine, storms, climb mountains with strength, never be scared, never give up because you have a loving partner for a lifetime next to you." I went to the window with open arms to see the city, wanting to hug the whole world. Life felt truly wonderful.

30

Dezső came in. His sculpted shoulders, strong arms, and those big blue eyes confirmed how much I loved him with every ounce of my being.

I showered and slipped into my nightgown, which I had received from my godmother. It had three different layers of lace. It wasn't see-through, but it subtly revealed the figure underneath. My face was unusually flushed and beaming. Dezső was standing in the middle of the room holding the half-opened bottle of champagne. When he saw me, he put the bottle down.

"You are breathtaking."

The cork flew out of the bottle with a loud explosion. He didn't look at it. The champagne was overflowing, but he didn't care. He took me in his arms and kissed me all over. His tenderness, masculinity, his caresses and whispers all triggered a series of unfamiliar feelings. To reach the highest point of pleasure and then freefall into two strong arms that will hold you until the end of time...is euphoria perceptible only to our souls. We didn't speak for hours. He was fondling me and kissing my tummy when my stomach started growling. He couldn't stop laughing.

"Stop it!" I said, pretending to be angry.

"I am dying of hunger and thirst with you. You didn't even let me drink from that champagne. It's all over the table."

Soon, we were both laughing. He looked at his watch.

"It's five already, nearly dinner time. Let's go to the dining room."

"I would like to have our first dinner in the Mátyás Tavern." (Very famous restaurant in Budapest.)

"Of course, how could I forget that, you mentioned it many times."

The Mátyás tavern was always full of guests, but we were lucky that night. I saw a few empty tables, and to my great delight, Kovács Apollónia was singing that night. I asked the waiter to seat us at the closest possible table to the band. Dezső slipped him 100 Forint and added that we were honeymooners from Slovakia. Shortly, the waiter walked us to the front table, across from the musicians. Two couples from Budapest gave us their table.

"It is a pleasure meeting you. We love the Hungarian sisters and brothers from Slovakia. You have a hard life there. We wish you a long and happy life!"

The night turned out to be unforgettable for all involved.

Dezső kept slipping one bill after the other in the violinist's bow. The first song my husband asked for: "Sweetheart, can you hear the music?" then "No one loves you like I do." Apollónia came to our table and sang to us. By the end, we were all singing together. I know many Hungarian song lyrics by heart. The guests were putting in their requests, too. I felt I had a second wedding celebration, better than it was at home. During one of the breaks, Dezső stood up and introduced me to the guests.

"This is my wife, Marika, and this is our first day of marriage. Yesterday she was a quiet, modest girl. Now I can't stop marveling at this vibrant, entertaining woman standing next to me. What am I going to do?"

The guests were laughing. An older gentleman said, "Take good care of her, my son, you have a great treasure in your hands. Love her and protect her."

The crowd was elated. The wine bottles we received as presents kept piling on our table. At two in the morning, the band, soaked in sweat, stopped playing. The restaurant was still full of guests. We had the waiters open our wine bottles and we toasted with everyone to the most beautiful day of our life.

It was four in the morning when we crossed the Chain Bridge, kissing with every step we made. When I got a chance to speak, I repeated the same question.

"Why do you think that old guy said you must take care of me because I'm valuable?"

"Because he is a wise, experienced, sharp-eyed man. He could see the goodness and infinite lust for life written on your face. You never give up. You are tenacious and you know what you want. What he said I have known for many years. That day you approached me with that tea, I knew you would be my wife. Modesty, reverence, and love were all glimmering in your eyes. I respected you and always treated you like my future wife, the mother of my children, and my partner for life."

A cold wind blew. He drew me close to him. "Was my answer satisfactory?" he asked.

"It was, and I am grateful to have found you. I will do everything in my power for our happiness. That is my promise to you. I will always stand by you, support you. What you just told me elevated me sky high. I love you."

Our days were exciting and busy. We went to museums and galleries, took late-night walks along the Danube, the Fisherman's Bastion, and Margaret Island Park, all very romantic historical places. We ate, drank, and rejoiced. Those days will always be unforgettable. On the final night, we wandered around the old part of Buda. There was a small wine bar in the basement. Dezső ordered our favorite Brassó-style roast pork, with a glass of red wine. We held each other's hands and said goodbye to Budapest.

The First Year

When I got back to work, my boss had moved me to a different job. "Come, I'll show you where your workplace is now."

There was a tiny booth in the corner of the quenching station. The job was very simple, inspecting all of the calipers and micrometers. I was to assess whether or not they were within tolerance levels. If not, I had to send them for recalibration or have them replaced. I knew I might surely go crazy in the booth without a window and nobody to talk with, but my boss arranged with the president of the Communist Party that I would be his part-time secretary, handling all correspondence.

He said: "Your new job will leave you with plenty of free time to do it. Consider it a promotion; the Communist Party trusts you. Be proud of that. The president of the party personally praised your Slovak language spelling."

He barely finished his sentence when the president called and asked me get to his office to type a report. When I came home and told Dezső, he didn't like my new job assignment, but he said, "Unfortunately, there is nothing we can do."

Dad's asthma was very bad. He sat in his armchair, wrapped in a blanket, when we got home from work. Mom worked the afternoon shift at the hair salon. I quickly emptied the ash out of the three masonry heaters. Dezső brought firewood and coal from the basement and started the fire. I heated the dinner that mom had made that morning. We chatted a little during dinner about our trip to Budapest. Dad interrupted a few times.

"Marika, are you okay? You seem sad."

"I'm just tired."

Dezső stoked the heaters and we went to our room, which used to be Dad's office where he designed and made unique, one-of-a-kind gold jewelry for acquaintances whom he trusted to not denounce him. While we were gone, they moved his desk to my parents' bedroom and bought an extendable sofa bed for us. The room looked like a storage place. The wedding gifts were in boxes in all the corners and on top of the cabinets. My parents offered that we stay with them until we get our own place from the factory or the city. Dad said, "Save your money, you will need it when you move out on your own."

It was still cold in the room. We got into our pajamas and jumped in the bed. Through the blinds, the neon light from the street illuminated the room with the tiny light strips, creating a terribly suffocating effect. We were watching the ceiling, covered up to our noses.

"Dezső, I think tomorrow I am going to submit a petition for housing at City Hall."

"Good idea. I talked with my boss about it. He said it takes two to three years to get an apartment, but families with children have priority. We are lucky to be able to live with your parents."

"We are, but how long can we live like this?"

"Things will happen. We just have to give it time."

"It is terrible that we cannot take charge of our own lives. We can't get a place, even if we have money in this state own everyting. We must live here until the city or the factory decides to give us an apartment. I have to work where they want me to work. I can't control my own life. What happens if I tell my boss that I am not a secretary?"

"Please don't."

He sat up, then said, "I went to the hiring office today and asked them if they need welders. The pay is almost double what I get now. In the socialist system, workers have the most rights. A worker cannot be downgraded, and I'm sure it would get us an apartment sooner, too. Starting Monday, I'll be a welder."

"Are you sure you will be happy there?" I asked.

"I'm doing it for a reason."

"Then I also had an idea."

"Tell me."

"If we have a baby, we can get an apartment much sooner."

Dezső started laughing. "So you are suggesting that we start making babies. You want to do it right now?" He looked around with a sad face. "We can't. There is no space for a crib."

"We can stack the armchairs on top of each other, unscrew the legs of the coffee table, and store the top behind the closet. Oh God, a baby would bring us so much happiness," I said happily.

"Marika, a baby needs proper conditions. Here we don't have it. You know that better than I do. I will get the apartment, I promise you. Then we will have as many children as you want. I want to bring our firstborn straight into our own home."

In the morning, I crossed the welding shop on my way to my booth. Thick smoke floated in the air and those flashes, that mysterious light of the welding, had a frightening effect on me. Above my head, the crane moved from one side of the shop to the other, making a squeaky noise. I ducked, as the bottom of a crane part was swinging above my head. Heavy, black curtains surrounded the welders. These people worked under terrible conditions. There was no air filter in place, so all of the smoke rolled towards the big entrance gate. I couldn't understand Dezső. He had said he was doing it for the apartment, but I doubted it. Dezső's boss had to recruit new members for the Communist Party. I read that in the party briefing. Knowing Dezső's way of thinking, he became a welder before his boss wanted to recruit him. I knew he would never be a member of the Communist party even if his political profile was to be destroyed.

"Honey, life is like a game of chess. You need to make your move, knowing what the other side plans to do. You cannot argue with the Communist Party leaders. They will destroy you. Smile and be dumb. There are hard times ahead of us. Mark my words. This year, 1968, will go down in history. People are unhappy. Dubček is trying to make life better for us, but he will fail. Russia will never let us be free."

On my way home on a cold afternoon, I stood in line at the vegetable store while Dezső was in line at the bakery. When I reached the door, there were five others before me when the salesperson announced that he was out of apples, oranges, and bananas. I walked towards the bakery when my father's friend, Jónás Pali, the Jewish rabbi, ran after me.

"I got you three bananas and four oranges," he told me.

"Thank you, Pali, it's so nice of you to help me with my grocery shopping."

"You know, an old man like me must find something to keep busy. I stand in lines and talk to people. This way, I get to know everyone and everything that's happening in the city. You can't get anything done in this world without connections." While we talked, Dezső came with the bread.

"There were only three loaves left and still thirty people standing in line. This will not end well. When people have money but can't buy food, the situation is bad."

* * *

I had loved my first job, but now I hated it. Lot of times I sat in the booth under the neon light, embittered and helpless. I got goosebumps when the phone rang.

"Comrade Imre, the typing material is ready."

For one week, I was typing in his office. After that, I got a desk with a new typewriter which was placed in my boss's office. It must have been unpleasant for the communist leader to have me listening to his conversations, witnessing that he didn't have any work to do other than chatting with the other communist leaders.

Our life was boring, like riding a train that you can't get off of. It's taking you somewhere, but you are not sure that you want to go that way.

In early spring, the snow melted, the trees blossomed, and lush vegetation appeared within days. The sunshine brought people out to nature. The city park was a natural forest. It had a small lake at the entrance, with a pair of swans. A small bridge connected to a tiny island that fit three benches and fifteen bushes of fragrant tea roses. In the park, between trees, people walked miles on nicely kept paths with hundreds of benches. Some people were reading, while others had picnics. The park was the only fun in our town.

The welding shop was behind with work; they had to stay overtime and Dezső volunteered. One month later, he came home with a framed diploma.

"I won the title of best welder." He casually put it on top of the closet. "This isn't very useful, but look what else I got with it?" He pulled out an envelope with five crisp bills of a hundred Korona.

"Congratulations! I am so proud of you," I said, gushing over his achievement.

Dad came into the kitchen. "What happened?"

"Dezső is the best welder in the factory."

"Way to go, son. Many just talk and do nothing but complain. I have no doubt that you will make a nice carrier."

Dezső and I agreed that the following day after work, we would go out to the park. However, the next morning, he called me and said, "I got some interesting supplementary work, related to innovation. It would be better if we go to the park tomorrow."

"No, I want to go today," I said unhappily.

"Is something wrong? You sound so angry."

"Nothing is wrong; I just want to spend time with you. Lately we barely meet. All you do is work, eat, and sleep."

"Alright. I'll come as soon as I can. I'll meet you on the island."

I got to the park, but every bench was taken on the island. I walked around, but I couldn't find an empty spot anywhere. Even on the grass were young couples sitting on blankets, with their children throwing balls, running around. I was listening to their adorable, carefree laughter. A few steps away, an elderly couple got up from the bench. I quickly went over, and as I sat down, I saw Dezső running. I waved my purse at him so he would notice me. He came but didn't sit down; instead, he analyzed me suspiciously.

"I know you, and I can feel that something happened. Tell me."

"You're right, something big happened. I am pregnant."

He opened his arms and shouted, "I'm going to be a father! We're having a baby!"

"Stop it, everyone is looking at us."

"I don't care. Everybody should hear this wonderful news. God, I'm so happy. I'm going to be a father."

It is amazing the range of emotions human beings are capable of experiencing. Sky high flames, the feeling of being in love, desire, yearning, uncertainty, and fulfillment are all experienced in our own way. Motherhood is a love rooted deeply in a woman's heart, which never fades.

My pregnancy was difficult. I threw up at least once a day. I lost three kilos, but the doctor reassured us that the baby was growing perfectly.

In July of 1968, people openly criticized the leaders of the country. In the pub, the men were planning a revolution. Dezső and Dad had long talks about politics.

"I am very worried about the kind of world our child will be born into. I don't think it's possible for us, the people, to win against the communists. We should learn from the 1956

Hungarian Revolution when thousands of people died and still lost the fight," Dezső told my father.

On the night of August 21, we were woken by a horrendous noise. I looked out of the window and saw a multitude of tanks approaching the city from the train station. The house was vibrating from the speed of the heavy chain vehicles. I got scared, and my hands were shaking.

"What's going to happen now?" I asked Dezső.

"I don't know. We'll see in daylight."

At five in the morning, Dad came knocking on our door. "The radio said that everyone should go to work. Marika, promise me you won't say anything. Don't be a hero. Heaven forbid something happens to you."

"Dad, I'm not a child." I immediately regretted saying that to him, especially in such an irritated tone. I could have hugged him instead, and promised him that I would take care of myself. I ran after him and kissed his tear-soaked cheeks.

"Please, forgive me. I am scared."

"I know. I am, too."

That morning, the streets were full of people rushing to work. When we passed the post office, two tanks blocked both ends of the main street. Inside the factory, the security guard directed everyone to the backyard. By this time, the majority of the workers were there. Two men rolled a barrel in front of the crowd. They helped the director step up so everybody could see him.

"People! Last night the Russian army attacked our country. We cannot tolerate this. We had enough of dictatorship. We want to be free! We must fight for our rights. The dictatorship is very strong like never before. People are sitting in prison for criticizing the Communist regime. Now it's time for justice."

The workers applauded.

"Give us weapons!" someone yelled.

"We can't fight empty-handed."

"We don't need weapons!" another shouted.

"Every communist must be hanged."

That got the crowd excited. Everyone was shouting in unison, "Hang them, hang them!"

"Over there! There's the one to blame." The president of the Communist Party ran toward the office building. Many young workers wanted to catch him.

The director shouted at them, "Stop! Stop! This is not the way we want to win!"

People cooled off. They liked the director. He was a firm, old leader with good intentions. He ran the factory according to the old system.

"Now you all go to your stations and do your work, as though nothing has happened. The city leadership is having a meeting in the City Hall. We will receive orders from them. We need solidarity and discipline to be able to win. I believe in the victory."

We clapped and cheered.

"Victory, victory, victory!"

I could barely get through the door, as all of the technical controllers were in the office. My boss held a little radio in his hand so we could hear what was going on in the country. In Prague, several people got shot. The Russian soldiers fired shots into the crowd in Kassa where women and children had died. My boss was very upset.

"I hope we won't have to wait long for the order to abolish the invading troops." No one expressed enthusiasm.

"Can't you see what's at stake here?" my boss questioned.

"What do you want? What can we do?" said a young technician, interrupting our boss.

"You should be happy that we can finally fight for our freedom. Now Dubcek will lead us to victory."

I couldn't figure it out. As a member of the Communist Party, he was speaking against his own kind. Or maybe he was a member of the party only for the perks?

He turned to me and said, "Why are you looking so surprised? Are you happy that the Hungarians want to reoccupy this land? Well, don't be, because that will never happen! Go ahead, say what you are thinking!"

"I'm scared. I don't want to give birth among tanks."

An old, gray-haired coworker put his hand on my shoulder and reprimanded my boss.

"What do you want from her? She is pale and her hands are shaking. Do you want her to give birth right here? I can tell you what I think. Our army and its soldiers are the only ones who can liberate us. We can't fight tanks with pitchforks." My boss turned red.

"You are with us or against us!" Then a coworker said. "All over the streets, there are big signs: FOREVER WITH THE SOVIET UNION. LONG LIVE THE COMMUNIST PARTY! This has been our parade slogan for the last twenty years. We have never had decision privileges. We live as slaves. Do you want to know what I think? You are a slave owner yourself, because only a week ago, you were supporting the Communist regime. Now you are pretending to be one of us. You better not rush into it, because you are betting on the wrong horse by joining us. There's no way we can win. Let us remember 1956, the Hungarian bloody revolution!"

"Shut up! Who are you to criticize me?" my boss asked angrily.

"I am an old, experienced man who is retiring next month. If I'm right, I will come back, look you in the eye, and you may kiss my ass if I let you."

Everybody had a good laugh.

"Shut your mouth! You drank your brains away. Mark my words. The year 1968 will go down in golden letters in the history of the heroic Slovakian people. We are not Hungarians who never won in history. You are losers. In 1956, America didn't come to help you. Why would they? Why sacrifice even a single life for Hungarians? We don't need help from anybody. We are proud Slovaks, and we can beat all our enemies. Our patriotism and resilience will make the impossible possible."

It hurt me to hear him shame Hungarians in such a way. What was even more painful was that we had indeed lost many battles. I still believe we, Hungarians, are a heroic nation. We stood on the plains and looked the enemy in the eye. We didn't hide in the mountains. We fought with integrity.

The unfairness of life had gotten me down so much at that point that I started sobbing. I didn't want to, but I couldn't hold it in. My boss looked at me, irritated.

"What is it now?"

"I am mourning the dead who have died in our country for no reason. I don't understand, I really don't, why it is necessary to take life and cause enormous pain to the ones left behind."

The silence in the office was deafening. I felt weak. I laid my head on the desk and cried. My boss picked up the phone. He called the supervisor of the welding shop. Dezső came and walked me out to the fresh air.

In the afternoon, due to a power shortage, every store closed and the factories dismissed their workers. Now the tanks and combat cars were parked everywhere. Armed Russian soldiers were standing in front of the Communist Party main building and the City Hall. Passersby showed their fists and shouted vulgarities at them. We could hear from afar, "Hang the communists!" In the corner, an old man leaned on his cane, talking to himself.

"Every communist must be killed. Hang them all! They don't deserve to live. They took everything I had; they destroyed my life. Now their time has come."

Dezső touched the man's shoulder.

"Please, go home before somebody hurts you."

"I know, but it would be so good to see them suffer. They have done terrible things to us. They deserve to die." Dezső and

I hurried home so we could get to safety as quickly as possible. Mom was in front of the house. Her face was flushed as she came running towards us. She had an envelope in her hand. "Mom, what happened? Calm down." Dezső read the letter. Mom hugged me, crying. "The army called up Dezső." My head was spinning. Dezső had to pick me up and carry me inside. Mom was holding my hand. I could hear her praying. Dezső was kneeling by the bed. I could hear his voice from a distance.

"My dear, gather your strength, everything will be all right." Dad brought our family doctor. He gave me a sedative and wrote a certificate for the factory, justifying a two-week medical leave. Dezső had to report to the police station at eight in the evening. All night I prayed for my husband.

With Dad, we listened to Radio Liberty. The transmission was very bad, but we managed to hear what was going on in the country. Novotny, our former president, went to Moscow. People were hoping that, if anyone could do something for our country, it would be him. On the streets, people were signing papers with their demands and sending them to Prague. I was home, so I didn't sign any petition and I did not talk to anybody. In the major cities, the college students raised barricades and the communists were hiding. The party headquarters and city halls were all closed. The stores were open, and we resumed work in the factories.

Our baby was growing well. My weight was still two kilos less than when I had become pregnant. I ate cream of wheat, toasted bread, chicken, compote, and omelets, nothing else.

The days and weeks went by. I had no news from Dezső. By early October, the leaves were already changing colors. In the morning, I first stopped in the office because I had been typing all day for the security management. However, on that day, my boss needed me. The radio was blasting the news. You could only hear fragments of words because of the loud crackle coming through the airwaves. My boss came to me.

"This is the report on our work here. I must turn it in today. It's quite long. Hurry up so I can hand it in at two o'clock."

I opened the drawer and looked around in the closet, but I couldn't find any typing paper.

"I have to go to the warehouse," I said.

"You sit down. Zoli, get paper from the warehouse. Bring at least five packs." He turned the radio louder. "In the capital... shhhhhh... with stones... shhhhhh... several people... shhhhhh... the tanks... shhhhh... through the barricades... shhhhhh... dispersed the demonstra... shhhhhh... Moscow discussion... shhhhhh... the Hungarian army is waiting for orders... shhhhhh... border... shhhhhh."

Jano turned the radio off.

"I knew it. I knew that the Hungarians would come in. They are waiting at the border, hoping to take over this land. Well, that's not going to happen. We will make sure to crush their pride. I hate Hungarians and their nationalism."

At this time, I was the only Hungarian in the office. Everybody looked at me. I felt no fear and looked my boss in the eye.

"I hate you!" he said.

"Because I'm Hungarian, or you have other reasons, too?"

He jumped up, shouting at me.

"Shut up! You have no right to speak. You are Hungarian with capitalist blood in your veins." All of the men in the office froze. I stood up, placed my left hand on my huge stomach, and walked dramatically towards my boss. I swear, everybody thought I was going to hit him. He sat down. I leaned on his desk with both hands so I could see him eye to eye.

"Don't you ever speak to me like that again, because I will claw your eyes out. Yes, I am Hungarian and proud to be one. This land used to be Hungarian, whether you like it or not. You came here. Even my great-grandfather was born here, and you..."

"Shut up!"

"I won't! I peacefully live here with you on this land. I respect every nation. I learned the Slovakian language. Many people can't even tell that I'm Hungarian. I know your grammar better than you do. The capitalist father you mentioned, he taught me discipline, respect, and reliability, among other things. In our family, hatred doesn't exist. We build our lives on love." I straightened my back and walked out of the office, my head held high. I had the last word, but I was feeling remorseful. Neither Dezső nor Dad would approve of what I had just done, but I had to do it. Let him humiliate me I felt I must respound.

The cold wind swept up the fallen leaves forcefully. Dark clouds were circling above my head. I was cold. I knew I should go back for my coat. Suddenly, from every side, groups of workers and office staff came out of the buildings. One of my coworkers stopped by my side and shook my hand.

"Well done. You were right not letting yourself be put down. I am Slovak, but I agree with you. After you left, Jano didn't say a word. He grabbed his papers and went over to the director's secretary. Come, we are all going to the square. Someone is giving a speech."

"I have to go get my coat. I'll catch up with you."

I knew it was not very wise to be in the crowd with my big stomach. I might get pushed, or hit, but I was so curious what would happen. I planned to stay on the sidewalk, by the wall. I could barely move along the main street because everybody was rushing to the square. I heard a great explosion. The ground shook beneath me. I stood by the wall and watched people running in the opposite direction. Not far away, in front of the Communist Party's main building, a cloud of smoke rose to the sky.

"Hurray! Hurray! We did it!"

A bunch of people stood on the roof of the Communist Party building, flying our flag. I realized that they pushed down from the roof the huge neon sign saying FOREVER

WITH THE SOVIET UNION. That was what had made the explosion. People shouted, "Come everyone, let's tear down the statue of Lenin!" Father Lenin, who had ruined our lives with his communist ideology, stood on a tall pedestal. The crowd attacked him, and with ropes, pulled him down. People were euphoric. In the square, on the streets, everybody was marching in place and clapping. An exhilarating energy, an unstoppable force, spread through the air. It was an unforgettable experience. Then, the loudspeakers went on.

"Everybody, come to the square. The city leaders have important news to share."

As I reached the statue, I saw an old man bashing Lenin's head with the stone from the pedestal. A woman in her fifties watched a man as he teared out the statue's arm. The woman looked around, then tried to lift it, but it was too heavy. She grabbed the fingers on the arm and dragged it behind her. The men noticed and mocked her.

"Ma'am, wouldn't you rather take home a different body part? I'll be happy to cut it for you."

The laughter was barbaric and vicious. I stood under the post office roof, watching what was happening. The chief of police was the first to stand on the podium, with the council members and city Communist Party leaders. At the same time, armed police surrounded the crowd. A postman stood next to me.

"I think we lost. There is no chance that we can take charge of our destiny."

"Why do you think that?"

"Look around. They are afraid. They have bad news."

The chief of police took the microphone. "Comrades! We have good news for you. The mayor will give you a detailed report of the last days' events."

There was unbelievable silence on the square.

The mayor said, "I am happy to report that we won the fight with small bloodshed. Dubček and his partners were insidiously working hand in hand with the capitalist organs. They wanted to take away our freedom. Dubcek's party committed treason; they must be punished! We are thankful to the Soviet army..." He couldn't finish his sentence. The crowd was heading to the podium, shouting, "Traitors, you are the ones selling out our country! Let's hang them!"

"Stop! Don't do anything you will regret!" By this time, the people had already reached the podium. Our leaders were running into the office building behind them. They barely had time to close the door before the crowds swarmed it, all while the armed forces stood in front of it. The first-floor window opened and the police chief shouted, "I demand that everyone go home at once, or I'll have you shot!"

I stood by the wall, watching the reaction of the people. The police raised their weapons, ready to execute the order. Nobody moved. The chief shouted again, "Get going, this is my last warning." Then a pouring rain started. The crowd dispersed to each of the side streets. A couple of minutes later, the square was empty. Nobody was willing to die or get wet for freedom. My boss was in the crowd, too. He wasn't keen on being a hero. I didn't have a camera on me. I could have taken a photo of the barricaded building, and the brave, patriotic heroes. It would be an interesting addition to Dad's newspaper clippings of the 1956 revolution in Hungary where thousands of people died on the streets fighting for their freedom. As I was standing there, the rain slowed. I still stood under the roof watching the office building when the door opened. The chief of police stepped out with his gun and looked around carefully. Then he motioned the leaders inside to come out. They ran in every direction, like rats in the streets. The only thing that mattered to me at that point was for Dezső to return home safely.

The rain stopped. A few drunken men were walking on the street. I could hear from a distance someone calling my name. Dezső was running from the direction of the main street. His coat was unbuttoned, his face red. I couldn't run. I just waited for him with open arms. He was crying. I was laughing. How differently we react to happiness.

"I searched the whole factory. I couldn't find you. God, you gave me a fright."

"I was standing here by the post office wall, under the roof. I promised you I wouldn't put myself in any danger."

I watched his weary smile. Something had changed him. Soon, we got home. My parents were at their friends' house. In the hallway, he helped me take my coat and boots off.

"Are you hungry?" I asked him.

"I'm not hungry. I'd like to talk to you before your parents get home."

"Is something wrong?" He was holding my hand as we sat down on the sofa.

"Dear..."

He stood up and went over to the window. I could hear my heart pounding. I definitely felt something disturbed very much my husband. Finally, he turned to me.

"We are going to America."

"Where?"

"America. The Russian troops are here to stay and the dictatorship will be even stronger than before. Nobody knows what the future holds, but we can be sure that it's nothing good. The borders are open for now. There is chaos everywhere. We can leave the country tonight and live in a free world. Very soon things will settle and then we'll be stuck here forever. I don't mean to be dramatic, but if I may quote Petőfi: IT'S NOW OR NEVER."

He was serious, but he didn't once look me in the eye. He walked towards me, but I stood up. I couldn't breathe. I opened the window.

"I don't understand what you're saying. This is our home; this is where our ancestors were born. Dezső, this is our country, why would we leave?"

"We have no country. This is Czechoslovakia. They hate Hungarians. The Russians and the communists will run this country. I know they will blame us for everything in the 'Felvidék' area."

"Blame us? We didn't do anything wrong. Why?"

"Primarily for being Hungarian, religious, and noncommunist. They will say you are the daughter of capitalists, and they will accuse us of hating the Russians."

"You're wrong."

He was more disheartened than angry at my words. "I am not. I don't want our children to grow up without freedom, with chains on their necks, being scared all the time. Do you?"

I was cold. I closed the window and sat in the armchair next to the fireplace. I looked at the framed family photos on top of my piano, those of my grandparents, mom, and dad. Then I glanced at the oil paintings on the wall of beautiful landscapes, flowers, and the woodcuts that Szabó Gyula the academic painter gifted me as gratitude for my help with his exhibits. I shook my head and said, "No, no, it is impossible for me to leave. I'm very sorry that I can't agree with you, but look at me. I can't take on the world in this pregnant state. We don't have anyone in America. We don't speak the language. Where will I give birth to our baby? On the streets? Only a month from now, he will be with us. I don't want to be homeless."

"Marika, I will do everything…"

"Please, let me finish. Maybe life is better on the other side of the world, but we wouldn't have anyone there. I can't leave everyone behind who loves us and whom we love. Who will we turn to for help?"

Dezső walked to me and knelt.

"Please, listen to me. I know what I'm capable of, and you and our son will have everything you need. I beg you, let's go while we can."

"I can't. Our roots are here. Our children need the family;

they would never meet their grandparents. That love is more important than anything. Do you want to take all that away from them?"

He slowly stood up. "No, I don't. I want to give my children a better future in the free world. I know the beginning will be hard, but I also know that one day, you will be grateful we left this country."

"I believe we can be happy here. I don't care about wealth. My parents were poor and we always lived happily. There is good and bad everywhere. Don't think for a second that America is a perfect world."

"That's true, but there are no communists, no dictatorship, and they don't lock you up for saying what you believe. You have no idea what the communists are capable of."

"I don't care. This is my home." I stood up. I was about to cry and I hated women who tried to win an argument with tears. I couldn't look at my husband. I felt sorry for him that I was being so stubborn.

Mom had brought the laundry in before the rain and put it on our bed. I went into the bedroom and started folding the clothes. Dezső followed me. He stood in the middle of the room watching me.

After a bit, he said, "Please sit down. I'd like to tell you a story. I was eight years old hiding behind my mother, clutching her skirt. I can still feel the numbness in my fingers from holding on so tight. I was terrified that day when my family lost everything during the time of nationalization. The police were beating our horses with whips because they wouldn't go out from the stable. My mother cried, and my father stood by the gate. I remember him saying:

"Sergeant, please don't take this one. He's too old, he will die on the road." He was my father's favorite stallion. The sergeant shot the horse without giving it a second thought. My father was a strong man, but he knelt down next to his beloved horse, stroked it, and wept. I stepped out from behind my mother and kicked the sergeant, pounding on his chest with my fists. My mother pulled me away when he pointed his gun at me. She stepped in front of me.

"Please, don't harm him. He's only a child," she said.

"I don't give a damn. He will end up hanging somewhere anyway." I got tears in my eyes. I could see the image before me."

I felt for him. I said, "Dezső, I know that terrible things happened in those days. The communists took everything from our family, too. They shaved my father's head and nearly beat him to death for speaking in Hungarian on the street."

"Honey, let me finish my story. They kicked my father, spat on him, and he died a week later. My mother was left alone with four boys. At the age of ten I was already reaping in the JRD (state owned agricultural cooperative) every dawn so we would have food on the table. We spent all autumn gathering twigs in our own forest for what we had to pay for, so we could have a warm room in wintertime. I will never forgive these things. I'm not telling you my story so you will be sorry for me, but because it could happen again. After sixteen years, I still see my father weeping, my mother's trembling hands, and the eyes of the dying horse. I want to forget this scene but it is so deep wound in my soul, in my heart I can' forget. The communists did that to us, and now they are getting the executive power. Fifteen years is a very short time in history. They confiscated everything from the people. We are equally poor now and the leaders squandered all. Look at what the country has become; it's miserable. They deserve to be hanged, but if we say anything, we will be the ones hanged." I stood up and hugged him.

"Dear, we must forgive in order to be happy. Anger will poison your life. You and I are strong. Even here, we manage to secure everything that our family needs. I don't care what kind of 'ism' we live in."

"That's where you are wrong. You cannot live in communism.

You cannot have your own desires. You cannot have your own identity, your own will. The idea that everyone is the same is nonsense. Yes, we are all humans, but we have different needs, tastes, and lifestyles. If I don't agree with the Marxist doctrine, I'm the enemy. The communist membership is worth more than a doctorate. There is no honor, no respect in this country. I can assure you, we are already on their blacklist."

I listened to his words, but I knew I was not going anywhere. I was thinking how to convince my husband to stay. For the first time in our relationship, I planned to go against his will. I loved him above everything. I had sworn eternal love to him only a year ago.

I spoke in a calm voice, "Who knows if everything you said will happen? And even if it will, I still want to live here. Trust me, there is a lot we can do in our own environment, with our strong will and with our friends. We can prove that we are not the enemy of our own country."

Dezső walked to the door. "You don't need to go on," he said. "We'll stay. I love you more than life itself. I will always stay by your side."

He opened the door and looked back at me. "I also promise that I will never hold this day against you. Whatever happens, I will not blame you for the consequences." I wanted to hug him, but he wouldn't let me. "I have to stoke up the stoves or the fire will go out."

I knew I hadn't won the argument, but that wasn't my goal. I knew, in this situation, my decision was the right one.

The following month, Dezső spent long hours in the factory. They worked on an innovation with the construction crew. Then he had a special welding project. In the evenings, he made sketches at home, trying to find alternatives. He truly enjoyed his work and our life continued as though nothing had happened between us. He could hardly wait for his son to be born. He kept his hand on my belly all night, and whenever he felt something, he put his ear on it.

Life in the city returned to normal. The tanks disappeared, but the people were scared. The Communist Party was in charge in the country. Our factory director was sitting in jail. Most of our engineers and other individuals from the leadership were downgraded to ordinary workers. If the Communist committee called somebody for a hearing, one could be sure something had been found to implicate them. I was on maternity leave, waiting for the baby to be born. I sat in the kitchen with Mom and Dad when Dezső got home. He looked at me with a worried face.

"Please, don't be alarmed about this," he said.

Mom stopped crocheting. "My God, what happened?"

Dad put his hand on Mom's shoulder. "Dear, let Dezső speak."

"Tomorrow morning at ten o'clock, the committee wants to talk with Marika. I tried to arrange it for after the birth, but your boss, who is the president of this committee, didn't approve it. It will be a short thing, they only have a few questions to ask you. They said it is very important that they talk to you now, because starting January first the factory will be under completely new management. Only trustworthy people can continue working in the offices." I was shocked to find that my boss wanted to talk to me. He knew that I did nothing against the Russians.

"Honey, you didn't sign anything. Please don't worry."

"That is true, but I could have a problem because my boss hates Hungarians."

"I know, but with your intelligence, you will answer their questions easily. The important thing is to stay confident. You can do this!"

The Hearing

The next morning, my footsteps were echoing in the empty corridor as I headed to the conference room. Walking up the stairs, I saw a few of my coworkers talking in front of the door.

"Hurry up, they are waiting for you," one said.

"It's five to ten. I'm right on time."

As I stepped into the room, I found myself face to face with thirteen committee members. They were sitting behind a long table covered with a red tablecloth, and each had piles of files towering in front of them. I said hello, but none of them bothered to answer. My boss, who sat in the middle, had become the new Communist Party president of the factory. A spinster sat next to him. I recognized her from the production hall; she used to clean around the machines. I didn't know any of the others. Finally, my boss looked at me.

"It was very important that we called you in for this hearing despite the fact that it is unpleasant in your state. We are aware of that, but the best interest of the factory must remain our top priority. We must find out who are the reliable people, who we can trust and work with. We will try to keep the hearing short." He turned to the woman sitting next to him. "Comrade Ilona, please address the first question."

"May I get a chair? I can't stand. I get easily dizzy," I interrupted.

My boss turned red. "Get her a chair!"

A young communist walked over to the back of the room, with slow steps. He looked upset about the trouble of getting the chair. I thanked him, but he did not answer. I took my time taking my coat off, then folded my scarf and sat down. I looked up to indicate that I was ready for their questions.

"Comrade, how did you feel on the night that the Soviet tanks rushed to our aid?"

"I was scared."

"Could you expand on that?"

"That feeling cannot be expanded. Maybe, let's say, I was very scared." My boss tapped the table with his pencil, and then asked, "What was your reaction? How did you act?"

"At home, I sat on the bed and held my husband's hand. In the office, I acted the same way as you did, if you remember it."

"Enough! This is a hearing, not a friendly chat. What I want to know is whether you passed judgment on the Soviet army."

"It didn't cross my mind. All my thoughts were focused on my husband. They had called him to join the army. I was so scared what would happen if he got killed."

"So you claim that you don't hate the Soviet Union, not even in your thoughts?"

"I don't hate anyone in my thoughts, words, or actions. Bring me a witness who ever heard me express hatred." The silence was tense. My boss spoke again, running his fingers through his greasy hair.

"You are Hungarian. You speak Hungarian in your home. Why? You eat Slovak bread."

"I work hard for the Slovak bread I eat. I am Hungarian because my parents are Hungarian. I can't change that. Since I live here in Slovakia, I respect this nation; I speak the Slovak language just as well as the Hungarian. I'm a hardworking, law-abiding citizen."

A bald man, whom I didn't know, looked up from his papers. He slid his glasses down his nose and gave me a scrutinizing look.

"Your father was a capitalist exploiter," he boldly said and just looking at me.

I started to lose my temper. "What's the question? Everyone knows that. It is not a secret."

"Indeed, everyone knows that, but what we don't know is whether you condone or condemn the fact that we took your father's scrounged up fortune, and now it belongs to all of us."

This knocked the air out of me.

"Answer my question!"

"It's hard for me to answer, because until the age of fourteen, I didn't know that my father had a fortune or that it had been taken from him. I was raised surrounded by love and I never felt that I was missing anything in my life. One thing is certain: my father is greatly respected in this town as one of the best professionals of our community. Having grown up an orphan, everything he had, he earned through hard work. He didn't scrounge up anything. He didn't get anything for free. He didn't steal and he didn't lie."

Comrade Ilona started tapping with her pencil. "We are not interested in your family history."

"Then don't pass judgment on my father if you don't know the circumstances. My father trained many apprentices in his profession. A few of them work right here in this factory and they can attest to the kind of man he was. Besides, those men are the best specialists in this factory. You can easily verify that." I took a deep breath, and then continued, "My father didn't take anything from anyone. He helped widows and orphans, and he made donations because he never forgot his past."

My voice quavered. I could feel my anger rising. I wouldn't tolerate anyone offending my father. I continued in a shaky voice, "Not every capitalist is a bad person, just like not every communist is a good one. Wouldn't you agree, comrades?"

The committee was in shock. One of the men spoke. "Your family's history clearly indicates that you were not raised as an enemy of the state."

"We still can't trust her!" my boss interjected.

"Let's take a vote. Who votes for?" I looked at the thirteen faces before me. They didn't know what to do.

"Nobody trusts her?"

Six men put their hands up. My boss smiled victoriously. I stood up, admitting defeat.

"Who is against?"

Three raised their hands, including my boss, the woman next to him, and the evil, bald guy. The woman jumped up from her seat.

"What's the matter?"

A member in the row asked.

"Last call, who abstains?" Four raised their hands.

"The hearing is over. The committee finds comrade Maria Imre trustworthy," Comrade Ilona announced.

I walked down the stairs sad, knowing that these people would be in charge of our lives. It was atrocious. As I was walking, I noticed my old, Hungarian coworker coming out of the personnel office. He looked at me inquisitively.

"Did they break your neck?"

"Almost, but in the end, they couldn't."

"Thank God. It would have been a shame. As of today, I'm retired. I thought I would say goodbye to our boss, but I won't. He is a very wicked and deceitful man. If you can, after your maternity leave, I advise you to request to be transferred to another department. That asshole will make your life hell."

"Thank you. I hope we will meet in the town, so I can buy you a drink and have a chat."

* * *

I was supposed to meet Dezső in the cafeteria, but he wasn't there. The supervisor shouted from behind the counter, "Marika, Dezső left a message for you. The new director called him to his office. He will meet you at home."

Mom and Dad were walking in front of the house when I got home.

"Good or bad news?" they asked.

"It's all good. Now the new director is interviewing Dezső. Hopefully he will bring some good news, too."

Two hours later, Dezső arrived. His eyes had a sky-blue sparkle, and his smile revealed something very good had happened.

"Honey, I heard the good news. I'm so proud of you." He kissed me and listened to his son's heartbeat. "Now, you guys make yourselves comfortable. I'll tell you an interesting story."

He pulled a chair next to the stove so he could face us.

* * *

Dezső began, "Today with Marika, we had a very dangerous, nerve-racking day. She did well, thanks to God. At eleven o'clock, my supervisor came to tell me that the director wanted to see me. I was sure it was some misunderstanding, so I didn't even take my welding apron off. What could the new director want from a proletarian welder? So, I went to the administration building and walked into the secretary's office. The nicest surprise of all was that it was Anna, the old secretary, who greeted me. She had a bright smile when she saw me."

"They didn't lock you up with the director?" I asked her.

"She laughed, and said, 'the night the tanks came in, I was taken to the emergency room with a gall-bladder attack. I had surgery that night and spent the critical next week in the hospital, so I wasn't involved in anything."

"Perfect timing. I was serving as a soldier in the army that time, so I didn't ruin my future children's political background. What's the new director like?"

"Hard to tell. This is his second week. He was relocated from Martin. He is a communist engineer with a very calm personality. He doesn't know anyone in the factory or in town. He's struggling to assemble a new management team," she shared.

"Do you know why he wants to see me?"

"He's been seeing many people every day."

"The door opened, and a middle-aged, short man stepped in. He had a warm smile. We shook hands."

"I'm Lipták Jozef, the new director of the factory," he said.

"I'm Imre Dezső, welder. I believe I can stand by my position in any circumstances," I told him, and he patted my shoulder.

"You see, Anna, this is the kind of person we need, with a healthy sense of humor. Optimism can heal the wounds of this country. Anna, will you please bring us two strong coffees? I have a bad headache."

"The office looked the same as before. We sat next to the coffee table. He picked up a thick file from the table; I could see my name on it. Then, he sat down across from me. He flipped through the papers. Anna came and put the two espressos, mineral water, and a bowl of crackers on the table. The director took a sip of the coffee and looked at me. He said, 'Yesterday evening this file landed in my hand. Do you know why?"

"I have no idea."

"Do you see all those files on my conference table? My secretary keeps bringing them over from the personnel office."

"He stood up and put my file in with the rest, then asked if I could see anything interesting about it."

"My file is the thickest," I said.

"Exactly. I thought, that's either a good sign or a bad one."

"That's true. I never thought there could be so much written about a simple man such as myself."

"Can you tell me why a qualified technician would become a welder?"

"I recently got married. We are expecting our first child and we need the money. Welders earn more."

"Interesting perspective. I see here that you also completed the three years' toolmaker apprentice school. At that time, you were already working on inventions for the factory. That's why they sent you to the industrial school. I can't understand how you can stand to work as a welder, where you can't use your brain."

"Sometimes the brain needs to rest. I have plenty to think about, planning my family's future, and I do enjoy welding. I don't mean to brag, but I am the best welder in the factory."

"Yes, I read about that, too. In the industrial school, you were the president of the CSISZ (Czechslovák Ifjúsági Szövetség). The school principal himself wrote a reference about you. You graduated with merits; you have exceptional organizational and strong communication skills. Now you are telling me that you enjoy welding. Forgive me for saying this, but I don't believe you. Your unfortunate political background derived from your parents' lives, which is not your fault, and it is not my focus, either. I believe you can be a great help to me, especially now that your wife's been found trustworthy by the committee."

"My wife is a smart, strong woman. I'm proud of her. We are expecting our first child in two weeks."

"Congratulations," he said, then finished his coffee, drank the water, and ate a cracker. 'You and I are quite similar, except that I'm 52 and you are 26. I don't think our country abounds with many young men like yourself, whom I can trust with one of the most serious job in this factory, running the military plant.'"

"He didn't take his eyes off of me. He wanted to read me, to see what was going on in my mind, but I didn't let him. I sat relaxed, sipping my coffee, then I had my water and ate a cracker. He smiled. My brain was computing. Should I accept or not? I knew that I was more than capable of doing the job. I thought to myself that if they ever fired me from this high position, because of my political view, then I could freefall into a pit so deep that I would never be able to claw myself out of it."

Dezső paused, and Dad interrupted, unable to take the suspense anymore. "Son, say you said yes."

"My pride and my ambition ended up winning. To stop torturing you, yes, I did say yes. I could almost hear as the weight lifted off of the director's chest. He stood up, extended his hand, and said: 'For me, a handshake seals the deal. I am confident that we will make a great team together. I will let the personnel office know that we struck a deal. Please sign the papers and I'll see you tomorrow morning at six.'"

Dezső continued, "I thanked him for his confidence in me, and before leaving, I asked for a favor. I told him how we are living in a tiny room in my wife's parents' house, and how we can't even fit a crib for our soon-to-be born child. I asked if there is any way he can help to get an apartment for us. He told me that soon the factory residences will be ready for handover, and he will, of course, look into it. Then we shook hands again, and now I'm here. What a day I had. In life, things can change in the blink of the eye."

THE NEWBORN

From the day Dezső accepted the manager position, our lives completely changed. He would leave home before five in the morning and not return until dinner. Seeing him happy and excited, I no longer felt guilty for not agreeing to escape to America.

On the first of December, Dezső barely made it to work on time. He wanted to stay with me because I didn't sleep well. Mom said, "With the first baby, it could take up to one, two days before the baby is born." By midday, I had strong pain, so I walked around the room, stopping by the window. Big snowflakes were falling. The pain was becoming more frequent.

"Mom, I think I'd better go to the hospital. Dad can't take me. There is over 20 cm of snow on the road."

We crossed the square, as I held, or rather clutched, Mom's arm. We were only two or three minutes away from the hospital when I nearly fainted. I had to kneel in the snow for a while, but, in the end, we made it to the maternity ward. The doctor said the birth would most likely occur during the night. The nurses were encouraging me to walk vigorously up and down the corridor to help open my cervix.

By eight in the evening, I couldn't take it anymore. I knelt in the corner of the room, grasping the central heating pipes. At ten o'clock, the nurse came to check on me. She said we were still far from the goal. It was midnight when I felt a sharp pain under my belly, and my water broke. Nine minutes past midnight, our son, Attila, was born. The date was December 2, 1968. When I held him in my arms, I could barely see him through my tears. The love of the mother knows no bounds. It is the most sublime and powerful feeling in the world. On the third morning, the doctor found everything to be okay and discharged us. Dezső called me, saying he would pick us up at noon because he couldn't find a taxi earlier than that.

"Why isn't Dad coming?" I questioned.

"Because we all won't fit in that small car."

"Mom doesn't need to come; we will meet her at home."

"She wants to come. Marika, it's already decided," Dezső told me.

* * *

Dezső carried his son, stepping firmly in the snow. Attila was wrapped so tightly in his wool swaddle that you couldn't see his little face. The taxi drove off, and at one point I realized, it had passed our street.

"Where are we going?"

"It is a surprise," he responded.

"Driving around the town in this cold with a newborn baby is not a good idea."

The taxi stopped. I looked out and noticed that we were in front of our factory's new apartment building.

"Welcome to our home."

"Wow!" I said, completely shocked. "You are the best!"

"You can't imagine how hard your mom and I have worked to have it all ready for today. Are you happy?"

"Yes! It's like a dream. In only three days, I have become a mother, and now we are walking into our very own home."

Our condominium was on the first floor. My husband, with a ceremonial gesture, opened the door.

"Honey, you should be the first to enter our little family nest," he said. As I walked in, I could see my mother's touch everywhere. The midday sunshine inundated the rooms with warm light. On the table were a big bouquet of red carnations and a bottle of champagne. I could see the snow-white crocheted blanket my mom made for the crib. Then, all of a sudden, I felt like I stepped into cold water. My slippers were filled with brown, sewer smelling liquid. I took a step back and noticed that our new home was standing in 10-15 cm of water. The carpets were floating on top, along with pieces of toilet paper and feces. The water waded through the open door and ran out into the corridor.

"Dezső, do something!"

"I don't know what to…"

He began throwing up and wanted to run into the toilet. That's when we realized that everything flushed in the nine floors above us came out of our toilet. I broke out in a cold sweat. I gathered all of my strength and went into the room. I opened the balcony door to create another outlet for the water. Although it was disgusting, I took the smaller rugs and put them up on the balcony rails. I looked around. Above ankle level, everything looked so beautiful. Then, the toilet started bubbling again, flooding us with more disgusting, thick water. I wondered what moron was flushing cleaning cloths or plastic baby food containers down the toilet. Dezső stood in the corridor, still vomiting. My parents were sitting with Attila on a bench close to the elevator. I walked to them, my slippers full of stinking water. It was disgusting. I sat down next to my dad. Attila was sleeping in his arms. Mom cried.

"I'm going to find a taxi. There is nothing to do," she said.

My husband came to us. "Dad, I will just run home to change. The disgusting water is leaking out of my shoes every time I take a step and I can feel the slime between my toes. I can't get into the taxi like this." Dezső had reflux again, but, by that point, his stomach was empty. I couldn't imagine how he would manage to get home in the freezing temperatures.

That evening, he got home at nine, and he was very depressed. The director gave him four men to dig up the soil around the sewer pipe. Cleaning the clogging took three days. We had to go stay in my mom's house. It was my first time experiencing the biblical Christmas story as a mother. I held our baby son and watched the flickering candlelight, the shooting star on top of the tree, the three kings, Mary, Joseph, and baby Jesus under the tree, all surrounded by the animals. It completed the historical day when our Savior was born. Everyone dressed up nicely. Dad and Dezső joined us at the table in suits and ties. The family is an immeasurable value, the cradle where we are safe, we love, where people rejoice, cry together, and stand by each other. The warmth of the home is where we return to rest, where our dreams are born and fulfilled. Dad often said to me:

"Marika, if you have a loving family, you have everything. Never forget our family. Use it as a compass! Raise your children with love, teach them to respect and value the principles of life. Love your husband as you love yourself. Believe me, wherever you may be in this world, family and your home are the greatest assets you can ever have."

By the end of March, we had finally moved into our apartment. I could hardly wait for the first evening, when I could make my husband dinner all on my own. We could talk, just the two of us, and tend to our son together. I loved watching Dezső's fatherly side, as he played with Attila.

I fell in love with him all over again. He brought me flowers with hidden messages. He became cheerful and attentive. I was a veritable wife and mother. I cooked, ironed, cleaned the house, took care of our house plants, and served my husband every evening as I had seen Mom do for my Dad. I set the table beautifully, with good food made with love. Dezső kissed my hand after meals.

"Blessed be these hands that prepared our meal."

We talked a lot. Sometimes we didn't agree on all matters. To Dezső, everything was simple.

"Honey, you over-complicate things," he would tell me.

"That may be true, but I enjoy it when I come up with different, unique things which reflect my personality."

"You are right."

"It's not about being right, I like discovering exciting possibilities. I know you enjoy my complicated solutions, too."

"Yes, my dear. Opposites attract." He laughed, then hugged and kissed me for everything. His blue eyes were shining at me all the time.

One April afternoon in the park, when Attila was asleep from all of the swinging, we walked over to the little island. Dezső kept glancing at me.

"Is something wrong?" he asked.

"What makes you say that?"

"Because I know you. You are pale, can't sleep."

I sat closely by his side and started to cry.

"Dezső, do you realize that in one week I have to go back to work? Attila will be raised by strangers in the nursery. My heart breaks."

"Being with other people will be good for him."

"How can you say that? He will catch every disease. He won't hear his mother tongue, only the Slovak language."

"Our son will learn both languages at the same time, which will help him greatly, later on in his life." We were silent. I didn't know what to say. This conversation was another example of just how simply Dezső saw everything. He turned to me and said, "Is there another way to manage this problem? What do you want to do?"

"There is nothing else I can do."

"You see my dear? You are over-complicating things again. Other children are doing just fine. Attila will love it, too."

"I'm also tormented by how things will work out with my boss, after everything that went down between us."

"I think you can have a fine relationship, as long as you want it. You are not a good actress because you can't hide it if you dislike someone. In this case, you don't have that luxury. Just be neutral. If you do your job well, everything will be okay."

"I am incapable of working with him."

"I have to remind you, we cannot afford to make enemies. One wrong word and we have a lot to lose now. It's a give and take. You are a smart woman who knows what she wants to achieve in this country. Please think about that. I'm sure you know what I am talking about."

"I know exactly what you mean. Yes, I must put up with him because I was the one who wanted to stay here."

He did not comment on my remark.

THE DISAPPOINTMENT

On Monday morning, to my great surprise, Attila was smiling in the nursery when the nurse took him from me. This was a positive start of the day that made me happy. I walked to the factory, and with forced optimism, I stepped into the office. It was a little early still, but my boss sat behind his desk. I couldn't see him behind the cigarette smoke and the newspaper he held in front of him.

"Good morning," I said.

He lowered the newspaper just enough to see who had walked in. I assume he said hello, but I could barely hear him, and then he went back to reading. I opened the drawer on my desk, but someone else's things were in it.

"Jano, which one is my desk?"

He put the paper down and looked at me odiously.

"You don't have a desk here."

"What do you mean?"

"How do you even dare to come into this office after what happened between us? I can't even breathe the same air with you."

"Well, you have to. I have the right to my job, by law."

"You don't have any rights. Go and get the other job because I don't have work for you." I felt humiliated. I stood before him, frozen. I didn't know what to do.

"Why are you standing there? Do you want me to kick you out? I hate you and all Hungarians."

I forced myself to remain calm as I sat down at my former desk. I called the director's office.

"Hello Anna, Maria Imre speaking. I have a problem. I would like to see the director. When will that be possible?"

"Come in half an hour, he can see you then." I went to Dezső's office. He was surprised to see me.

"Is it that bad?" he asked.

"It is."

I told him what had happened. I couldn't even see any sign of anger on his face.

He went with me to see the director. When we arrived, the director greeted us. Dezső immediately got to the point.

"Director, I would like to introduce you to my wife, Maria."

"Dezső, call me by my name, as always. I'm pleased to meet you, Maria."

"With regards to a very unpleasant matter…"

"Say no more. The president of the Communist Party told me what happened."

"Can I tell you my side of the story?"

"You could, Maria, but there is no point to it. He doesn't want to work with you. Nobody can force a Communist Party leader to do anything that he doesn't want to do. Believe me, that will end up hurting you. Between you and me, it's very disappointing that this is the behavior of a communist leader, but this man can ruin your future. The law is on your side, but I recommend you just peacefully step aside, and I will find you a different job."

Dezső turned to me, but before he could speak, the director put his hand on Dezső's shoulder.

"Dezső, there's nothing else I can do. My authority is less than that of a communist leader. I hope this unpleasant matter doesn't ruin our relationship. Shake my hand, no hard feelings."

They shook hands. I walked to the door.

"Goodbye. Thank you for your advice," I said.

There was no irony in my voice. For me, what had happened was a valuable lesson. My husband knew long ago that in this system things work like this, but I didn't believe him.

In the corridor, he hugged me. He felt sorry for me, and that annoyed me.

"We will talk it over at home," he said.

"I don't think there is anything left to talk about."

I knew then that I must prove at all costs that the system was not going to destroy me. The director found me a job, folding blueprints. It was very offensive, but I got paid very well.

THE NEW BEGINNING

In the afternoon, I picked Attila up from the nursery. When he saw me, he raised his hand and almost flew into my arms. It was a cloudy day. Pushing the stroller, submerged in my thoughts, Jónás Pali, the rabbi, walked toward me.

"Hello. I took some pastries and bread to your apartment. I baked them myself for our synagogue."

"Thanks, Pali, you are such a good friend."

"What's wrong? You look very embittered."

"I'm in a lot of trouble. I lost my job. I want to leave the factory, but there is nowhere to go."

"Come. Let's sit down in the coffee shop."

I told him in detail everything that had happened to me. He was famous for helping people. The Germans had killed his entire family. They had a big bakery. Pali's mother convinced him to join the army since there he could hide from the Gestapo and have a better chance of staying alive. When the Germans occupied the town, they evacuated Pali's entire family into the yard. They had to bring out the wood tables and shelves, and pile them up. The soldiers set a fire. The family stood around it and they got shot. Pali came home and found his daughter's half-burned shoe in the ashes. That's all that was left of his family. He ran out to the street with yellow stars all over his clothes.

"Shoot me. I'm a Jew."

People thought he had lost his mind. A couple of families hid him in their basements or lofts. When the war ended, he got the rabbi position in my town. He believed he was meant to stay alive, so he could make the world a better place. He was close friends with my father. I knew him from a very young age. He was like my grandpa.

When I told him my story, he took my hand. "Don't worry, I'll find you a job that they will envy."

Attila started fussing.

"Pali, I have to go. Thank you for listening."

* * *

When I got home, Dezső was already waiting for us. I hugged him with a smile.

"What happened?"

"I told Pali my story. He said he'll find me a good job."

"That's great."

A week later, I sat with Pali in our favorite coffee-cake shop at four in the afternoon waiting for someone who would get me a job. Pali ordered three brandies, three coffees, and a slice of cake for me.

A handsome man walked in. He must have been a well-known person because many people waved at him. He gave them a smile and came to our table.

"Let me introduce you to Maria Imre, she is a Regina girl."

"I'm Velky Vlado, the marketing vice president of the restaurant company," he said as he held my hand. "We have met before, don't you remember?"

He laughed loudly. Pali was surprised.

"You two know each other?"

"I have to tell you this story."

He sat down and raised his glass for a toast.

He said, "I moved to this city when I was nineteen. I had two jobs, one of them, delivering newspapers early in the morning. At that time, a machine shop owner on the main street was already in his office. He was famous for being a good professional and a very strict man with his apprentices. I took his papers to the office. He praised me, shook my hand, and gave me a tip."

"He told me to be proud of myself, as I was a young man who was already up and working at five in the morning. He said I would surely be a successful man. After that, every time he was in his shop, I stopped in his office and he gave me a tip. One day, we met on the street, as he walked towards me with his daughter in his arms. He proudly introduced me to his one-year-old daughter. That was you. We are no strangers; we've known each other over twenty years."

Vlado laughed. He slurped up his coffee and broke off a piece of cake with his hand.

"Let's get to the point. You are in luck, Maria. Someone just retired from the technical department. He was in charge of the maintenance and acquisition of restaurants, hotel equipment, and kitchen appliances. I believe that job fits you like a glove. The technical director is my friend. I'm sure we can offer you this job. Do you want it?"

"Yes, very much."

"Tomorrow afternoon around three, come to my office. Fero, your future boss, will tell you the details."

He broke off another piece of cake and drank his mineral water.

"I must run. I'm already late for a meeting."

"Vlado, thanks for your help," Pali said.

"Pali, it's nothing compared what you did for me."

"Connections are what you need in this country. Maria, do you see that big gate across the street? That's where you have to go tomorrow. The Restaurant company executive board is in the Orava courtyard. You will work there."

* * *

The following year was full of events. Dezső worked on a prototype. In autumn, the factory engineers tested the winch system for tanks, in the presence of military officers. The invention worked perfectly. They celebrated in the STAR restaurant. The director raised his glass to future successes.

"We discussed with the management what reward you should get for your excellent work. A diploma for the professional merit and 2,000 Korona bonuses or…? I had an idea, and there is something else that would make you happier."

He placed a crane engine startup key in front of Dezső. He looked it, then at the director. Everybody laughed.

"No. I am not giving you a crane; I just didn't have any other key around. Imagine this is a four-bedroom condominium key."

"Thank you. You are right, this make me very happy, but I have one request. I would like to be on the highest floor in the building. I don't want to swim in feces." The director had a good laugh and told the apartment story to everybody.

When Dezső came home, he waltzed with me around the room.

"Now we can start working on a baby girl."

"Yes," I agreed.

I loved my new job. My boss and I were the same age. With all of the colleagues, the technical department worked together like a family. From the start, they involved me in serious, responsible jobs. We remodeled an old pub into a four-star bar. After much planning, I got the green light to buy all of the technology and furniture for it. I worked a lot, but I enjoyed it. One day, before the grand opening, I sat down in the bar and closed my eyes. When I opened them, the place gave off a very elegant impression. There was a round fountain in the center of the room, and paintings of vibrant tropical flowers decorated the walls. The tables for two were under the palm trees, while the booths along the walls were ideal for larger groups.

Vlado came in and told me, "You did a good job. I like it. I'm sure tomorrow will be a big success. I'm happy for you."

In the morning, I went to the bar to see if everything was ready for the grand opening. The waiters were arranging various cookies on platters. Others were preparing shots of vodka for the toast. I felt that the WINTER GARDEN would be a favorite place for many people. I still had two hours until the opening ceremony. Dad hadn't been feeling well for days. Their house was nearby, so I decided to check on him. I found Mom crying in the kitchen.

"Dad coughed all night. I am very worried for him."

When I stepped into the bedroom, Dad forced a smile on his pale face.

"How was the opening?"

"It will be at ten o'clock."

"I wish I could be with you."

"When you feel better, I'll invite you for a glass of Hungarian peach liquor. Isn't that your favorite?"

"It is." He coughed again. Mom gave him warm tea with honey and lemon.

"Dad, I am going to call the doctor. If he can't come, then we'll take you to the emergency room."

By the time I was able to talk to the doctor, it had gotten late. The invited guests were already inside the opening. Dezső waited in front of the bar. The security guard was nervous.

"Everybody is looking for you. The director already started his speech."

I could see the director waving at me. He said, "Let's welcome comrade Maria Imre. I would like to thank you for your hard work. You really have done a wonderful job here. In the name of the Restaurant company board, I give you this letter of recognition and a bonus. Keep up the good work. Now, please, enjoy the party. The bar is open until noon, and all food and drinks are on the house! After that, we open the door to the public."

The guests cheered enthusiastically. Vlado came to me. He said, "I'm sorry you weren't here when the guests stepped in. They were all in awe. Everybody loves it. Now, let me bring your attention to a private matter. Lately I've been seeing your husband in the company of Kati in the grill bar. She is a dangerous woman, slender, barely girl. I've been watching them for a while now, and she is laughing and flirting with your husband."

"Don't be silly. Kati is my best friend."

"Whatever you say. I'm only warning you."

He ruined my mood. How could he even think such a thing of my husband? I went over to our table. Kati hugged me.

"I've been waiting for you. Congratulations, the place looks amazing; we will be coming here for coffee. I have to catch the bus now, though. I made a big grocery shopping for my mother."

"We actually have to go, too; I have to take my father to the doctor."

"Give him my best. I'll bring over some honey tomorrow that my parents prepared for him." I sat down for a few minutes and had a coffee with my boss, his wife, and Dezső. When we got to my parents' home, we found Mom kneeling by Dad's bed.

"He's gone. How am I going to live without him?" I knelt too and rested my head on my father's chest. There was silence. Childhood memories, hugs, and carefree laughter all flashed through my brain. I could hear his voice say, "My darling Marika." I couldn't catch my breath between my sobs. Dezső helped me up and kissed my father's hand.

"It is going to be hard without him. He was an exceptional man," Dezső said. The old Hungarian families of the town and many of my coworkers, even Dezső's director, came to the funeral. Reverend Tóth Zoltán, who had been my father's friend for forty years, said the last words on behalf of our family.

LIFE AND DEATH

I visited my father's grave daily, bringing Attila with me. I felt like half of my soul had wandered somewhere with him. Dezső empathized with me, but I wanted to be alone with my memories.

On a windy, cold, autumn day I left Attila with mom and went to the cemetery. I sat on the bench when I saw Pali coming up the hill. He looked serious as he sat next to me.

"I must talk to you. Don't get me wrong, but what you are doing is wrong. Sitting every day next to your father's grave doesn't make a point. You must face it: the one thing in life that we cannot change is death. Death is irrevocable. It is an immense pain to lose someone we love, but no matter what we do, we cannot bring them back. Neglecting your family is painful to them. They are alive; they need you. If your father is looking down from heaven, he must be sad. You are very selfish now. Think about it." I felt ashamed. I shivered in the cold wind.

"Let's go home. This wind goes right through our bones." We walked down the hill, without talking. Before we went our separate ways, I took Pali's hand and said, "I am very grateful for your true friendship, for all of the advice and help. I behaved badly. Dezső never hurt my feelings."

"Your husband loves you unconditionally. Cherish it."

When I got home, Dezső and Attila were playing with toy cars. They smiled at me.

"Can I play with you?" I asked. They both jumped up and hugged me.

"Dear, your hands are frozen. Come, Attila, let's warm

your mother's hands." He was rubbing my fingers with his tiny hands. Dezső turned away and wiped his tears with his sleeve.

"Mommy, is that good? Should I do more?" I picked him up.

"You did a very good job. I love you very much."

Dezső left the room and returned shortly. He said, "For days, I've been waiting for the right moment."

He took a key out of his pocket, dangling on a heart-shaped keychain.

"I got our condominium key. We can start packing."

"Oh, that is great news. Please forgive me for the way I behaved. I am truly sorry."

"I love you very much. I am glad you came back to us."

I looked at the heart-shaped key chain. It said: "Key to the loving home."

CHANGES

Saturday morning arrived, and we were ready for moving. As we were on the first floor, it didn't take long to carry the furniture and boxes downstairs. The challenge came in getting everything up to the tenth floor. The elevator wasn't working until everybody moved in. Luckily, we had a lot of help. Dezső's friends from the factory, my coworkers, Kati, Mom, and I were the moving group. Everybody admired our new home. There were three bedrooms, a living room, a kitchen, and a bathroom. The large windows gave off a lot of light. Mom just stood and marveled. It was late night by the time we got everything upstairs. We were exhausted. Our helpers told us the payment for their help could be a delicious dinner, once we were settled.

I kept my word and prepared a real Hungarian dinner for our housewarming party. We had such a good time. I will always remember how the Hungarian and Slovak couples chatted and laughed together. I was worried because the Hungarian hatred really took on after 1968. My husband often said: "The politicians are who turn people against each other."

When everybody left, I felt sick. I whispered the wonderful news to Dezső, "Our baby girl, Zsuzsika, is on her way."

We were happy and young. Sometimes I felt everything was happening so fast for us, and I wondered how we got so lucky when so many people suffer around us.

My pregnancy was easy the second time. I ate everything and felt good. From spring to autumn, we took daily walks in the park, which Attila enjoyed. He learned to count, adding and subtracting to ten, and he couldn't wait for school to start in September. Dezső ran his shop with expertise. When he didn't have enough qualified workers, he often worked on the machines himself to make sure that the fitters didn't have to stand by with a shortage of parts. In his shop, following through with the plan was the very strong law. In the military section, there was no such thing as missing targets, as the leadership would immediately suspect sabotage.

I loved my job. Working with people of different backgrounds was fun. I got to know all of the managers and employees of restaurants, bars, pubs, and hotels, and this gave me great connections, exactly as Pali had told me. They relied on me a lot and I did my best to fix their broken appliances. I got many bottles of hard liquor as tokens of their gratitude.

Summer ended, and Attila went to school. This time, the maternity leave was a blessing for me. I was able to walk my son to school, helping him with homework.

It was already mid-September, and there was still no sign of the big day. Dezső was carefully listening to our baby's movements since there was not kicking, but rather stretching in my tummy. On the morning of September 19, I decided to go to the hospital for a checkup. As I was getting ready, I felt a sharp pain in my belly. I sat down, waited a couple of minutes, and the pain increased. I knew I must get going. I couldn't stay at home alone. I waited for the elevator when my neighbor walked up, panting.

"Don't wait. It's broken. I've been gone ten minutes to get bread. I came back from the store, and now it is not working."

"This is bad timing. I am on my way to the hospital."

"Should I call an ambulance?"

"No, thank you, it's faster if I go downstairs. I don't have time to wait. Thank God the hospital is only five minutes away." I sat down on the stairs every time a strong pain came. When I reached the ground floor, I felt better. Ten minutes later, I walked up to the maternity ward. The moment I rang the bell at the door, I felt my water break. The nurses took me into the delivery room and a few minutes later, at 2:25 in the afternoon 19th September 1974 our second son, Csaba, was born. When I held him for the first time, he had the cutest smile on his face, and in the first minute we bonded when he held my finger with such strength. He looked like an angel with blond hair.

The elevator was still not working when we got home. The broken, spare part was expected to arrive in three weeks. People in the building were very upset. Some family members had asthma. A woman on the eleventh floor had surgery; she died by the time the ambulance got to her. Dezső filed a complaint in the City Hall. He came home outraged.

They told him that if we didn't like it how things are, we could move out. There were hundreds of other people who would gladly take our place, even without an elevator. Dezső was angry, ranting about the system. For me, it was a big problem to get down and up daily. I had Csaba on my arm, held Attila by my side, with a schoolbag on his back, when we walked to the school. After dropping him off, I climbed back up to the tenth floor with Csaba and some grocery shopping. In the afternoon, I went downstairs again with Csaba to pick Attila up. My whole body ached. I felt like my stomach was about to burst. Sometimes we waited for Dezső at Mom's, so he carried Csaba up the stairs. Finally, at the end of October, the elevator started working. I can't say how happy I was. I took my sons for walks in the park every afternoon.

Around that time, Dezső was coming home grumpy. He didn't talk, and he spent lots of time with the boys. In Attila's room, he built an electrical train track on a big table. The train collection had four locomotives and many different railroad cars. He created tunnels, mountains, he bought houses, trees, and made roads and bridges. It was a very relaxing hobby for him after a nerve-racking day. Attila played for hours with his father. I set the table and went to check on the boys.

"Daddy, are we going to work on the board after dinner?"

"Not today. I'm tired. But we'll continue tomorrow."

During dinner, I shared the good news with him. My mom had decided to retire. She wanted to take care of Csaba and Attila while we were at work.

"I'm glad," Dezső said. "She always knows how to help us." He sat on the balcony looking far away to the snowy mountains of Tatra. It was in his nature to rethink problems before he talked about them. Once he said, "Please forgive me. I am not good at complaining. Once I process my worries, I'll share them with you. I want you to raise our sons in peace. You have a great burden on your shoulders, taking care of our family. Your hectic job is already too much to handle."

After we got into bed, I kissed him. I said, "I'm not sleepy. If you feel like talking, you could tell me about your day."

"I'm worried. Today, your former boss paid me an unexpected visit. He acted as if we are best friends."

"He never had a problem with you."

"He is a very evil man. He said he just stopped by to congratulate me. The Communist Party approved giving me the Best Department Manager title for the year 1974. He said that he knows the director already told me, but he would like to be the second to wish me the best, and how he often thinks about me. He mentioned that a talented man such as me would be welcomed and honored in the Communist Party if I decided to become one of them."

"I told him that for the time being, my work in the factory and my family life, raising two little boys, occupies most of my time, and that I am afraid I wouldn't make a valuable member of the party. The other thing is, I don't know enough about the Communist Party's principles to be able to stand by them. I said I will continue to study and when I am ready, I will let him know."

"He said, 'I hope that day will be soon. Just so you know, there are many people who want to join the party, but to be a member is a privilege. Not everyone has the honor to be accepted.'"

"Then, he smiled smugly as he closed the door behind him. I'm worried. This man has infinite power. Who knows how my director will react if this spineless thug pressures him into getting me to be a communist. I tell you now, that will never happen."

"The director protects you. You are a key person to him," I said, trying to calm his nerves.

"Maybe, but I am not sure."

In November, I organized a surprise party to celebrate our wedding anniversary. I invited our three friends couple, including Sanyi, who grew up with Dezső. He was a gynecologist. They often had good laughs about their childhood experiences. We had each other over for dinner or got together in the park to have fun with our children. Kati came, too. She really was my best friend a Slovak girl, lived with her parents in the hills north of our town. Amazingly we were like sisters. Dezső took the boys in the park. When he came home, we stood in the hallway.

"Happy anniversary! We wish you both health and a long life in love and prosperity." We toasted with champagne. Dezső stepped out and returned with a bouquet of red roses.

"I thought my wife forgot this special day, I wanted to surprise her. Honey, I wish us many years of happiness. I love you very much." After dinner, we sat in the living room, had some beers, and carried on with our conversation until two o'clock in the morning. The topic was politics. We women went to the kitchen, talking about girlish things such as cooking and fashion. Kati suggested that we do the dishes.

"It will be nice when we wake up in the morning and the kitchen is clean."

At first, I resisted, but everyone wanted to help. I turned the faucet on, which made a hissing noise. No water came out. Sanyi came to the kitchen.

"Girls, I couldn't flush the toilet. There is no water."

"I know. We were just about to do the dishes."

Dezső came in, "What's happening?"

"We don't have water."

"That's great. It's freezing outside. I bet the radiators are cold."
Our guests left. I put warm blankets on the boys. We crawled under the down duvets, and Dezső mumbled something about the system before falling asleep. I was awake for a while. My thoughts returned to the day when Dezső wanted us to escape to America. I had heard the men talking earlier that evening, and noted how Sanyi said the very same things about our society that Dezső talked to me about ten years before.

Sanyi said, "The only thing left to do in this country is to flee. If I could, I would leave empty-handed, in one pair of pants, but I can't get a passport. You know, we were born in a wrong time and a wrong place."

I told myself it wasn't true. We stand in line for everything, but we are not hungry. We have a beautiful condominium and good jobs. Our family is happy. Sanyi said nothing is secure here. I think that nowhere in the world is a promise to have all the best in life. But I became worried. What would happen if Jano set his mind on destroying Dezső? There would be nothing I could do.

I shivered; it was very cold in the room. I knew we would have to go to Mom's for breakfast, as it was impossible to stay in our home under these conditions. We had to keep bringing up buckets of water from the basement and heating the bedroom and kitchen with electric heaters. I moved Csaba and Attila into our bedroom. After weeks, we still didn't have water. My mom told me:

"I think it would be wise to stay daytime in my condominium, and at night the boys can sleep here. I have room for them. You and Dezső have the heater, you can survive in your place until the water problem gets solved."

Her condominium was on the third floor. The water pressure reached that level. January was extremely cold, so we stayed with my mom and slept on the floor.

Dezső's shop had an inspection from Detva. After work, they had lunch and one of the engineers talked about the Hrinova weir, where the cement wall cracked. Our water came from there. When the water started to leak, they immediately released the water; otherwise, when the wall broke, the water could flood four villages. They were trying to add in a new wall, but they said it might take six to eight months until it would be fixed.

I was vacuuming when Dezső arrived home, panting.

"What happened?" I asked, concerned.

"The elevator stopped working and we are not going to have water until September. It is impossible to live like this. In only a month you are going back to work. We can't handle this."

"Don't be angry. Until they fix the elevator, we will stay with Mom."

The situation became tragic. Due to a lack of the spare part, the elevator didn't work for two months. On February first, I went back to work.

New Turning Point

On my first day, I had a warm welcome from my boss and coworkers. After a brief chat with everyone, Fero, my boss, invited me for a coffee.

"Come, I have something important to talk to you about."

"Fero, you can tell me anything, as long as I have my job."

He laughed nervously. "I'm in trouble. I need someone urgently who has good organizational skills; I had you in mind."

"Fero, I love my job. Please let me keep it."

"Listen to me. Just try it for one month. While you were on maternity leave, we went through three auto park managers. They all left after a one-month trial period. It is a hard job, I'm being honest with you. The auto park is the heart of our company. All the work must be on time. The food has to be delivered from the main kitchen, the bakery, and the deli to the schools, factories, small restaurants, and buffets."

"Fero, stop, I can't do it. I have a family to take care of. I am a mother of two little boys who I want to raise in peace and love. I can't argue with raff guys every day."

"Maria, there is no doubt in my mind that you can handle these people. You have an interesting approach and style. You respect everybody and that makes them respect you."

"Fero, no matter what you say, I can't take this job."

"As children of the old Hungarian families, we must stick together. Help me. This job isn't hard when our cars are in good condition but unfortunately is big shortage buy auto parts. I tell you why I want you to take this job. The supervisor of the main auto parts distribution was your dad's best friend.

That man will bring down the stars for you. He will get you everything you need for our cars. Then your job will be very easy to handle. I will give you the highest salary." I shook my head again, saying no, before he said, "You know, I had three other applicants for your job and I hired you just because Vlado told me to. Now is your turn."

"Okay, I have your word. I get my old job back after one month when I don't like this one."

"I promise."

* * *

Kati was appalled by my decision when we spoke. "I don't think you know what you got yourself into. Not long ago, one of the drivers threw a snow shovel at our director; he dared to tell him to shovel faster and not to be late. He said, 'I'm a driver, not a snow shoveler! When it snows, the company should hire people to shovel the snow or build garages!'"

"Kati, after one month, I can get my old job back."

I quickly learned how to fill the delivery orders for the drivers. The most important part of my job was scheduling the early morning trucks, which delivered all of the breakfast items to the city buffets and factory canteens. Before noon, the transportation of the baked goods and lunches took place. Every day, all of the food was to be delivered in time to over fifty places. My major responsibility was keeping the cars in good condition. I got my own office with phone, a coffee table, two armchairs, a desk, and a cabinet.

Afternoon, Fero and I went to the parking lot to meet the drivers.

"Comrades!" Fero began, "I asked for this meeting because I would like to introduce your new boss, comrade Maria Imre."

"A woman?"

"Yes, a woman. She is a good organizer and a hardworking woman. I believe you will find common ground for solving all of the problems we have. You know, recently, our company incurred great losses because of late deliveries. The factories and schools can't sell our products after lunchtime or after breaks. We must be on time. This is the main goal. Mrs. Imre, would you like to say a few words to the drivers?"

"Yes. I am starting this job with great optimism. I would like to ask you all one thing: let's try to work together from day one, so that our common focus is finding solutions. I will utilize all of my knowledge to facilitate your work, providing everything you need for your vehicles. It is very important that the cars are operational at all times. When we watch out for each other's best interests, we can be successful."

There was silence, and then they started clapping. I shook hands with everyone and invited them the next day after work for coffee in the Orava restaurant to talk about problems and solutions. With my boss, I went back to my office.

"This will work," he said. "They already like you. If you get some tires and starters for the cars, you will be a star."

"Fero, it was over ten years ago when I saw the auto parts distribution supervisor. I was a child." I looked at my watch. I was half an hour late to meet Dezső. He was waiting on the street. I grabbed my purse and ran. My husband stood on the sidewalk. He ran to me. His blue eyes sparkled. I knew something good had happened. He handed me a bouquet of red carnations.

"Congratulations!"

"How do you know?"

"What?"

"Why did you bring me flowers?"

"Because I love you and I managed to buy a parcel in the outskirts of our town called Vidina. We're going to build a house."

"Wow, we are? Do we know how to build a house?"

"Not yet, but we can learn."

I noticed our friend, Sanyi, waving from the opposite sidewalk.

"Hello, hello! Are you deaf?" he asked. "I've been shouting

forever. I saw a bouquet of flowers and figured out you must be celebrating something."

"We are going to build a house! Dezső bought a parcel. Can you believe it?" I said, excitedly.

"That's a wonderful idea. This deserves a toast. My wife is working an extra shift and my mother-in-law is visiting. We don't get along. Let's go to the grill bar!"

Just then, one of our company's drivers walked in our direction.

"Congratulations!"

Dezső turned to me. "What happened?"

"Today I became the manager of the auto park."

"That is the best news! Do you know how hard it is to find someone to haul construction materials? The city doesn't have a transportation company for private people. You guys are so lucky."

Sanyi raised his glass.

"All the best! I have a friend, a great construction engineer. His name is Lajos Setény. He teaches at the house builder technician school. Talk to him. He can design and help you build your house."

CHANGES

The next morning, I visited the supervisor of the auto parts. He wasn't in the sales area. I had been waiting for a while, when a warehouse worker asked me if I was a friend of his boss.

"Of course."

"He is in the back of the warehouse."

He opened the door for me with a sign that read, "JUST FOR EMPLOYEES." I heard laughter from the tire storage area.

"Good morning!" I said.

The boss, who I used to call Pista bácsi, reprimanded me sharply.

"Who let you in here? Who are you?"

"I'm Regina Sanyi's daughter." He opened his arms and hugged me.

"Wow, you're all grown up! Look at you; you look like your father! We were good friends, may he rest in peace. You sat a lot on my lap at the park restaurant when you were a little girl. Those were good times in the Hungarian club. Tell me, what brings you here?"

"I just became the manager of the auto park in the Restaurant Company. I came to ask you if you can help me to get some parts, tires for my vehicles."

"You will get all the help. Who am I going to help if not the daughter of my good old friend?"

"Thank you. I brought some vodka, as a token of my appreciation."

"Come, maybe I can find the order your predecessor brought in. He was such an arrogant guy. He said to me: 'Boss, you give me a ring when you have my order ready.' He's still waiting."

The corkboard was full of papers. He looked through them. "I got it! Let's see what I have in my warehouse to give you, so your boss can see how well you are managing the auto park. I don't like him. His father is Hungarian and he won't speak Hungarian. Well, it doesn't matter. I'm helping you, not him."

He read the list, and then said, "I give you all the tires and half of the other different parts that are listed here. The rest of it I'll prepare for you next month. I don't want our collaboration to look suspicious. From now on, write down whatever you need so I can order it. Tomorrow morning, send a truck and we'll pack it up. Don' tell anybody about our connection."

"Thank you, I'm very grateful."

"You are very welcome. I would also like to bring to your attention that you have a driver who does car repairs at home. I know him well. He is a very talented, humble man. Have him do the maintenance on your cars. He can take a lot of problems off of your shoulders. His name is Palo. He's driving the big Tatra truck. Okay, girl, I'm rooting for you!"

After work, the drivers and I had our first meeting. I noted how they were neither dumb nor arrogant. Their helpfulness surprised me. I felt great about our collective work.

I got to my mom's by dinnertime. Everybody looked so happy.

"Marika, we decided with Dezső, you will move in with me. We can make my living room your bedroom. I can watch the kids, do the cooking. You don't have to pay rent, electricity, gas for your place which is unusable. All that money you can use in your new home. What do you say?"

"Oh, my dear Mom. I am speechless. Thank you."

After dinner, we went home. The entrance hall was dark. I tried to turn the light on, but the bulb must have been out. The elevator wasn't working. We didn't even get irritated.

"Let's take the kids back to Mom."

Other tenants came walking up the stairs, cussing. Dezső moved to make room for a man with two small children in his arms. He stepped aside, not seeing a bucket of water someone had left there. He tripped, and his foot got stuck in the handle. He lost his balance and Csaba flew out of his arms and fell. I scooped my son up as he screamed terribly. People came to help Dezső, but he couldn't stand up. I ran with Csaba to my mom's, she lived across the street. I called Sanyi. A few minutes later, he was by Dezső's side. He called the ambulance. I went with Csaba to the emergency room. He had a big blue bump on his forehead which looked very bad, but otherwise, he was fine.

That night, Dezső was the only one sleeping from the effects of the painkillers. Csaba woke, crying, several times. Mom and I took turns calming him. At dawn, I fell asleep and woke up to Dezső moaning from the pain. I called Sanyi and he brought over a strong, injectable painkiller. I was late for work. The truck I sent to the warehouse was already parked in front of my office. My boss and the director were staring in amazement at the loading area. They wanted to get answers from the driver.

"I don't know. All I was told yesterday that first thing in the morning I must go to the auto parts warehouse and look for the manager. They opened the big gate and loaded my truck."

When they saw me coming, my boss waved.

"I knew it; I just knew that you could pull it off!" The director leaned to me. "Did you get tires for my Volga too? They are terribly worn out."

"Yes. We can change them today."

"Thank you." Fero came to my office. "You are amazing!"

"It wasn't my merit. One thing is sure. In the future, we are not going to have problems with auto parts. Now, we must focus on the organizing side and on how we treat people."

"I don't understand."

"Yesterday afternoon, I had a meeting with all the drivers.

They were happy to voice their opinions. I found out that you had promised them overtime bonuses, which you never paid. That's why they don't want to work night shifts and Sundays. That is a disgrace. If in the train station the cars are not unloaded in time, we pay three times more penalty than what it would cost us to pay the drivers' overtime. I am telling you right now, before I start my work, I don't make promises that I can't keep."

"Alright, we will think of something."

"I have to go now. My husband fell down yesterday. He can't walk. Something is wrong with his spine. I'll come back as soon as I can."

"Let me know if you need anything. My wife is chief nurse at the rehabilitation."

"Thank you. Dezső's friend is a doctor. He is with him."

We had painful weeks. The elevator again stopped working. The German manufacturer sent a maintenance group to assess the situation. They found that the elevator wasn't installed properly. It was expected to take six months before it would be operational again. There was nothing left to think about. With no water, no heating, and no elevator, we had to move in with Mom as quickly as possible, so we did.

The weeks passed, and Dezső's condition was the same or worse. After each physical therapy session, he was in intolerable pain. Mom feared he would be paralyzed. Kati came to visit Dezső and brought him a well-known osteopath's name and address. He lived far from us, in a small village.

Kati said, "Dezső, you should go see him, I'm sure he could help you. I know two women from my village that had to be carried to him. They couldn't walk. He realigned their spines and they walked out after seeing him. This old peasant man has helped everyone he ever met. He treats his patients on his kitchen table for free."

Dezső was willing to try anything. When we got there, people waited in front of his house. I heard incredible stories about the old man's talent. A lady asked me, "What are you here for?"

"I brought my husband. He's in the car. He can't get out; he has a bad back problem."

"The old man, Józsi, will surely help him."

The lady went into the house. A few minutes later, Józsi came out and went to the shed, returning with a rickety hospital bed on wheels.

"Whose husband is in the car?"

"Mine."

"Come, I put him on this bed."

I watched as the hunched old man reached under Dezső's armpit, with the other hand under his bottom, and pulled him out of the car to put him on the bed.

"Ma'am, you better stay here. I'll let you know if I need you."

The lady came out and whispered, "Józsi bácsi is working on your husband's spine. He was appalled. Whoever was treating him didn't know what he was doing. Six of his vertebrae are dislocated. Good luck to you. God bless!"

Late in the afternoon, Dezső came out, holding on to Józsi's arm, as he walked towards me.

"Your husband must sleep on the floor for weeks. Often, you should put cold and hot packs on his spine. With all of the physical therapy, they pushed his vertebrae so far apart, it was difficult to realign it. I tortured him quite a lot, but he will be better within a few days. I rarely have such a young patient with this kind of big problem. He is a strong man, very resilient to the pain. God bless you both!"

Dezső slept all the way home. At Losonc, he got out of the car.

"I am not in pain, just feel a tension," he shared.

* * *

In the morning, a beautifully set table waited for us. Mom cut thin slices of Hungarian salami and sausage, and she got fresh rolls and all kinds of vegetables to serve.

"What are we celebrating, Mom?" She was glowing with joy. My question filled her eyes with tears.

"The fact that Dezső can walk again and I can see him smiling. That is such a blessing, so we must celebrate and praise the Lord for it."

THE GREAT UNDERTAKING

My husband has gotten better, and we could continue to follow our dreams. Later that day, I had a meeting with Lajos, the construction engineer. He and Sanyi were waiting for me in the grill bar at four o'clock. I put in an envelope all of the sketches that we had made. Building our house was going to be complicated because our land was on a steep hillside. If we succeeded putting my vision into reality, we would have a unique house.

I met Sanyi, Lajos, and his wife at the grill bar. Sanyi introduced us and left.

"I'm going back to the hospital, I'm on call today. Marika, how's Dezső doing?" he asked on his way out.

"He is well; he's going back to work next week. It's amazing what that old osteopath was able to do with his spine."

"I heard about him, but, as a doctor, I wouldn't trust him with my life. He doesn't know about human anatomy."

"Don't be silly. He would have been imprisoned long ago if he had paralyzed anyone. In the hospital they know anatomy, but they can't heal."

"Alright, alright. Are you cooking something delicious these days? We could get together."

"If I get a decent piece of meat, I'll give you a call."

After Sanyi, left, Lajos got to the point immediately.

"Do you have any vision of the type of house you want?"

"Yes. We've been planning it for months. Here is the floor plan we drew of all three levels. I like different, unique creations. If you see our land, I think you will agree that the plot requires a one-of-a-kind solution. We would like to push the house into the hillside so you can only see one and a half stories from the street side, but all three floors from the backyard. Here are the sketches." He looked at them attentively. I ordered coffee and asked if he or his wife wanted a drink.

"Yes, a new construction deserves a toast."

He was flipping through the sketches, shaking his head.

"Your drawings are amazing. Do you have experience in construction?"

"No, we are just good at drawing. Dezső and I went to the industrial school in Kassa, so we know technical drawing."

"I see. What you drew here can be executed with specialized professionals. The reinforcement of the bridging, the one-and-a-half level deep foundation will need serious insulation against humidity. The balcony is too long; it will be difficult to manage with only two pillars, but not impossible. That needs a lot of steel which has to be bent and bound professionally." He ran his fingers through his hair a few times. "It's a very daring undertaking."

"We are not primitive people; we have pretty serious technical backgrounds, especially my husband."

"Ok. I can help build your house. It is an interesting project."

In April, we started the groundwork. It is unbelievable how many connections I needed to get an excavator and bulldozer. For five liters of vodka to the excavator operator and three liters to the bulldozer operator, the job was done. After all the dirt was moved, the steep hillside turned into a beautiful, three-level garden.

That evening, we feasted our eyes on the sight of our new home. I could picture the rock garden and steps between the levels. I wanted to have flowers fruit trees and a big vegetable garden.

I said, "Dezső, I have an idea. Do you remember those five cracked concrete steps by the condominium? I will find out at City Hall if we can get them for scraps. It would be a great solution to put them in between the terraces. Can't you picture that?"

"You are a genius. Yes, I know what you are talking about, but what I don't know is how on earth you got this idea."

"I've been here once or twice before. I can remember things from my previous lives." We had a good laugh. Then Dezső stood up. I looked at him. The starry sky, the light of the crescent moon, revealed his strong shoulders and accentuated the sparkle in his eyes. He took my hand and drew me to him.

"Is it possible that I married a worldly being?"

The next day, I went to the construction department of City Hall. There were a couple of people in the office. I told them my inquiry.

"Ma'am, we received orders to get rid of them a month ago, but we had nowhere to put them. For a bottle of Borovička, I'll send the crane to load the truck with those stairs. Just give me your address."

For the next two years, we worked with super human strength. We were tireless and happy. Our goal became more attainable by the day. I truly realized what humans are capable of when they really want something. I thought a lot about my father during this time. He always said: "In life, everything is possible. It is up to you how hard you willing to work for your dreams." I carried bags of cement, worked with a pickaxe, and helped with digging the foundation. What a sublime feeling it was to be able to do it all! Dezső and I made big progress every day. He did all of the plumbing, along with the water system and heating. We carried the heavy radiators; I held the windows until Dezső built them in. In the mornings we went to our jobs, and in the afternoons, we worked on the house. Mom cooked for us and took care of the boys.

Lajos was a big part of our success, and we became good friends. He came to help without being called. Dezső made a rebar bending press for the reinforcements for all of the bridgings. He made the concrete mixer. It was so big that I could pour three bags of cement or lime in it. I'd shovel it full of gravel or sand and the result was six wheelbarrows of concrete. I also mixed the plaster for the entire house. Dezső installed the doors and bathtubs, as well as the toilets. The neighbors were amazed by what the two of us were able to accomplish. We called for help with what we couldn't do ourselves. The walls were built by masons. Dezső passed the bricks to them while I mixed the mortar. The tiles in the bathrooms, as well as the kitchen and marbles on the steps, were done by one of my driver's brothers, while I did the grouting. A good friend installed the electricity. Dezső had installed the plumbing and water system in his house. This is how construction was done in socialism. The government did not permit anybody to work privately and the builder companies did not take jobs from private citizens. There was a big penalty to do side jobs for income. This is why the alcohol was worth much more than money on the black market.

Getting the building materials was a nightmare. I stood in line at four in the morning, at the gate of the brick factory. My driver and I, along with a handful of other private builders, wore asbestos gloves to quickly unload the bricks coming out of the oven. Dezső couldn't leave the factory; his work was more complicated than mine. My boss gave me a certificate, authorizing me to use the company trucks. In the delivery note, I put the origin and destination of the cargo and the driver filled in the distance in kilometers, so I could pay for the gas.

The following year, in October, we were ready to move into our new home. It was the greatest event of our lives. Now we planned to turn the house into a loving home. My mom helped me with the decorations. She gave us several paintings, statuettes, along with old-school, hand-cut crystal bowls, all which she got from my dad.

Before Christmas, I went out shopping for gifts with a purse full of money and came home empty-handed. I got many bottles of alcohol for helping people take home furniture, kitchen appliances, and all kinds of heavy stuff. The drivers got tips, and I got bottles. I thought, I should go around too with bottles of alcohol myself, visiting the stores with which I wanted to have connections. I told my husband about my plan, but he got upset with me.

"I'll be so humiliated if somebody wants to get a favor from me with a bottle of vodka. It is humiliating to be bought with alcohol," he said.

"Nobody is buying me; they buy my services. We have so many bottles; we hardly have a place to store them. Let's put a bunch of them in the car. You drive and I'll tell you where to stop so I can wish happy holidays to a few store managers. I tell them what I need, that's all."

Everyone was happy to receive my cognac or vodka and made notes of things I needed. The butcher waited for me every Friday, after closing time. He told me how much I owe him and at home, I looked at what I got. There was often pork chops, roast beef, and at other times, he'd pack chicken and veal. In the shoe store, they set aside winter boots for my sons, and in the toy store I was able to get remote controlled toy cars and electric train sets. I delivered my bottles every month to the grocery store. The manager put in paper bags items that ordinary people have never seen. My husband constantly worried what people might think about us.

"I don't know. This is the kind of world we live in. I receive and I give. Besides, I pay for everything. The Communist Party leaders bring guests to the restaurants and eat for free. The president of the party loads up his car at the dairy factory with butter, sour cream, cheeses, as if it was his personal pantry. They fired the person who took a photo of him doing it. They don't care what people think."

Soon after, Dezső had an idea to mark an X on the four corners of the labels of every bottle. It looked like they had been printed like that.

"From now on, I'll check every bottle that you get. I have a feeling nobody drinks the alcohol. They just pass it on whenever they need something. This is why I don't understand this charade." Over a year later, a well-known surgeon needed a refrigerator hauled to his house. He came to my office with a bottle of cognac and Dezső found the X on the label. The bottle had been traveling from hand to hand for a year to end up back in our hands. It was unbelievable! Dezső was correct in his thinking.

One afternoon, Pali came over. Dezső was in the basement, installing a gas pipe to the stoker. I was washing dishes in the kitchen when I heard his voice.

"Is anybody home?" he asked.

"Pali, we've missed you," I replied. He looked around.

"You've done a perfect job here. Honestly, I didn't think you could pull it off. This required enormous willpower."

"Pali, even for me it seems unbelievable, but when you truly want something, it gives you incredible strength. Achieving something you are determined to do is the greatest feeling of all. Reaching my dreams makes my life worth living. My father taught me that. Unfortunately, he's not here to see what we were able to achieve."

"No doubt, a true aristocratic lady wouldn't have been able to do this," he laughed.

"Pali, I would love to be a fine lady. My mom is that way. Can you imagine me fainting at a cuss word, complaining, and being fragile? I can't afford to do that because we wouldn't get anywhere."

Pali was holding his stomach, still laughing.

"You can't help it. Your father's blood is running in your veins. Nothing will make you lose your ground. Nothing broke him either."

"Where is Dezső?"

"In the basement."

"I want to have a word with you," he said.

"Something bad?"

"Not yet. He had a fight with your former boss."

"Why?"

"He went to Dezsõ with the communist membership signup sheet and Dezső, well, I don't know the details, but the outcome was that Dezső threw Jano out of his office. The city Communist Party secretary told me this. Everybody is talking about it."

I froze.

"Your husband is valuable for the factory, but my advice is to not play with fire."

Just as Pali finished his sentence, Dezső came in.

"Hello, Pali, good to see you! Marika was worried for you. Are you feeling better?"

"When you get as old as I am, nothing goes smoothly. But let's change the subject. You did a beautiful job here. Many people are talking about you and this house you built."

"Anyone can do it with hard work and determination."

"You are right; but these days, people like to wait for the government to get everything because doesn't cost money. In this regime, nobody works hard and they are satisfiedwith basic things. But when somebody wants more and works for it, then many people envy and hate those who succeed."

* * *

By December, winter had really set in. The snow and icy roads made work more difficult. One of my drivers got into a big accident. At the train station, many cars full of beer waited to be unloaded. The transportation of the orchestras from Budapest and Bratislava for Christmas and New Year's was a long and difficult drive. I didn't have enough cars to do everything. The drivers worked day and night. At the last minute on New Year's Eve, I got a phone call from the train station saying that we got three more cars of Pilsner beers from the Czech Republic. On this day, we only worked until noon, getting ready for the festivities that night. I went to my boss to arrange some compensation for the drivers; otherwise, I would never find people for the job. Fero promised that he would give them 100 Korona per person. This way the job was done. On payday, my phone rang. It was the accounting lady, calling about four drivers, demanding one hundred Korona that had been promised to them.

"What's the problem?" I asked.

"I didn't receive any authorization." she replied.

"I'll go to my boss right now."

Fero's office door was open. Four angry maintenance workers were confronting him. They were refusing to work Sundays for free. Fero was about to explode with rage.

"It is part of your duty! We all want to build our socialist country to live better here!"

"If you don't pay, we won't work. This is not a capitalist country where workers are exploited."

I was standing there. I didn't want to interfere, but my boss noticed me.

"Why are you standing there? What do you want?" His voice was so irritated, it offended me.

"What do I want? I want my men to be paid immediately, just like you promised. I don't lie to my people; my men are not used to that."

Fero shouted with anger. "The rumors were true about you! Now I can see the capitalist blood in you. Don't you ever forget that you don't have any men here. This isn't your company."

"You don't forget that I care about this company as mine, so you should consider yourself very lucky for that! Besides, you took everything from the capitalist exploiters and gave it to the people. I am the people; everything here is mine too! Until my drivers get paid, we are not working, and come Monday, I quit."

I went into my office and slammed the door behind me. A few minutes later, Fero came to see me.

"You were right," he conceded, "but from now on, when you have a problem, let's discuss it in private. I value your work ethic, but it cannot be detrimental to me. I called accounting. The drivers have been paid."

"Thank you."

Fear

I woke up in the night to the sound of pouring rain and wind howling outside. The trees were cracking under the window and my bed was shaking too. I noticed Dezső flinging his arms as he thought he was fighting with someone. Tears rolled down on his cheeks, and his hair was soaking wet. I touched him, but he didn't wake. I held his hand.

"Dezső, did you have a bad dream?"

"I can't breathe. I have to go out to get some air."

"It's raining," I said, handing him a glass of water.

He began to tell me about his dream. "We were in Darnya with my mother and my father. He was still alive. I stood in front of the gate. Csaba was in my arms, Attila by my side. You were picking wildflowers on the hillside and waved to me with the bouquet.

He told me that he could hear me shouting. "I'll be right there!" was what I yelled to him in the dream.

Then, he continued, "The sky turned dark and the police appeared on horses between us. You were running toward me. I could see the flowers fall from your hand. The horses stepped all over them, and then you were gone. Attila ran between the horses, looking for you. He kept calling for you. I heard shooting. The old stallion stood tall in front of the chief of police. Then, my father hugged his dead horse. I stared at his glassy eyes. I have the image in my mind of the old horse's eyes, looking up to the sky as my dad cries."

As he finished, he took both of my hands and kissed them.

"My God. I can't survive if I lose you."

On this day, my mom took the boys shopping. We were

106

alone. Dezső read the newspaper on the sofa. All day, he was quiet. I felt we must talk about his worries. We always shared our thoughts about everything, except politics. I felt I had no right to criticize the communist system because I wanted to continue to live there, but I knew we must break the wall of political differences between us. I still could not understand Dezső for feeling the same hatred for communism as he had twenty years before. My mother-in-law would spend her days crying because the communists ruined them. Her sons drank away all their money, even their mother's pension, and communism was to blame for their misery.

My family was very different. In my young age, I learned the history that they taught in school. My parents never told me that what was being taught was a lie. I was never told to hate anybody. Dad taught me that if I worked hard, I could achieve much in life. There will always be some people who earn their bread the easy way, and others the difficult way. Studying hard, and gaining knowledge and discipline, are the strongest weapons in life. Live smartly and cautiously. Don't be a hero; our communist leaders are so powerful that disobeying them may bring tragic consequences. I try to live by my father's advice.

I was proud of my husband. He was an extremely smart man, with morals. He was a very strong man, an upright person, not hiding his beliefs, but I knew he shouldn't do it in a way that put him in danger. He must think toward the future for his sons.

I made coffee and sat next to him. I didn't know how to start the conversation.

"What's on your mind?" he asked.

"I would like to be part of your thoughts. Maybe I could help…"

"Unfortunately, you can't."

"You have to know I'm by your side, no matter what. Now, I have more experience, and I must admit, I was wrong in the past. Everything is a matter of experience and a person's point of view."

He turned to me.

"A few days ago, your former boss pissed me off. I had a meeting with two of my craftsmen, drawing and explaining the stages of the project. That idiot barged into my office and demanded that I dismiss my workers because he wanted to talk to me right then. I didn't have time. I was in the middle of solving essential problems. You know what that moron said? In this country nothing is more important than the work of the Communist Party. For me, I told him, completing the plan is first."

"He stood there like a pile of shit. I remembered when he asked you if you were waiting for him to kick you out. So, I said the exact same thing to him. He turned red. He knew what I was talking about and left. I think a lot about life lately. I admire the political awareness that your father instilled in you. I am scared of what the future holds for me."

Dezső told me how he waited for some remarks from the president, but nobody bothered him the rest of the day.

Later on, he helped me a lot carrying big rocks to our rock garden. On the lowest level of the yard, he built a sturdy pigsty and a henhouse. We bought twenty chickens, ten ducks, and two pigs. Every day I brought home large aluminum containers full of food leftovers from the Orava restaurant for slop. We planted the garden with vegetables, thirty different dwarf fruit trees, lots of roses, and different flowers. The house surroundings started to look very unique.

That summer, we didn't plan a vacation. Sanyi bought a little weekend house by the Ružiná Lake, and we often spent weekends with them. The children enjoyed the water; we cooked good food and relaxed next to a glass of wine.

Meanwhile, Pali hadn't been feeling well. We met once a week, after work in the cake shop. He didn't complain, but he was low-spirited. Kati's father also got sick. The doctors removed half of his stomach, as he had first stage cancer. Sometimes I had lunch with her and summed up whatever was going on with our families.

One Saturday morning, Sanyi called us to spend the weekend with them next to the lake. Sanyi's wife, Eva, and I started to cook cauldron goulash. The dads and the kids went down by the lake. Later, Sanyi and Dezső sat down with two chilled Pilsner beers at the big oak table. The goulash was quietly boiling, and I opened a bottle of wine. Eva and I joined the guys.

That was when Sanyi turned to Dezső and asked, "How is your mother? Is she feeling better?"

We were surprised, and responded, "What happened to her?"

"She fell down the stairs. You haven't seen her?"

"We don't go often to Darnya, I don't get along with my brothers."

"My mother told me, they don't treat her well. They drink a lot. You could try talking to them. Maybe they will listen to you more than to the village folks."

On the way home, Dezső told me, "If you don't mind, we could visit my mother tomorrow."

"I like the idea; finally the boys will meet their other grandma."

The next day, when I saw the church tower of Darnya, my heart raced. The moment we pulled up by the house, several people came out of the pub. My mother-in-law stood next to the gate. She greeted us in a loud voice so people in front of the pub could hear her.

"What a great surprise! The long-lost son finally found his way home." She didn't look at me, just hugged her son and seized him up.

"You are very thin, my boy."

"Mom, let's go in the house. I didn't come here to put on a show."

By that time, many people were standing in front of the pub.

"Dezső, is that you? You've turned into nobility; you don't even want to look at us anymore?"

We got into the hallway. Attila handed his grandma the bottle of wine. My mother-in-law looked him up and down.

"You look exactly like your father when he was your age. What's your name?"

"Attila."

"That's a beautiful name."

"Mom, here is our younger son, Csaba."

He walked toward her with flowers, but when she opened her arms to hug him, he started crying with fear. She had no teeth, and her head was covered with a black head scarf. Her face froze.

"Look at him. He hates me."

"Mom, he doesn't know you."

"He hates me. I bet his mother taught it to him."

"Mom, we all love you."

She held Attila's hand and said, "Let's go to the pub. I'll buy you something, anything you like, for the present you brought me."

We stepped into the living room where Dezső's three brothers watched TV. The eldest turned around.

"Sit down and be quiet. We're watching a very good movie."

Csaba moved over to his father's lap. I hoped Dezső could get him to like his mother.

The movie ended. The brothers didn't look at us, and they left the room. Dezső opened the strange, black curtain. Attila came in with his grandma behind him.

"Show what I got you."

"Look, this is American bubblegum. Good people are making it in America."

"I introduced my grandson to everybody. They said he is handsome, just like his father was. Come, my son, to the kitchen." My mother-in-law looked at me. "You stay here! Keep your boy so he doesn't scream when he looks at me."

A couple of minutes later, they were back.

"My son told me you like coffee. I'll make some for you." I could see that Dezső was fuming. Csaba sat on my lap again, held my neck so tight, he nearly strangled me. My mother-in-law came back with the coffee.

"It's not healthy to spoil a child."

"Mom! My sons aren't spoiled."

I felt very uncomfortable.

"I love my sons. My father taught me that, in life, everything can be achieved with love. Love is the best way to shape a child's soul. I love and respect you. I want you to know that I love your son more than my own life."

I watched her face, but I could see that my words had no effect on her. Her hands caught my eye, as they were resting in her lap, all wrinkled and cracked from working in the garden. I wanted to hug her and express my gratitude, but her sharp voice broke the silence.

"Don't talk to me about love! Every time I look at you, my heart breaks that my son is living with a woman like you. Nail polish, mini skirt, you look…"

"Like a beautiful woman, who is the best mother and a hardworking, attentive, loving wife. Our life together is happy. Nothing can come between us, because we are one. We share our thoughts, joys, sorrows, money, bed, and body. Please remember that!"

I wished that I could whisper her: hold your son in your arms; be happy because he is happy.

"We are leaving. Don't forget, you are always welcome in our home. Anything you need, call us. We will come and help. I told you in the kitchen, we love each other unconditionally. You should try to be happy for us and not trying to divide us."

He wanted to hug his mother after these words, but she turned away from him. When we got into the car, Attila asked his dad, "Why is grandma upset with you? She doesn't love you?"

"When you grow older, I will explain to you. She loves you."

Soon after, school started again. At that point, we had two sons in the elementary. I got a call from the vice president of the Communist Party, asking me for a meeting.

"I would like to have a word with you, comrade Imre, and

get some answers in a delicate matter. Every year the city hall sends us a report on how many children went to school and which school they are attending. I was surprised to see that your children are enrolled in the Hungarian school."

"May I ask, what is the problem?"

"Why did you put your sons in Hungarian school? You are ruining their future."

"Why?"

"Your sons will never be equal to those who attend Slovak school. They must learn to write and read in the Slovak language. Studying the history of our great nation is very important."

"I would like to point out that Hungarian schools teach the Slovaks' language and are for Hungarians. If Hungarians send their children to Slovak schools, there will be no use for Hungarian schools. Just out of curiosity, have you ever met anyone who went to a Hungarian school?"

"No, but our statistics show, that graduates of Hungarian schools don't have half of the knowledge that the students have from the Slovak school."

"Look at me. I completed my entire education in Hungarian schools. We have known each other for years. Do you find me dumb or intellectually inferior to the rest of the Slovak population?"

He was surprised by my response.

"I'm convinced that it is very useful for my children to study in their mother tongue," I continued. "I read about this in a psychology review. My father put me in a Hungarian school in the fifties; it was quite dangerous to be Hungarian at that time. I don't understand why it's a problem if Hungarians are Hungarians. The more languages and cultures we know, the more it benefits our society."

"Hungarians don't like Slovaks."

"That is not true. I am raising my sons as Hungarians because that's what they are. Their names are Attila and Csaba. We live in Vidina, where there is not a Hungarian soul in our

112

neighborhood, but they love us and we love them. My sons are playing with the Slovak boys like they are brothers. The Hungarian school teaches students intensively the Slovak language, as well as hard work and diligence. Minorities have to work harder to be successful. They educate valuable people, who love this country and will build it as their own."

"Look, comrade Imre, you have the right to choose the school you want. Thank you for coming in and lecturing me on the education of Hungarian children. I will transmit your opinion to the Board of Education, when I have the chance."

A few days later, we witnessed an interesting conversation. The boys were in the library, playing with the trains. Dezső sat at the kitchen, reading the train catalog. I was cooking when it caught my attention how quiet it was in the room. I curiously stuck my head in to see what was happening. Attila spoke softly to his brother.

"Dezső, come. Our sons have secrets," I said.

We stood behind the door. Attila's seriousness, as always, was funny. He explained things like an old man. "I have a big secret. Promise you won't tell anyone. Then, I'll share with you. Give me your word."

"Okay, I won't tell," said Csaba.

"I need your word."

"You have my word."

"Today my teacher told us that Daddy isn't our father."

Csaba's little face got sad. I will never forget that sweet, alarmed face.

"Lenin is our father, but we mustn't say that at home."

"I don't want that man to be my daddy. I want Dezső to be my daddy. Your teacher is lying! I know that Dezső is my daddy!"

Csaba screamed between his sobs. He tended to call his father Dezső. When he started speaking, his first word was "Dezső". It had stuck because it was cute and Dezső liked it. We didn't wait long before stepping into the room.

"Who's lying?"

Csaba jumped into Dezső's arms.

"Attila's teacher is lying."

"Teachers don't lie." Attila was sitting on the floor, his head bowed.

Dezső was earnest as he said, "Attila, come sit next to me. What your teacher said is not a secret. I will explain to you after dinner what she meant." He hugged him and opened the train catalog. "Look at this engine. Do you like it? Should we get it?"

* * *

When early December arrived, we slaughtered our pigs. The next day, we invited the families of Lajos and Sanyi to a pork feast. Everything tasted delicious. The sausage, stuffed cabbage, roast, and my mom's great cookies made the evening special. The greasy food called for good wine. We had a wonderful time until Éva brought up politics. She was angry with Sanyi because he didn't want to be a communist.

"He is going to ruin the future of our children."

Sanyi reprimanded her coarsely. "I told you already, I won't be kissing any asses!"

Ani looked at Sanyi disapprovingly. "We are communists; it's time you all knew that."

The blood froze in my veins. We all stared into the air.

"See Sanyi, they are clever."

Lajos spoke up. "If I may, I'd like to tell you my story about why I became a communist. I am a village boy. I was born in a crummy, clay house. Even my great-grandparents were peasants. They worked for landowners and earned barely enough to put food on the table. When everything was nationalized, we had a better life. My parents worked for government-owned land for a good salary. I was a good student and the school recommended that my father send me to college. If it wasn't for the regime change, I would be working in the fields in my village now. I am grateful to the communists for what they did for the poor. As a communist, I help where I can. I never harm anyone."

The situation was tense. Sanyi was disappointed.

"You shouldn't have hidden what you believe in," Ani interrupted.

"We had no choice. You hate communists."

I got upset.

"Ani, that's not true. We have our own reasons why we didn't become communists. I accept your views. I have no reason to become a communist. This regime destroyed my family and on top of that, now they are going after us just because we are the children of former capitalists."

Dezső continued to eat the stuffed cabbage roll like nothing happened. We looked at him, then he said, "I agree with my wife, you are grateful to the communists, you have a reason. I don't hate you, but I condemn the communist ideology. I want to live in peace. I don't want to join people whose ideology I don't share. I'll never become a member of the Communist Party, even if they skin me alive." At that point, I took a bottle of wine and topped off everyone's glass.

"Let's drink to our friendship and to always preserve the love and respect we have for each other!" I said.

* * *

In spring, Dezső suggested it would be nice to go for a summer vacation.

"Where would you like to go?"

"To Venice, Rome, we could check out your ancestors' country. There is a bit of Italian blood in your veins. I already mapped it all out. Hungary, Yugoslavia, Italy, and Austria."

"It's too late to arrange it now. People who want to get to west Europe must submit their application in January."

"You could try. You have many connections."

I filled out the applications and submitted them. Two weeks later, I came home and found Dezső sitting on the balcony. He said, "I didn't get my passport. The factory management didn't approve my application leave the country. You did, so you can go to Venice by yourself."

"Don't be silly, I'm not going anywhere. Next year, I'll make the necessary connections and then we can have a guaranteed summer vacation."

That summer, we spent all of our weekends at Sanyi's vacation house. We took walks in the forest and swam with the kids in the lake. We had our meals at the nearby restaurant. It was quite a relaxing time.

When we returned home early from our stay because of the rain, Mom stood in front of our house, chatting with the neighbor.

"Thank God you came home early! Two hours ago, Dezső's brother came with the taxi. Your mother is in the hospital in Rimaszombat. She had a stroke and is asking for Marika. You should go see her."

An hour later, we were at the hospital. When we stepped into the room, the doctor had just covered my mother-in-law's face.

"My condolences," he said.

Dezső's eldest brother came charging at him like a rooster in a cockfight.

"Where the hell have you been?"

"Shut up, or I'll smack you across the face," Dezső replied.

The other brother fell to the floor, crying hysterically.

"Mother, why did you do this to us? How will we live without you?"

He kept repeating it louder and louder. Several nurses came to check on him and suggested giving him a sedative. Dezső looked, without tears, at his mother's pale face. He kissed her forehead.

"Enough of this circus," he said to them. "Please act like

men. I will stay with you to arrange the funeral. Marika, please go back home, order a wreath in our name, and a bouquet for our sons."

"We need wreaths, too, for each of us," one of the brothers said.

"Why three? You can put all your names on one wreath."

"Who are you? You have no right to decide…" another brother said.

"Darling, just get the wreaths. I'll call you tomorrow morning and we will talk about the details. You could order some cold cut platters and some pastries. We'll have a small reception after the funeral. My mother's relatives from Miskolc will come to say goodbye."

On Tuesday morning, I went to Darnya to clean the house so we could seat the relatives. Before the funeral, Dezső's brothers several times sneaked out from the house and went over to the pub for drinks. At two o'clock, three gypsy musicians showed up asking for me. They wanted three hundred Korona to play my mother-in-law's favorite songs on the way to the cemetery.

"Who called you here?"

"Your brother-in-law."

"If he hired you, then he should pay," I said.

Dezső came out of the house. "What's the problem?" he asked.

"Do you know anything about this singing business?"

"I don't, but don't fight next to my mother's coffin. How much do you want?" he asked the man.

"Three hundred Koronas, my lord."

"Just pay them," Dezső told me.

"I don't have the money. I spent over one thousand already for the wreaths and the food."

"This is all I have. Take it or leave it," Dezső said, taking two hundred and sixty Koronas from his wallet.

Around this time, they brought the coffin out of the house. We followed it to the hillside cemetery. Very few people came from the village, but from Miskolc, eleven relatives escorted my mother-in-law on her last journey. The reformed pastor said a brief eulogy. At the end, I whispered to Dezső that the kids and I should go ahead to set the table. I didn't want my sons to see their uncles' behavior. One of them grabbed the shovel, yelling that they shouldn't throw the soil on their mother. Another one lay on the dirt, crying like he lost his mind. As we started walking, Dezső joined us.

"It is unbelievable what alcohol will do to a person. My brothers have completely shed their humanity. The people in the village won't even speak to them. My heart aches that I couldn't say goodbye to my mother. I'm sure she wanted to ask for your forgiveness.

I thought about how I believed his mother was a cold-hearted, insensitive woman. I came to the conclusion that it didn't matter anymore.

We returned to the house and set the table. From the restaurant company, I had gotten three tasteful platters and three big boxes of pastries. I arranged all of the food nicely, and by the time I finished slicing the bread, the guests arrived. I liked them. They were pleasant, intelligent people. They praised our sons for their impeccable behavior. Then my brothers-in-laws arrived with a bunch of their drunken pub friends.

"Come, we have delicious food here."

At first, they were shy and only put a few things on their plates, but as they got into the drinking, they became brazen, loading fistfuls of salami and ham onto their plates with their bare hands. It was a truly disturbing sight. The guests from Miskolc said goodbye and made us promise to visit them. Dezső and I walked them out and put our boys in the car. We told them that we would be back in a few minutes. On the way back to the house, I couldn't hold it in any longer.

"Dezső, why did you leave that vodka and brandy I brought on the table so your brothers could get drunk on it?"

"I'm sorry. I wasn't paying attention."

"When we go in, before they completely lose their minds, we must settle the funeral expenses. I bred the bills for their wreaths and the cold cut platters. The rest I received for free. By the way, I saw the invoice for the coffin in the kitchen. My father's casket was three hundred Koronas, your mother's one thousand. She had an extra pillow, a silk interior, an extra blanket, and a carved wood coffin. Do you think this abnormally high price shows your family's love for your mother? Your brothers abused her, and now an expensive coffin is good for your conscience. I am shocked you agreed with this choice, and I hope the expenses will be split in four."

I stepped into the room. One of the brothers' friends lay on the floor, holding the empty bottle of vodka over his mouth, trying to squeeze the last drops out of it. The twin brother slept on the chair. Only the oldest brother, Gyula, was sitting at the table, repulsively licking the plate, like a dog. I asked the remaining guests to go home.

"In this house, only I can give orders!"

"Then come into the kitchen and pay your debt."

He jumped up from the chair and smashed it to the floor with such force that the pieces flew around the room.

"You won't get any money! For over a decade you didn't care about our mother. Besides, we don't have any money. Ha, ha, ha!"

He burst into a deafening laughter. The drinking buddies were applauding him. I took my purse and left. As I walked out, Dezső stood in the middle of the room, speechless. I got into the car and waited, but he didn't follow me. I drove off. I almost got out of the village when I saw him in the rear mirror standing in the middle of the road. I turned around.

"Dad, we are glad you're coming home with us," the boys said.

I drove home in silence. The next week passed, but we did not talk. I wasn't able to forget that brutal, arrogant behavior that I had never before experienced in my life, all while my

119

husband just stood there. He brought me flowers and talked to me, but I just listened.

One day he said to me, "The days are passing and you are shutting me out of your life. I want you to understand that you can't argue with a drunken person. I didn't want to have a fist fight with my own brother on the day of my mother's funeral. It wouldn't fix what happened. We never ever go to Darnya. My mother is dead. She rejected me, but her loss is painful to me. Marika, you saved me from my own family. If I hadn't met you, I don't know where I'd be now. If you feel I've done something wrong, I am sorry."

"You did not do anything wrong. Somehow, something brooked in me that afternoon. I believed love awakens love in people, even in animals. I joined your family with love. Unfortunately, your mother was mean-spirited and your brothers are not just mean-spirited, but wicked."

"I know the wound of the soul is very painful. I hope I can heal it with my love. I am yours."

We both shed tears.

* * *

In early January, the topic of summer vacation came up again.

"Marika, let's go to Italy with the children. We need some relaxation."

I wasn't in the mood to make connections to get the traveling papers we needed; I wanted to live a simple, quiet life. Fighting and being disappointed just made me embittered. I told Pali about our plans and asked him if he knew anyone at the passport office who could help us.

"I do know many people there, but that is not enough. From the passport office, the applications are sent for approval to the workplaces and to the City Hall. Without those approvals, their office cannot issue passports. If you want to travel to west Europe, you have to be very trustworthy."

I filled out the applications and told Dezső to make sure to mention our travel plans to the director, since the permit to leave the country largely depends on the employer.

On Monday morning, Dezső arrived at his shop where the director was waiting for him.

"I have an important issue to discuss with you. Let's go to your office," the director said.

He sat down in Dezső's chair and put the file that he carried on the table. It was clear he was in a bad mood as he looked at Dezső, who stood puzzled in the middle of his office.

"Sit down; we have important things to talk about." Dezső pulled a chair from the conference table and sat down, facing the director.

"I received an assignment from the president of the Communist Party. I believe it was a year ago that you kicked him out of this office. He told me about it at the time. I know that you are angry with him for treating your wife disrespectfully, but not even I, much less you, can afford any kind of anticommunist behavior. Since then, I've been asked several times to recruit you to the party. I found many excuses to justify why I haven't done it. You work a lot of extra hours, you wouldn't have time to attend meetings, your young sons need you, and so on. I kept trying to avoid this unpleasant conversation. I also stopped Jano from coming here personally, because I knew that it wouldn't end well."

Dezső sat in front of him, very relaxed, almost like he didn't care what the director was talking about.

"For years, we've been working together in an amicable relationship, yet we never became friends. I think I know why, because you don't become friends with a communist. I'm sure you have your reasons for it. You are the only manager in the factory who is not a communist member. Please make your decision wisely." He opened the file, and said, "Please sign it."

"I can't. I work hard. I am an outstanding professional. I don't want any party privileges. When my job requires me to be a communist, I will resign and go work as a welder."

"It's not that simple anymore. You are in a bad position because everybody knows that you are against us."

"I am not," Dezső said.

"But you are not with us, either. What are you going to do if you can't be a welder?"

"I will leave the factory."

"The party has long arms. They will destroy you. I want to help. Dezső, I respect you. Don't destroy your life."

He took a pen out of his pocket, and again said, "Please sign it." Dezső stood up. He and the director locked eyes for a few seconds. Then, Dezső took the shop keys out of his drawer.

"I resign today with four months' notice. That should give you enough time to find a good communist to replace me."

"You can't do this! We are going to squish you like a bug! Do you understand? We will ruin even your children's children. We have the power to do it."

"I know, but nothing can change my mind."

Dezső told me the story. I wasn't surprised. Somehow, I knew one day this would happen.

We had a devastating three months. His job application was rejected by every factory in our town. Toolmakers and welders were in great demand, but nobody wanted to hire him. I told Pali about our situation. He shook his head.

"This is a very serious situation. They will break him. I can't understand you guys. Are you so dumb that you don't know it's not good to piss against the wind. It will all end up on your pants?! Dezső must understand what these people are capable of doing." I spent many sleepless nights trying to find a solution, but for the first time in my life, I felt helpless. There was nothing I could do. The Communist Party held the reins of Dezső's and our family's fate.

122

I was terrified. I met Pali on the street one day, and he told me, "The communist leadership gave Dezső's name to every company. Nobody is allowed to hire him. Jano, your former boss, is convinced that he can force Dezső into the party. If not, he will have to work as a cleaner in his shop. I ran into Sanyi. He told me he joined the Communist Party last week. He did it for his children's sake. Tell that to Dezső."

In the afternoon, I had a lot of work to do. My phone wouldn't stop ringing. Vlado came into my office. He motioned that he'd wait until I finished the call. He got a paper from the shelf and jotted something down. By the time I finished the call, he had folded the note and put it on my desk.

"I came to say goodbye."

"Where are you going?" I asked.

"Stop pretending you don't know. The whole town's talking about me."

"I don't care about gossip."

"Well, this time you can believe it, it's true. The Communist Party kicked me out of town because I cheated on my wife. I'm getting a divorce and marrying this young reporter. She's pregnant."

"What are you going to do?"

"I'm still communist; they transferred me to the town of Velky Krtis, not so far, forty minutes' drive from here. I'll be director of the service corporation. Hairdressers, cleaners, sewing shops, funeral homes, gravestone makers, carpenters, flower shops, auto mechanics are all under its umbrella."

"Interesting. The Communist Party promoted you for the director as punishment."

"They need me there. Maria, I'm happy. Can you believe it? I'm 65 and going to be a father!"

"I congratulate you."

"Thanks. I didn't want to leave without saying goodbye, and perhaps I can help your husband."

"How do you know about Dezső?"

He laughed.

"You know, the members of the Communist Party know everything. I hate those who abuse their power. Jano is one of those. He is an arrogant, self-absorbed, spineless man. It's dangerous to give power to people like him. Slovaks have a saying: 'If you put the dog shit in a mason jar and put it up on the shelf between jams, it's going to think it's a jam, too!'" He laughed at his own joke.

"Here is my new phone number and the address of my office," he added. "There are not many specialists in the town of Velky Krtis. I want to put my own people into leadership positions. I can give you and your husband great jobs, with excellent pay. Losonc has no say in hiring Dezső, because this town is in a different county. When they do, I don't care."

I told Dezső about Vlado's job offer, but Dezső stayed quiet. He was a broken man. I watched him and remembered when he said: "You have no idea what the communists are capable of."

NEW HOPE

On Friday, Dezső came to see me in my office. He sat in the armchair; I was making delivery notes for the next day. My boss stood in the open door.

"The director called. He wants a truck now for his daughter to move."

"It's Friday afternoon. Everybody wants to go home."

I was angry with our leaders, thinking they were entitled to everything.

"Don't be upset. I wrote a check for three hundred Koronas. Send Palo. That is good money for one afternoon."

Dezső watched as I assigned the next day's work, distributed the gas slips, and listened to the problems encountered that day. I took notes of the condition of the cars, which car needed an oil change, who wanted to take days off next week. Before long, we were finally alone.

"Mom took the kids for ice cream and invited us for dinner."

"Oh, that's good. I'm so tired."

"I thought we could talk about Vlado. I don't have any other choice; we can go see him on Monday."

Vlado waited for us at ten in the morning. In the management building, an old man sat by the door. He wasn't in a good mood as he pointed with his finger at the open notebook.

"Write your name here, and the address and the name of the person who you are visiting."

Vlado came down the stairs and said, "You don't have to do that. I'm so glad you decided to come. Pista, remember these two faces. These people are my friends and the door to my office is always open to them."

As we stepped into the secretary's office, I was surprised to find a tastefully decorated space. On either side of the window, there were beautiful, large palm trees. Next to the window, on a table, there was a modern Italian coffee machine that caught my eye. Even the telephone had an interesting, atypical, square shape. The secretary wore no lipstick or eye shadow, but her exceptionally warm smile gave away her intelligence.

Vlado led the way into his office as he turned to me.

"What do you think?"

"I'm impressed. What can I say? It must be easy to have creative thoughts in this beautiful surrounding."

"You know me well. I enjoy stylish things. This town is very behind; the leadership wants to create jobs. People are poor here. The Communist Party and the town council gave me the green light to do whatever I feel is necessary to lift up the life in the town. There's plenty of money to do that. What I don't have, unfortunately, are good professionals. I've already arranged to open an apprentice school. I'm thinking locksmiths, welders, operators for the milling and lathe machines. A year from now, we have to open a factory, specializing in shoemaker's tools. We have a large contract with a Czech shoe factory."

Then, he said, "Oh, I apologize, please have a seat. The secretary will bring us coffee."

He poured Napoleon cognac in glasses. We toasted to a successful future. Vlado told us the history of the area. Long ago, the locals used to work in the coal mines. Then, the mines were shut down because of the poor quality. By this time when we were meeting, a company started a huge winery. The surrounding, rolling hills were great for growing grapes. The majority of the town spoke Hungarian, so that's why Vlado was looking for managers and key workers who spoke both Slovak and Hungarian.

"First, I'll take you around town, and then I will show you the building under construction, which will be the factory.

Dezső, I would like you to be in charge of the factory. We have to start production a year from now. Until then, we have to bring all the machines, install them…"

"Is the equipment included in the five-year plan? Have they been petitioned at the ministry?"

"No, but that won't be a problem. I will help you make connections. I presume you already know that, in this country, if you have connections, you have everything."

Vlado winked at me.

"Vlado," Dezső started, "I am no good at running around, gifting bottles. If this is part of the job, then unfortunately, I can't take it."

"We can talk about it later."

We stopped in front of an industrial building. Trucks were parked all around. Installation teams for electricity and water, along with bricklayers, were doing the finishing touches. We looked around and came back to the car.

"Dezső, my offer is this: if you take the job, I will pay you twice what you were making in the military factory. I value your knowledge. What do you say?"

"From a technical standpoint, I can do this job, but I told you I will not be running around Prague, giving out bottles from one ministry to the other. I can't do that."

"Don't worry. I will take care of that."

"Vlado, this is different from buying a stove or a potato peeling machine."

"I know, but don't forget that I was the marketing vice director in the restaurant company for fourteen years. I handled every acquisition and every sale. I have incredible connections. Your job is to set up the shop and start production."

Vlado could see Dezső thinking, so he continued, "You can't find a decent job anywhere. I am not taking advantage of your situation by offering you a big job with little pay. I need a man like you."

Dezső was quiet.

"Here's one more offer to you," Vlado added, trying even harder to convince Dezső to take the job. "I want to show what a good businessman I am. I know that you haven't been able to get your passport for years. If you start production next September, I'll make it possible for your family to go on the Italian trip you've been dreaming about."

"Then I accept your offer," Dezső finally said. "I will start the production in time, you have my word."

On the way home, Dezső wasn't excited about his job as we spoke.

"I don't know why I am not comfortable with Vlado. And I hate traveling. Prague, Bratislava, and the everyday commute. We won't have family life for the next year. "

I knew Dezső was right. He had frequent business trips, but they were successful. Vlado made valuable connections that made it possible to get all of the machines.

At my job, everything continued as always. Nobody asked about my husband. Only Kati knew where he worked. During this time, she often spent the night at my home. It was great. Our friendship deepened, and the boys liked her. This way, the evenings without my husband weren't boring. One evening, she told me that the communist leader in our company asked her about Dezső. I found it interesting because they usually know everything.

Hearing about the Communist Party gave me chills. After twenty years, my file still read "NOT TRUSTWORTHY," only because my father was a capitalist. The regime actually robbed him, and yet I was considered untrustworthy. These thoughts made me furious.

In the time when my office was busiest in the afternoons, Fero came in.

"We have to see John, our Communist Party leader."

"Can't you see how busy I am, and at four I have a parent-teacher conference."

"We have to go."

"Okay, let's go. Have him write the delivery papers, make him schedule the jobs for tomorrow, or nobody has to do it. Stop the whole life because the Communist Party leader wants to see me."

"What's wrong with you?"

"What's wrong with me?!"

"You, as a boss, are not capable of telling your communist comrade that it would be better to meet, let's say, in the morning?"

"Fine, fine, I will call him and say that we will be in his office tomorrow morning."

During this time, Dezső was in Prague. He was not coming home for another two days. In the evenings, on the phone, we always shared our activities from the day, but I decided not to tell him about the meeting. I knew he would be worried for me.

LIFE GOES ON

I tried to act normal in the morning when the drivers came to my office, although my heart was jumping out of my chest. I wanted the earth to open up and swallow me. I wondered how I might act with our communist leader as my door opened.

"We are not going to the meeting. He doesn't have time, but he will call me when he does. Maria, what is your husband doing now?"

"Working."

"Is it true that Vlado hired him?"

"Yes."

"He can have a big problem."

"He will find a way to sort it out. Vlado is a very intelligent communist member," I responded.

I was about to step out for lunch when my phone rang. It was Vlado.

"Hi, I'm here at the courthouse. What are you doing?"

"I'm getting ready for lunch. Vlado, why are you calling?"

"Meet me in the coffee shop."

"Something happened to Dezső?" I asked worriedly.

"No, I need to talk with you."

When I arrived, the coffee shop was almost empty. Vlado sat at the table behind the masonry heater.

"You look pale," he said to me.

"I didn't sleep well. Tell me what's happening."

"I've made a great deal hiring your husband. He is a wonderful man, with a good personality. He is really centered. It's a pleasure to work with him. They love him in the ministry, too. The two of you are a perfect match. Whenever he talks about you, his entire face lights up, I can tell how much he loves you."

"Vlado, I'm assuming that's not what you want to talk about."

"You're right. This morning, the police arrested the manager of the lapidary and gravestone shop. He was stealing money. He made tombstones without registering them and put the cash in his pocket. The undercover police watched him for a long time. Now I need a Hungarian speaking manager immediately. This shop makes the most money for my company. Making gravestones from granite and marble is the best business in town."

He took a deep breath and continued, "You'd be perfect for that job. You could design unique tombs. The customers will love you. I know you would love it, too."

"Vlado, I have family obligations. I am raising two boys, my husband is barely home, we have a beautiful home here. The restaurant company can hold me for three months."

"In compliance with the labor laws, you can work for me tomorrow. You have the right to immediately follow your husband, if he is employed outside of your county. Do me a favor."

An inside voice told me to take the job. I thought to myself how God sent Vlado at this exact time. He was my savior.

"Okay, I'll help you."

"Thank you. I knew you to be a real friend."

As I was steeped in my thoughts while back at work, Fero walked into my office.

"Come, John is waiting for us."

"Before we go, I need to tell you, I'm resigning."

"You can't be serious."

"Ever since my husband was chased out of this town, I barely see him. He leaves home at 5 AM. and, most days, he doesn't make it home for dinner. We have children, but we don't have family life."

"I don't understand. You love your job. We love you."

"My family is more important."

* * *

I slept well. I didn't even notice when, in the early morning, Dezső stood next to my bed with a huge bouquet of roses. Vlado told him the news, and he drove straight home from his trip.

"If Vlado keeps his word, then next year I will take you to Italy for our second honeymoon. I also thought, if everything goes well, we can sell this house and buy another in Velky Krtis."

"Ambitious plans, I love it."

I was excited about my new job. I smiled when I imagined walking among graves, with measuring tape in hand. I thought to myself how my friends would make fun of me. I also thought it was funny.

We sat on the balcony watching the sunset. Dezső regained his optimism.

"Let's go to the Star restaurant for dinner," he said. "I'll take you out dancing! I can't even remember the last time we danced. Was it at our wedding? Anyway, it was long ago. I'll invite Sanyi and Lajos with their wives."

We had a lovely time, laughing and joking; we were sizzling with lust for life. The restaurant went dark. We could only see the light of a cigarette, in front of the orchestra. In the mysterious dim light, and the smoke of the cigarette, the singer sang Dezső's favorite song: "Don't ever say it's over, that there is nothing left for you, there is always something new, just keep waiting for a miracle and never say it's over." We slowly danced to the music. In his arms I was again a twenty-year-old girl, yet I found myself still in love after all those years. I couldn't feel the passing time; I was thirty-eight, and Dezső forty-two.

On the first day of my new job, we headed out to Velky Krtis in the sparkling sunshine. We passed Gács (Halič) castle, through the mountains and forest. It was a beautiful ride, and soon, we arrived at our destination.

Vlado waited for me in front of the lapidary building. We went into the office, from there to the shop, where Vlado took me around. It was crazy loud. A block of marble that was the size of my office was sliced for slabs. On the other machine, a worker in rubber boots and rubber apron polished a big granite plate. In the warehouse I saw two black marble slabs and a couple of candle holders.

"I don't think I can make the monthly plan with these resources."

"I am sure you will get all the granite you need. Make the good connection in the big warehouse in Zsolna will help. You should plan a visit there soon, so you can personally meet the manager."

My first week was hard. People flooded my office. They wanted to order gravestones. The news got around that a new boss was in town, but I didn't have anything to sell. They brought all kinds of alcohol and money to stuff my pockets. I was shocked. I encouraged them to come back three weeks later. Until then, I would try to get some slabs.

I got along very well with the workers. They told me how the business worked. When a job was finished in the cemetery, they got tips.

"You will get money, too, when the customer is happy with a nice piece of headstone. It is an unwritten rule, just like tipping the barber."

One week later, I was mentally prepared to go introduce myself in the main granite and marble warehouse. The workers helped me complete the list with all of the names of special marble and granite.

Friday afternoon, while organizing my office, the phone rang. It was Vlado.

"The Communist Party secretary is heading to your office. Be nice to him and promise him everything he wants. That is the kind of treatment they like."

A few minutes later, a middle-aged man arrived. He extended his hand for a handshake as he addressed me in Hungarian.

"Welcome to our town. I was glad to hear we have a new

professional manager in our lapidary shop. Vlado has a good instinct for hiring qualified people. I met your husband. He is a real professional. My name is Kovács Zoltán."

"Maria Imre. Take a seat. May I offer you a cup of coffee?"

"No, thank you. Drinking coffee is like being an alcoholic in my case. I drink it all day long."

"What can I do for you?" I asked.

"I come to you with a huge request, which I know, won't be easy to fulfill. In two months, it will be one year since my eighteen-year-old son passed away in a motorbike accident."

He sat quietly for a while, fighting his tears. I almost started crying myself, seeing the pain of a father who lost his son. I poured a glass of mineral water. He drank with slow sips.

"I apologize. Unfortunately, time doesn't reduce the pain. When I realize that the situation is permanent, the helplessness fills me with such despair that I can't control myself."

"I am truly sorry for your loss. It must be awful for a parent to lose a child."

"Thank you. My wife and I thought that, for the one-year anniversary, we would like to make a pure white marble gravestone for him. I know, it's almost impossible to find white marble, but here is this envelope."

"Please, don't give me money."

"I ask you to take it and use it to bribe everyone you have to. That is how we can reach our goal. Without money, nobody will give you anything, believe me. I can't cover my son's grave with hundreds of Korona bills."

He stood up. "Give me a call when you can start the work. We will plan the exterior of the grave together." He left without saying goodbye, leaving the envelope on the coffee table. A few minutes later, Dezső arrived, in a great mood.

"Guess what? Vlado received a permit to get me a work car! A Skoda. We can use it to commute. He was getting tired of me using his Volga for business trips."

I told him about my meeting with the Communist Party secretary. I opened the envelope; it had one thousand Korona in it.

The day before my business trip, I packed five bottles of vodka in a box and split the money into two envelopes with the thought that maybe I would have to give money to the manager and the warehouseman. I dressed professionally, in a nice suit, high heels, and carrying a stylish briefcase. I asked the driver of the truck to watch the entrance of the warehouse building. If I came out, he must bring the box in.

I stepped into an office with at least ten men present, all right in the middle of a big argument. A fat man was shouting, sitting at his desk.

"I already told you! The warehouse is empty!"

"It cannot be empty; I've been waiting here since yesterday afternoon. Last night a truck full of marble drove into the warehouse. I saw it with my own eyes."

"You did, but it is an order for a Soviet monument. Come back next week. Maybe we´ll get some granite from Italy."

"I don't care, I am not leaving. How can I make the plan, when I don't have anything to work with?"

"I'm calling the police!"

In the mayhem, everybody headed to the door. I stepped aside so they could leave. The man at the desk arranged his papers. I stood and waited for him to notice me. He finally looked up.

"What are you waiting for? I said the warehouse is empty!"

"I am not interested in the warehouse. Are you the boss here?"

He looked at me and said, "No. What do you want from him?"

"I need to talk with him."

"Who should I announce?"

"Comrade Imre."

He knocked on the boss's door and closed it behind him. The manager, Comrade Novák, came out, wearing very thick lens glasses, squinting at me as if he couldn't see me clearly.

"Please, comrade, come in."

He was sweating as he pointed at the chair.

"Did you come from Banská Bistrica to do an inspection?"

"No, I came from Velky Krtis to meet you. I am Maria Imre, the new manager of the lapidary shop."

His face turned red. He didn't know what to say. I got one of the envelopes and put it on his table.

"I brought this for you, in hopes that we will have a successful collaboration. I have five bottles of quality vodka in the car, too."

He smiled. His yellow, gappy teeth looked like a crummy rake.

"You are very good at business negotiations. I've been working here for over ten years but nobody has ever frightened me like you."

"I apologize. It was not my intention."

"Your calmness and appearance are similar to those inspectors who are always finding something to fine you for. Tell me what would you like from my warehouse?"

"Everything you can give me. Especially what others can't get."

He laughed out loud. "Is your truck covered?"

"Yes."

"I like lady managers. They are astute. Please, wait for me in the outside office. I will check my warehouse stock."

"Where should we put the bottles?"

"Bring them here, in my office."

The manager gave the driver instructions, how to get through the backyard from another street into the warehouse. He emphasized that only special buyers know this secret entrance.

"Comrade Novák, there is one more thing I would like to tell you. If you give me my monthly order, I'll give you every month the same amount of money you got now."

He shook my hand. "Okay, call me with what you need. I don't want you to send me a list. We will get the slabs ready before the truck gets here."

136

He loaded the truck with beautiful white marble slabs and various sizes of black, gray, and maroon granite until it was completely full. I acted as if it was the most natural way to do business.

"I hope you are satisfied, comrade Imre."

"I am. Thank you."

"Drive safe! Next time, we could go have lunch together. That will be fun."

I got in the car, pretending not to hear him. The truck had a heavy load, so we drove slowly on the hilly road. I was meditating about the system we have in our country. I was amazed about what five hundred Koronas could do.

The next morning, Vlado called my office.

"Was your trip successful?"

"I got some slabs."

"I'm coming now. I promised nice granite to my friend. The Communist Party secretary gets what he wants?"

"I got everything."

The secretary hugged me when he saw the beautiful white marble slabs. We designed a very attractive headstone and grave covering. He talked about me everywhere. The days that followed brought endless rows of people lining up in front of my office. I couldn't keep up, writing orders and cashing invoices. In four days, everything was sold and we had work for two months.

One afternoon, an old lady came in to the office. She wanted a smaller granite headstone for her husband. She had been to this office many times, but the previous boss never had a granite slab for her.

"You know dear, I am poor. I can't afford an expensive headstone, but now in my village, the bartender in the pub advised me to come again. He said, 'Auntie Mariska, I'm sure you can get a gravestone now, because a lovely Hungarian woman took over the lapidary's management.'

So, this is why I came in again. I would like to get a medium size, gray, speckled kind. My husband was a very good man. He deserves it."

"Come with me, Auntie Mariska. I have a slab that got chipped on the corner during delivery. We can cut off a couple centimeters, then it would make a beautiful medium size slab for you."

"My dear, this is beautiful. My God, it would look so nice on my husband's grave, but I don't know if I can afford it."

"Let me add up the numbers for you."

I drew the sketch, wrote down the text that was to go on the slab. In a few minutes, the invoice was ready.

"It costs eight hundred Korona, with installation included."

She started crying. "The previous boss couldn't do anything under three thousand Korona."

Three weeks later, we installed the headstone on her husband's grave. The next morning, she was waiting for me in front of the office.

"I couldn't sleep all night! I am so happy to see my husband's beautiful gravestone!"

She counted the money in her lap and gave it to me.

"My dear, I made you something as a surprise. I hope you accept it. I knit sweaters, vests, and scarves to supplement my income a little. Many customers don't take the leftover yarn. I used those to knit you a sweater."

She took the neatly folded, hand-knitted sweater out of her bag. Without exaggerating, it looked like a cardigan out of a fashion magazine, with beautiful color coordination, and impeccable, detailed handiwork. I teared up as I thanked her. I wore that sweater for years and remember that sweet old lady.

In July, before production started, over two hundred people came to the grand opening of Dezső's factory. City leaders, the Communist Party's powerful members, people from Prague and Bratislava, from the ministry, and many invited guests of Vlado's high connection circle attended. They toasted with champagne in Vlado's and Dezső's honor. Vlado loved to celebrate himself. In his speech, he praised Dezső's organizational skills and work ethic.

"There is no such thing as impossible to comrade Imre Dezső. If the eight-hour work day wasn't long enough, he'd work all night, just to keep his word. He never once looked for excuses, only solutions. He is truly a man of his word. I present him with this certificate and envelope, as praise and gratitude."

Vlado hugged him energetically. I smiled because I could see on Dezső's face that he was anxiously waiting for this circus to be over. Everyone knew him as a reserved, humble man. I admired him for that. He lived happily in two different worlds. One was where he lived with me and our family. The other place was his very private world of numbers, rules, and logic. The innovations, coming up with non-existent ideas, made his life complete. We were so different. I had always been led by liveliness, emotions, laughter, lust, and the choice to strive for a better future. I swept Dezső along with me, flying high in the sky, holding our breath, enjoying the view and the feeling itself, which many have never experienced. I would free fall from great heights and then soar again with full force to reach something new high above. I could laugh and cry, know how to win and how to lose. These feelings cannot be expressed in numbers. What makes a painting, a statue, or an opera beautiful? Nobody knows. It either touches us or leaves us cold.

It is rare for two such different people to walk together happily on the same path. Dezső loved my world. He fully enjoyed it, but he never invited me to his world of numbers. Only once did I catch a glimpse of his cherished world. He talked about the future when he would be a renowned inventor.

"I know that one day I will discover something that thousands of people will need. I feel it in my heart, in my brain, that knowledge which solves the unsolvable. Then I will fulfill my destiny."

We planned our trip to Italy for the first two weeks of August. We got our currency request approved, but our passports hadn't arrived yet. I wasn't worried because Vlado had promised us.

Most days, Dezső and I had lunch together in my office. I brought cooked food from home in containers. I heated it up on a little hot plate. He called me if he couldn't come or he would be late. I was out in the shop, writing down the measurements of the slabs to be invoiced. I proudly looked over our works. We created more and more unusual, unique, and modern styles. From the main warehouse, I always got whatever number of marble slabs I ordered. I didn't even drive there; I just put the bottles in a box, with five hundred Korona in the envelope. Vlado was amazed at what my collective was able to accomplish. Sometime we made the plan up to 200%. I looked at the big clock on the wall and rushed to my office. Lunchtime was long over. I called Dezső's office. The phone rang for a long time before the warehouse supervisor picked up.

"Dezső went to see the director, maybe an hour ago."

I knew they were interviewing skilled workers for the shop. That was probably the reason why he was late. I found out from my husband, after work, that the postman brought him registered mail.

He told me, "I could feel there was bad news inside when he gave it to me. I opened it. Neither the Communist Party nor Vlado signed our visa application. The reason was because there was plenty of work waiting for me until September with hiring and training new people. They couldn't risk not having the factory ready for production in September. It said, 'Please comrade Imre, understand our predicament and kindly postpone your vacation request till next year.'"

THE BARE REALITY

Dezső told me how he went to Vlado's office. He stood in front of the bar cabinet when he stepped in.

"My friend, so glad you came. I need a drink."

"I didn't come to drink. I got a letter from the president of the Communist Party."

"What did he say?"

"That none of you signed my visa application."

He grabbed the bottle of vodka and took a big gulp. "I'll explain everything."

"I don't need your explanations. I promised something. I kept my word, you didn't."

"Dezső, I don't want to argue with you."

"You don't want to argue with me? You have no reason to. I am a reasonable man."

"You are out of your mind! Are you implying that I am not? I took you in from the street! If it wasn't me, you would be rotting in the gutter now!"

Dezső walked toward the door. Vlado grabbed his arm.

"Wait! You don't know me. I am a man of integrity. I give you something bigger than Italian vacation." He took out a thick file from the cabinet.

"This is a luxury trip to Russia. Moscow, Stalingrad, Leningrad. It's only for ministers and communist leaders. This is my gift to you."

"Thank you, but I don't want to go to Russia."

"Dezső, don't ruin yourself. You can have all the knowledge and degrees in the world; you can wipe your ass with it. This is what you need!"

He took his Communist Party membership booklet out of his pocket and waved it in front of Dezső's nose as he left.

* * *

I sat in my chair, arranging invoices by numbers, when my office door opened.

"Vlado, this is a surprise. What brings you here this late afternoon?"

"I was nearby in the flower shop; I need to send flowers for name days to my friends in the city hall. I have to keep the connections alive."

He looked around my office. "This furniture is very old. It looks awful. It is a shame you make the most money for the company and your workplace looks bad. I will buy new furniture for you."

He was nervous. He gave me a bouquet of yellow roses he hid behind his back.

"I brought them for you."

"Why?" The question unwillingly popped out of my mouth.

"I had an unpleasant argument with your husband earlier, which I regret."

"Then you are in the wrong place. You should go to him."

I smiled, but Vlado remained serious.

"I am not at my best today. My wife left me with my son. I am desperate. I was so stupid. I have been drinking all morning. I´m arrogant when I am drinking. I offended Dezső terribly."

"What happened?"

"The Communist Party leaders recommended that I not sign your trip to Italy. The party in Losonc is convinced that you wouldn't come back. I didn't have the courage to take the risk. I too feel how much Dezső hates this system."

"What do you want me to do?"

"I have never met a man like your husband. Whenever your name comes up, his eyes light up. He loves you, respects you.

142

If you ask him to do anything, he will do it. Tell him to forget what I said today. Will you do that for me?"

"Okay."

He shook my hand and ran out of my office. He held his head in his hands, looking as though he was on the brink of insanity.

At home, Dezső was silent, and very disheartened.

I tried to calm him by saying, "I am sorry about what happened, but we can't change that. Life goes on. I admit I was wrong in 1968. I didn't realize how freedom is so important in life. I thought, when we work hard, we can achieve anything. After twenty years of hard work, we have what most people around us haven't even dreamed of. I'm scared to show how proud and happy I am because I feel any day, we can lose everything. I'm worried. Please don't make things worse with Vlado."

"Marika, I don't blame you for anything. You were about to become a mother and you were sheltered from bad things all your life. Those who love don't assume bad things."

"Dezső, I think we still have enough strength to start all over. I will find connections that will get us out of this country. You were right, this country isn't ours. Promise me you will make peace with Vlado. Everyone must think that we are happy and content."

The next day, Pali was taken into the hospital with a heart attack. The doctor told us: 'Mr. Jonas is very strong. Fortunately, he got to us in time.'"

We sat by his bed. He asked about Dezső's work.

"Pali, I successfully prepared the factory for September production, but Vlado didn't sign our visa application."

"Kids, please stop this passport nonsense. You are never going to get it. The more you push for it, the less likely you'll get it. I don't want you to leave the country. I don't want you to ruin your lives. I know families who never made it in America. It would be suicide to leave. Freedom! Gibberish! What are you going to do with freedom when you have nothing? Go and have a vacation in Balaton or Bulgaria!"

"Pali, we are not safe here. My father was beaten..."

"I know, you're a Regina girl! As you said, they kicked and beat your father, but he raised and never give up. You followed his advice. You fought and worked as hard as a man. You both reached the top. I don't get it, I really don't. Your whole life has been governed by the notion that they took everything from your families. You wanted to show this regime doesn't matter in terms of whether you'll be successful. I have to tell you, you are extremely successful. Now what do you do? Want to leave and leave everything to them voluntarily! I feel sorry for you, I really do. I hope you come to your senses. If you disagree with me, please don't tell me because that will make me so angry, I can get a bigger heart attack. I'm tired. You should go."

Saturday morning, I went shopping and ran into Kati. Her dad died not long ago and now her mother was in the hospital.

"Kati, stay with me while Dezső is in Prague. It's been a long time since we've had a good chat."

"I would love to do that, but I must feed the pigs. We have a few chickens. Mom's little dog is depressed because she's not home. Let's go to the Winter Garden, we can talk there."

We sat down under the palm. I looked around. The place brought back many nice memories.

"Kati, I haven't seen you in so long. Maybe you are married by now."

"I'm not, but I tell you, for the very first time in my life, I am very much in love. If it will last, I'll tell you more about it."

She reached for my hand.

"We are very good friends. I'll be honest with you. You look very tired. Is something wrong?"

"For the past year, Dezső has been away constantly, on business trips. Mom helps me a lot, especially with the kids, but his absence completely throws our lives upside down."

"Is Dezső cheating on you?"

"No, Dezső always loves me. We are both exhausted."

"Then, you should go on a vacation. I went with my boyfriend to Italy in May and it was marvelous."

"We wanted to go, but didn't get the visas."

Kati was in disbelief.

"Why?!"

"We are untrustworthy."

"What moron would think that you are not coming back? Your house is here; you guys are driving a big Italian car, and you have good jobs. I'll look into it. We can't achieve anything in this country without connections. Jano, your former boss, is the one who ruined your resume."

"Kati, don't worry. Summer is almost over."

"Italy is beautiful in autumn. In the past years, you just worked. Forgive me for saying this, but as a friend who loves you like a sister, I disapprove of your lifestyle. You are completely burned out."

She looked at her watch. "I have to go meet the doctor in the hospital," she said as she got up to leave.

UNEXPECTED CHANGE

O ne day, in the late afternoon, we were on the street, chatting with our neighbors.

"Dezső, are they coming for you?" our friend Tibor asked tensely as he glanced behind us. I turned around and saw a police car stop in front of our house. A police officer got out from the driver's seat and a handsome man stepped out from the front passenger seat. He opened the back door. Much to my surprise, Kati stepped out with ravished hair, her eyes swollen from crying. The handsome man came to me and asked, "Can we go into the house?"

Dezső walked in front of me with Kati. He opened the door. In the living room, the two men looked around.

We had a beautiful home that only our close friends had seen. It was one-of-a-kind, and it truly reflected us. It had beautiful carpets, a leather sofa, armchairs, lead crystals bowls, vases, and oil paintings on the wall. The dining room and living room were separated by a big marble fireplace.

"You have a quite nice life here out of town," the policeman said.

Kati pointed at the handsome man. "This is my boyfriend, Suchár Peter. He works in the Communist Party leadership. And he," she said, pointing to the other man, "is Mlynár Gustav, the head of the passport department."

"Kati, what happened to you?" I asked.

"Please forgive me; I didn't want to come here."

The policeman jumped at Kati's words. He said, "We came here with a special request. My cousin Peter and Kati had an intimate relationship. Kati is pregnant. Peter has a wife and three sons whom he will not leave, no matter what. If this gets out in town, Peter loses his job."

"This is not about my job. I love Kati, but I must be realistic. There is no way I can leave my family for an unborn child. I can't build our happiness on my family misery. We must break up. This is the only solution we have. We know that you have a close friend who is a gynecologist. Can you talk to him and arrange for Kati to go one night and take care of…"

Dezső jumped up. I had never seen him act in that way.

"Do you think I will ask my friend to do something illegal that could get him taken to prison? What makes you think that I'm a rotten, spineless man? What if Kati dies on the table?"

"Dezső, I want to keep this little life forming under my heart. I can raise him alone. Nobody has to know who the father is," Kati said.

Mlynár arranged his collar as if his uniform was too tight.

"You all say that, but then blackmail the guy all his life."

Dezső stood up.

"Please, sit down, I have a decent proposition," the policeman said. "This paper," he said, pulling it out from his packet, "is an official request for an abortion. We'll submit to a nine-member committee. They will analyze the reasons why the woman doesn't want her pregnancy. If you sign this request, stating that you are the father, they will perform the abortion. You are a married man, with two sons, who doesn't want this baby. You are nobody, I mean an unimportant man. This action is not going to hurt you anyway."

We were speechless.

"We are not expecting you to do this for free. As soon as you sign this request, I will immediately grant your family a two-week visa to Italy, which I have denied in the past."

I'll never forget this scene. A voice inside me said that this was our chance, the chance that we had been waiting for. We should grab it. Dezső squeezed my hand.

"I'll sign it. We love Kati. She doesn't deserve to be treated like this."

"Comrade Imre, come to my office tomorrow morning at ten. You sign the paper and I'll give you the visas. Kati, are you staying or coming with us?"

"I'm coming; I have to see my mom in the hospital."

Before they left, Kati whispered to me, "Marika, I loved him madly, believed every lie he told me. Now I am scared for my life."

They left. I looked at Dezső and said, "We are not coming back, right?"

"Right."

* * *

Dezső made a trailer, to be able take more stuff and pack comfortably for camping. He welded all my jewelry (most of which my father had made me) into the hitch of the trailer. That was the only thing we could take with us. We were careful and made sure nobody saw any unusual behavior, because the smallest sign might make the police take back our visas.

The day of our departure was looming. I often saw Dezső walking in the garden, looking at the tree full of apples. Later, he was in the living room, holding the big crystal vase he had given me for our first anniversary. In the evening hours, he played with the boys on the train panel. We both were saying goodbye to our past, especially our youth, when great things had happened, but we were ready for a new beginning.

I made a last quick trip to town. While shopping, I ran into a restaurant manager who was a good friend of mine.

"Tibor, good to see you, you look so good! How do you do that?"

"I spent one month on a Greek diet. We haven't had a

vacation in five years. My wife said she would divorce me if we didn't go to the Mediterranean Sea area. I admit I needed to rest. Are you going anywhere?"

"Yes, to Italy. Drive around Rome, Venice, camp on the beach."

"Were you able to get currency on the black market?"

"No."

"Then your money you get from the bank won't even cover the fuel. We had to give up visiting a few landmarks. I give you advice – get some green coffee. It sells well over there."

"What if they catch us at the border?"

"I can talk with my buddies. For three bottles of vodka and some beers, you can take across anything you want."

"You really mean that?"

"We are friends, aren't we? You helped me out many times."

"We are leaving Saturday, at noon."

"I'll give them a call. Whoever comes to your car, just say you have a message for XY from Tibor. I'll call you about who to look for."

* * *

Dezső signed the petition for abortion at the police station and we got our visas. I waited for Kati to call me, but she didn't. I went to the restaurant's management building and asked the guard to call her out. A few minutes later, she ran down the stairs with tears in her eyes.

"Kati, don't cry. We are not upset with you. You are not the first or last one who believes in true love."

"Thank you for all that you have done for me, I've already been in front of the committee. Peter arranged it so they didn't even ask me anything – just signed the paper."

"I'm glad."

"I have very good news for you. My mom had the surgery; she is recovering nicely at home. We talked about my baby and agreed we will raise my child together. He will be just mine! I am not going to tell anybody I am keeping my baby."

She hugged me with the joyfulness of a little girl.

Two days before we left, Mom wanted to come help me cut the roses.

"I know you are very busy. Two weeks ago, I saw your garden is neglected. Those beautiful roses need to be trimmed."

"We'll pick you up on the way home from work," I said.

Mom waited in front of her condominium. When we got home, I made fresh lemonade and took it out in the garden. I wanted to tell mom about our vacation plans. I put the jug and glasses on the table, under the balcony. Mom headed to the roses with the garden scissors. She looked back, and her pale face reflected immense pain.

"Could you bring the wheelbarrow so I can put the branches in it?"

"Yes," I said, wondering what made her so sad. When I stopped next to her, she straightened her back and looked me sharply in the eye.

"Do you have anything to say, something important to share with me?" she asked.

"Noooo."

"In that case, I'll tell you a piece of news. In fact, I shouldn't tell you."

"Then don't."

My heart pulsated so fast, I almost stopped breathing. It was in this moment I felt my mom had found out the story about Kati's pregnancy. In my little town, there were no secrets. Somebody from the committee had to spread the news, saying that my husband was the father of Kati's child.

"Mom, come sit down. We can talk in the shade."

"What's to talk about? That you allowed a snake into your home? How a woman like this doesn't die of shame. But that is not as despicable as how your husband acted. Conducting himself in such a shameless manner!"

"It's not true."

"Not true? The whole town's talking about it."

"That doesn't mean it is true!"

"You know about it?"

"Yes, and if you trust me, then you believe this is an evil gossip. I never lied to you. People are envious. We couldn't get a visa for years and now we finally did. Someone came up with this crazy gossip to throw dirt on Dezső and cause me pain. People are jealous of us. Mom, I swear on my children's lives, Dezső would never do something like this."

Her eyes were filled with tears.

I continued, "There is something else I want to talk to you about. Dezső and I have wanted to leave this country for many years. We were persecuted for many things. We had problems being Hungarians, for our capitalist background, for not being in the Communist Party. We are scared of threats and the anxiety of being destroyed by them. We want a better future for our sons. They will live in a free country. We'll leave tomorrow and we are not coming back."

Mom poured herself a glass of lemonade and drank it.

"Marika, you have everything. What more do you want? You've been working like an animal for the past eighteen years and now you want to give it all up."

"Mom, what you are talking about is only money. The freedom…"

"Please, darling, freedom is nothing but a concept. What do you do with freedom when you are homeless?"

"We won't be homeless. We are not afraid of hard work. In that world, you don't need to suck up to anyone; you don't have to be afraid to say what you think. Over there, I won't be an untrustworthy enemy just for being the daughter of a capitalist family. Mom, this isn't about me. It's about my sons. I envision a better life for them, different from the one our family has had for the past decades."

"So far, I always supported you in everything. God as my witness, if I knew that you would have a better life, I would pack your bags myself. I am scared for you. Life is difficult everywhere. You don't speak German or English. You're going to pay an enormous price for your dream of freedom."

She took her freshly pressed handkerchief to dry her tears, but they kept rolling down her pale cheeks like little pearls. I rested my head on her shoulder.

"I love you, Mom. My whole life you supported me, you watched over me, you tirelessly helped me all the time. Try to understand, I am a mother too, I want to do everything I can for the happiness of my sons. I promise you, a few years from now you will be with us, in a better world."

"God bless you. I pray that you have the strength and good health to start all over again. I'll be missing you very much."

The next morning, we made a plan. I took Mom and the boys to her place. From there, I went to the bank to get the currency. Then I planned to drive to Velky Krtís, close my shop, pick up Dezső, and pull the trailer home from his workplace.

When I parked my car in front of the bank, many people stood in line and the bank was still closed. One hour later, I still waited outside.

My son Attila, by that time fifteen years old, ran toward the bank.

"Mom, come home quickly!"

He took my hand, pulling me from the line. He was sweating and looking scared.

"What's the matter?"

"Two police officers came to grandma. They are looking for you. You must go to the station immediately."

"Go home and tell grandma not to worry, everything is alright. I'll get the money and go straight to the police."

The bank door opened, and before I went in, I squeezed Attila's shoulder.

"Don't worry. I'll meet you at grandma's place."

"But grandma said they will lock you up. I want to stay with you."

"Grandma is afraid of the police. You don't have to worry."

The money exchange took a long time since we planned to travel through four different countries. I stuffed the currencies into my purse and rushed out of the bank. I stopped by the car wondering what to do next. I had the passports. Maybe it was all a trick and they were going to take them from me. I decided to not take the car. Instead, I rushed over to the police.

As soon as I said my name to security, they immediately knew who I was and sent me to room number seven. An old police officer sat behind his desk, two ashtrays in front of him full of cigarette butts. I could barely see his face from all of the smoke in the room.

"Take a seat there."

I sat down in the chair in the middle of the room. I felt chills. Absolute panic had gotten to me. The door opened, and a younger, high-ranking officer stepped in.

"We looked for you at your workplace; we talked to the director and to your husband. We've been in Vidina, at your house, even looked for you at your mother's place. We need to interrogate you on a very important matter before you go on your vacation."

The phone rang. The old officer picked up.

"Great! Bring him here in room seven. Comrade Imre, will you please go to the side room? We have someone we need to talk to urgently before we talk to you."

As I went into the other room, they locked the door behind me. A thin ray of light came to the room through the small window close to the ceiling. The room was empty and very silent because of the cushioned door. It took all of my strength to fight my tears as I thought how unbelievable it was that this was happening to me. I paced around the room for quite a while; my legs were shaking when I heard the key turn in the door.

"I apologize for leaving you here, but the person we interrogated has, indeed, solved our investigation. It has come to our attention that your lapidary shop always has beautiful marble slabs available, which is rare these days. In the city Kassa, somebody robbed a big marble and granite warehouse. The robbers took over two hundred thousand Korona worth of marble slabs. We suspected you being in connection with them. We assumed that is how you managed to get cheap merchandise and sell it for a high price, keeping the money for yourself. Your director gave us all the invoices issued from the main warehouse."

He seized me up.

"The boss of that warehouse has very good taste. He must like you a lot, giving you materials in such quantities."

I wanted to respond to his disrespectful comment, but now, at the last minute, I could not afford to pick a fight with anyone.

"We are glad that you didn't get involved in this dirty business," he continued. "Your director would be very disappointed; he really stood up for you. Earlier we talked to a comrade who gave us the information we needed. They already apprehended two robbers. Now we can close the investigation. We hear you are heading to Italy. Have a nice vacation. I'll come see you when you return. I would like to make a nice gravestone for my parents."

I left the police station and ran to my mom's place. She opened the door, shaking.

"I thought I would never see you again!"

"It was a robbery of marble slabs; they thought I had purchased some. It's all sorted out now. I am going to my shop. When I come back, I'll pick up the boys and go packing. Tomorrow at noon we must be at the border."

The boys asked if they could come with me, and I said yes. As we passed the castle, dark clouds were gathering above the mountains. By the time I got to the top, there was thunder, lightning, and hailstorm the size of bird eggs crashing on my car. I had to stop. The deafening banging and the howling sound of the wind were frightening. Within minutes, the rain started pouring, and then the sun came out. A beautiful rainbow appeared before us. I got out of the car and cleared the ice drops off of the windshield. The rays of sunshine reflected in all of the dents that the hailstorm made on the car.

I got to my shop and immediately saw something was wrong. Water streamed out through the gate. A worker lay under the tree. He mumbled something; he was drunk.

"Boys, stay in the car. I will close the shop and we'll go to your father."

I rushed in and turned off the water. At the back gate, two workers were throwing up. Three of them sat on the ramp. They looked at me with distorted faces.

"We've received some vodka and wine," one said. "We didn't work today, just cleaned the shop. We had a couple goodbye drinks before our vacation."

"Leave the shop immediately. I don't want to see anybody when I come back."

I shut down the main electricity switch, the water faucet, and closed all of the gates and doors. The oldest worker approached me.

"Boss, we are very sorry."

"You guys disappointed me greatly."

* * *

Dezső ran to me when I got to his work.

"You can't imagine how I felt when the police called me. It's unbelievable, all the things we have to go through.

Mom called. She said what happened. The poor woman was laughing and crying at the same time. Later, Vlado called to say that everything was sorted out."

"Yup, it is a hectic day; I have a very bad headache."

"Let's get the trailer and rush home. We can have a good, strong coffee."

Because everything was arranged at the border, I packed winter clothes, jackets, and blankets. I put some family photos in a box. My heart broke for every keepsake that had to be left behind. I used to think I couldn't live without them, but life produces interesting situations. The trailer very quickly became packed to its maximum capacity.

Dezső went to get fuel. The kids and I had fun trying to close the top of the trailer. By the end, all three of us were sitting on top of it, trying to press down all of the things. During this great endeavor, Dezső came back. The terrified look on his face made me laugh.

"Honey, what is all the stuff that you packed?"

"Everything that we must have."

"Do you think about the fact that we must open everything at the border? Please take out the less important things."

"Relax. We won't have to open anything. Tibor, the manager from the restaurant close to the border, arranged that nobody check us at the border."

"Marika, please, let's not risk anything. I don't want to push our luck."

"I know you don't like these kinds of arrangements, but we don't have enough money to survive. When winter comes, do you think we can walk around in T-shirts and sandals? Be a little pragmatic."

"Ok, whatever you think is best for us. I might have a stroke from all this stress. I can't imagine how they won't check our car but unpack every other one. Have you thought about that?"

"I have not; Tibor is trustworthy. He asked me for many

favors in the past, so now, he does one for me. Believe me, if I feel any danger, I wouldn't do it."

I put three bottles of vodka in a box and planned to pick up two cases of Pilsner beer from Tibor.

In the morning, I prepared our last breakfast. The boys ate with a hearty appetite and talked about their vacation plans. Dezső put a few bits of omelet on his plate and went to the balcony. I packed sandwiches for the road and filled two bottles with the Losonc famous mineral water. Dezső and the boys loaded all of the food into the trunk of the car. I stepped out from the kitchen; Dezső was drying his tears, waiting for me in the entrance door.

"Are you ready?"

"Yes."

I walked to the car; I could hear the keys as Dezső locked the door. It would be nice to have a good cry, but in front of the boys, I had to look happy.

"Everything will be alright. Now we will stop at grandma's place, say goodbye, and then we are off on our big trip."

We had coffee with Mom. She laughed when the boys asked her what present they should bring her from Italy. She was a very strong woman.

"I will leave it up to you. Surprise me!"

Next to the car, Mom hugged us all.

"Come home if you don't feel your life could be better there. I'll pray for you."

We didn't cry. Our hands were shaking when we hugged for the last time. I got in the car. Dezső drove off immediately. I caught a glimpse of Mom in the sideview mirror. She buried her face in the apron and her whole body shook from crying. She raised her arm for a last wave. My tears were flowing in silence.

At the border, many cars were in front of us. I could see how the cars were separated in two rows. Whoever was traveling to the socialist countries went to the left side where the border police checked their passport, stamped it, and let them go. In the front of the building, on the right side, were benches. Next to them, cars were lined up which were headed for the west side of Europe. From these cars, people were unloading their stuff on the benches. Finally, it was our turn. The border patrol sent us to the bench.

"Unload your trailer and the trunk before the border officers come to you."

They were all talking in a group while we started opening the doors. I didn't know what to do.

"Why are you standing there? Open the trailer!" one of the officers scolded me.

I walked toward him. In a low voice, I said, "I am looking for Józsi, I have a message from Tibor."

He lowered his voice, too. "Okay." He turned to the others and tapped Józsi on the shoulder, saying, "Tibor sent you a message."

Three of them walked over to our car. I opened the trunk. One took some boxes with food out to the bench. The other took our passports, and Jozsi looked inside the car.

"Sir, what do you have in those boxes?" he asked very loudly, in an official voice, so everybody could hear him.

"Alcohol."

"You can't take that much alcohol with you. Turn around and take it back, or I'll have to confiscate it."

This time people were sorry for us. This theater that the police officer was playing was very dramatic. I told him sadly, "Just confiscate it."

Józsi and his colleague took the boxes into the custom building. The officer who checked the trunk was looking into the boxes, playing his role so the special treatment wouldn't be obvious. Józsi came back with a blank paper.

"This is your certificate for the confiscated items. I am sorry, but we must obey the law. Drive safe."

The barrier opened, and we were in Hungary. The boys were amused that the officers forgot to check the trailer.

In Balassagyarmat, my mom's birth place, I watched the familiar streets where I would never walk again. We came upon the Ipel River when a sharp noise came from behind the car.

"Dezső, pull over. I'll take a look."

"I can't stop here. It is the border area. Look at the signs."

"Just for a moment."

I stepped out and saw we had lost one screw from the license plate on the trailer. It was hanging, scraping the ground. I tried to push it back, but I couldn't. I stood up and a border patrol guard was already standing next to me.

"Do you know it is prohibited to stop here?"

"Yes, but our license plate broke off."

"Where are you heading?"

"Italy."

"May I see your passports, please? I will wait until you put your plate back."

Dezső straightened, but we didn't have a screw. He found a small stick on the ground and tried to use it, but it broke. I had few pairs of stockings in the glove compartment to use, in case my sandals were uncomfortable. I took one and ripped it up. We used it to tie the plate back on the trailer.

We crossed Hungary without stopping. Close to the Yugoslav border in the Csárdás restaurant, we had our last dinner.

"What should we eat?"

"Túróscsusza! Pasta, cottage cheese, and bacon, a Hungarian specialty."

I looked at the folk woven tablecloth and the red dotted tableware. These were to be our last hours on Hungarian soil. I wondered if I would ever have the chance to return to my beloved land again.

It was past midnight when we got to the Hungarian-Yugoslav border. The tall towers surveilled the area with reflector lights. I saw armed soldiers between the trees and the customs building, basking in the reflector light. The border was heavily guarded because it fell between the socialist and capitalist states. Two soldiers stood by the entrance, pointing their guns at us. Through the glass walls, we saw four officers' playing cards. On the sofa, two others ate a big goose or turkey thigh. They wiped their greasy hands and came out to us. I opened the box by my feet so they could see the Pilsner beer. I stepped out of the car and came face to face with a smiling Hungarian officer.

"Good evening or morning?! I see that you're coming from Slovakia. Do you speak Hungarian?"

"We are Hungarians from Felvidék."

The Yugoslavian officer said something, pointing at the Pilsner beer.

"We brought this beer for you. It goes nicely with your delicious dinner."

"That is very kind of you, Mrs."

I stepped aside so he could take out the box. He handed it to his Yugoslavian colleague and stamped our passports.

"Thank you for the beer. Enjoy your vacation!"

I couldn't believe it! The danger was over! Dezső looked exhausted. The boys were asleep. I waited for an encouraging hand squeeze or a smile. I was disappointed. I imagined when we successfully survived this day, we would laugh and cry together. Dezső's childhood dream had just come true but he was quite.

The sun was coming up. I felt a huge emptiness inside me. From that day on, we had nothing. It was only the four of us, going into the unknown, where nobody waited for us. We stopped in a small parking lot, on the side of the road. Dezső stepped out of the car and stretched.

"I am hungry and tired. We can have breakfast here and then I need to sleep for a couple of hours. We can be in Italy by tonight."

We spent five days on a campsite next to the Mediterranean Sea. The boys enjoyed swimming, taking long walks in the beautiful bay among the cliffs, and watching the Italian nightlife. We visited Venice. Our sons had fun. With Dezső, we were worried. It was unbelievable how differently we now saw the situation. Here, in the foreign land, where we couldn't understand the people, we felt the bare reality. We were alone. We couldn't even ask for help. It was a devastating feeling. Could we responsibly decide we were capable of making a good living where we couldn't speak and didn't know anybody?

On the fifth day, after breakfast, Attila and Csaba went down to the beach. I cleaned up after breakfast. Dezső stayed with me.

He said, "Since we left home, I've been constantly thinking about our future. Why we should stay and why we should go back. I feel I have an immense responsibility on my shoulders. I can do great things in America. If, within a few years, we are able to open a machine shop, I can teach the craft to my sons, and then the Imre Company will be world famous. We both know, nothing can be achieved without sacrifices. I have faith, resilience, and knowledge to achieve my goal. The new beginning will be extremely hard, I am ready for it. It's true we are losing twenty years of hard work back home, but I think we can create something even bigger in a free country where knowledge and hard work make us successful."

I felt he was not sure what to do.

"Marika, if we are not on the same page and you are not convinced that you can take on the difficulties of starting all over, then we should go back. Don't do it for me. That will break your heart in the long term. I want you to be happy."

"Dezső, I follow you. You are the head of our family; the final decision is yours. The future of our children is just as important to me as it is to you. I am ready for any sacrifice. I'm not a complaining woman; I'll work hard hand in hand with you to survive. I promise you, if your plan doesn't come through, I will never blame you for it. We'll do everything possible to secure the best future for our family."

"Then, we pack and take off to Germany."

THE ROAD TO FREEDOM

The next morning, the boys didn't understand why we were cutting our vacation short. Dezső told them we were running out of money and wanted to see some famous landmarks on the way.

The traffic through the Alps was slow. Many travelers headed south and north, with boats and trailers. Csaba asked his father to stop because he was hungry.

"Our destination is an hour away. We'll have dinner there," Dezső said.

Beyond a curve, we saw the German flag and the border station. I was nervous because we didn't have visas for Germany. Far from us, a border patrol guard directed the traffic with his tiny German flag. As we got closer, we could see those who showed their passports through the open window he directed to the left where they stamped their visas. On the right-hand side, German cars drove through without stopping. Dezső joined that row and we easily got into Germany. A few minutes later, we found a picnic park. I got fresh bread in Italy, and two of our own cans of roasted pork were our dinner. Dezső took a picture of our sons. Attila was sixteen, Csaba ten.

"Daddy, why did we come to Germany? Was this part of our vacation plan?"

"No, it wasn't. Boys, this is a historical moment in our family's life. Your mother and I decided that, if we ever got the chance, we would go to America. We want you to grow up in a free country where there are endless opportunities."

Attila's face lit up. "I want to see America!"

Csaba turned his big blue eyes at his father. "How long are we staying there?"

"Forever."

Csaba's eyes immediately filled with tears. "I'll never see my grandma again?" he asked.

My eyes filled with tears too. "Of course you will. Grandma will come soon and live with us."

"But I want to see my friends, too. I want to go home. I love my home."

"Csaba, you will be very happy in America, I promise you. Sometimes in life we make difficult decisions. We give up things for a much better goal."

Attila interrupted me. "What happens when we don't like America? Can we go home?"

"No, we can't," Dezsõ said. "America is a very special country; many people want to live there. It's going to be a great honor if America accepts us and gives us a new home."

"Your father is right," I said, backing up Dezső's words. I looked up to the sky. The stars were shining above us. We all hugged each other and I said a short prayer.

"My Lord, I pray to you, please gives us strength and health to walk on the path where there is peace, love, and success in front of us. Please bless us. Amen."

PART TWO

FAREWELL, EUROPE!

We reached the outskirts of Munich, slept in the car, and ate leftovers for breakfast. Desző anxiously looked for a police station for legalizing our stay in Germany. He parked the car, and with great self-confidence, along with the dictionary and our passports in his hand, he walked into the building. We waited for a long time until he came back. His forehead was beaded with sweat, and he had a hopeless look on his face.

"It's not a simple task to settle in this country. They sent me into five different offices. I tried to explain what I want, but nobody understood me. What should we do now?"

"First we must sell few of my jewels; we barely have money. I'll try exchanging in the bank all of the remaining currencies for Marks."

We pulled up in front of a jewelry shop. I put two pair of earrings and a bracelet on the counter. A very ladylike, sympathetic woman greeted me, and without telling her what I wanted, she called somebody from the shop behind the store.

The broken gold price was low. I didn't have another choice, so I said okay. I teared up and took the money. Selling my father's custom-made jewerly for so cheap was painful. I walked to the door, but the man called me back. He took a 100 Deutsche Mark bill from the register and gave it to me. The lady hugged me. It's a terrible feeling when people feel sorry for you, but I was grateful for their kindness and generosity.

I found a bank around the corner. I laid all of our leftover money – Italian, Yugoslavian, Hungarian, and Slovakian – on the counter. The teller separated them and exchanged them all. Now we could survive one week at a campground. I hoped we would find an emigration office; otherwise, we would have to return to Slovakia.

While I was exchanging the money, my family window-shopped nearby in front of a toy store. Csaba ran to me.

"Dezső promised me while we are in Germany, I could start a Smurfs collection." All his life, he had called his dad Dezső, his name having been his first word when he was a baby. Since Dezső liked it, he allowed it to continue, and it created a very special relationship between father and son, almost like friends.

The Smurfs were displayed in the store window on a panel that showed cities, hills, forests, lakes, and bridges. I watched Csaba with his nose pressed against the window, staring at the Smurfs. I wanted to cheer him up.

"So, which Smurf should be the first in your collection?"

"The mountain climber."

"Let's go get it for you."

In the store, we found out that if we bought five Smurfs, we would get two for free. We decided to get them. Attila got bored; he went out to look at different store fronts. He waved to us while standing in front of a jeans shop.

"When can I get an original pair of jeans?"

I looked at the prices.

"Not in the near future."

"Mom, please take a closer look at them."

He pulled me back. Dezső and Csaba walked away.

"I told you, we can't afford it now."

"Can't you see what I see?"

He pointed to the corner of the window. It read: WE SPEAK HUNGARIAN.

"Oh! What would we do without you?"

"Dezső, come back. Look what your son found!"

He squeezed Attila in an embrace.

The store owners were an elderly Jewish couple. We became friends with the woman, Ilona, immediately. She got the phone book and called the Tolstoy Foundation. Then, she wrote down their address, explaining to us how to get there. Dezső mentioned to them his qualifications and his plan to work in America in some kind of machine shop.

The shop owner, Pista, said, "I know somebody in California who owns a medical equipment repair shop. He escaped from Hungary in 1956, the time of the revolution, at the age of 17. He didn't achieve much, but I can give you his address. If you're ever in California, he can help you if you are in need."

He tore a piece of brown wrapping paper and wrote down the name, phone number, and address.

We easily found the Tolstoy Foundation. Linda, the Hungarian couple's daughter, took our case. Filing papers for the German authorities and the American Embassy took a long time. It was late afternoon when we got the address for a hotel for refugees and a month's worth of an allowance for food. This amount would come to us every month from the German government. It is amazing how West Germany handled political refugees.

We said goodbye to Linda when Csaba whispered to me, "I'm very hungry."

Linda hugged him and said, "You didn't have any lunch today?"

Csaba was shy and very quietly said, "No, we had just breakfast."

Linda took a heavy box out of the closet. "We have these packages for families who are traveling by car through the country, but I give it to you. It is late for food shopping. Take it to your hotel room."

In the hotel, we got two rooms next to each other. The bathrooms and a fully equipped kitchen were at the end of the corridor. I enjoyed my first shower with fine, apple scented German soap and shampoo. That night we slept like babies. At ten in the morning, Dezső gently stroked my shoulder.

"Good morning, my sunshine."

At first, I didn't know where I was. He sat next to me, laughing, with his blue, sparkling eyes. I don't know how he managed to grow younger overnight. He dragged me out of bed, with a mischievous smile.

"Look, I set the table for breakfast. The boys are hungry."

"In twenty years, you never set the table!" I said.

"See? This is what the western air does to me."

We had wonderful food from the box Linda had given us. During breakfast, I suggested going into town.

I told myself to let go of the stress, humiliation, and pain we lived through in the past. I knowingly wanted to not look back, but rather to plan for our future the best I could.

We had no plans and no goals. Wherever our steps took us was where we would go. Chasing each other on the bank of River Isar was fun. Buying roasted pumpkin seeds, popcorn, and chocolate dipped ice cream made our stomachs messed up, but it didn't matter. We joked and laughed like never before.

For the next four months, I don't recall any exciting memories. We met a family from Hungary: Pipo Misi, his wife, Erzsi, and their daughter, Kristina. Attila, Misi and Dezső went together to study English. Kristina spent her days playing with Csaba and the Smurfs, or we went to the nearby playground. Erzsi and I shared memories while we watched the kids. One day, I came back from grocery shopping to the hotel when the doorman waved at me. Next to him, a well-dressed lady reached to shake my hand.

"My name is Isabell. I heard you came from Hungary."

"We came from Slovakia. We are Hungarians from Felvidék."

"I personally like the Hungarians from Felvidék and Székely areas in Romania. You guys have a hard life in those states, which developed a strong backbone in you. I am looking for a trustworthy, intelligent housekeeper. The woman who worked for me left for Australia. Our house is big. Do you think you could help me?"

"Gladly."

We had a long chat about my family and why we left Slovakia. Isabell told me about her first years as an immigrant in 1956 when it had been the Hungarian bloody revolution. They barely escaped from the Russian secret service. Her husband was one of the organizers. At that time when we met, they lived a very private life because they were still in danger. Many times, it happened that people disappeared, because the undercover communist agents took them back to Hungary and jailed them.

We were just about to say goodbye when Dezső came downstairs. I introduced them.

"Mister Imre, my brother is building his house in the outskirts of Munich. Would you be interested in working for him?"

"Yes, I would like to."

"We have to be very cautious; we can't let anybody come close to us. My husband has a high position at the Hungarian Free Radio which is against the Russian dictatorship and the communist regime. Please don't talk about us with anybody."

"Of course."

After all of the lazy days, we were happy to safely earn some money. Isabell and her husband László often invited us for dinner. We enjoyed each other's company and developed a close relationship.

It was a big surprise when we got our interview appointment with the American Embassy in Frankfurt in November. I got excited for the early hearing because many families in the hotel had been waiting over a year, and still waited. At the same time, I got nervous about what would happen if they denied our political refugee status and we couldn't go to America. My husband absolutely believed America was waiting for him with open arms.

We got interviewed in separate rooms. The main interest was about the reasons why we didn't want to live in Slovakia, and what kind of problems we had there. In the end, I got two final questions: Was I a member of the Communist Party? Had I denied my Hungarian ethnicity to get ahead in Slovakia? My answer to both questions was "no".

I then got escorted to a beautifully decorated living room, with a table full of food, coffee, and soft drinks.

"Your husband will come here once he finishes his interview. While you are waiting, there are magazines, and please enjoy our buffet."

Soon, Dezső came in with his interviewer.

"Your family has a big chance to get very soon to America. There is a great demand for qualified, educated people. Generally, the immigration approval can take two years. I am sure you will get the political refugee status soon."

On the second of December, we celebrated Attila's sixteenth birthday. We missed my mom. I often thought about her; she was without any news from us. We were afraid to contact her, thinking that the authorities might find out where we had gone.

In early February, we got our approval letter from the American Embassy, allowing us to enter the USA. That was an unforgettable day; all of our worries were gone. The choice was between Chicago and New York. These were the two cities with the highest demand for my husband's profession. Dezső's dream was to go to California. He told me he must talk with Linda, how maybe she could help.

One night, he came home late with lipstick on his cheek. I had to laugh when I saw him.

"Where have you been? Look in the mirror, what's that on your face?"

"You got me! I wanted to surprise you. On the way home, I bought flowers for Linda. She hugged and kissed me on the cheek."

Attila looked at his father.

"Why did you give her flowers?"

"Well, this is the secret that I didn't want to tell you before I had the result. I asked her to arrange California for us. I told her I had back problems and how the cold weather is not good for me."

"What did she say?" I asked.

"She didn't promise anything, but she will call the embassy."

A couple of days later, the door slowly opened, and a hand appeared, holding a sign: CALIFORNIA. Dezső jumped into the room, making funny faces. He theatrically bowed before me, then handed me an envelope and a handful of tropical flowers.

"This is my last bouquet to you in Munich. Linda arranged California for us! On Monday, we go pick up our papers and flight tickets in her office. Then, we get suitcases from a warehouse, new clothes, basically everything we need. This is a gift from the German government to political refugees who are leaving this country."

Isabell and Laci invited us for a farewell dinner. They gave us five hundred dollars as a goodbye present.

"Put it to good use. We wish you all the best!"

The last evening with our friends, we had a nice dinner. Saying goodbye, even though we had only known each other for seven months, was hard. They all came with us to the train station where we hugged and wished each other lots of luck.

I sat on the soft, cushioned seat in the train and cried. It was painful to leave Europe. At the same time, I felt happy that America was giving us a new home. The bullet train was speeding toward Frankfurt. Dezső stood by the window. He couldn't see much in the dark and at that speed, but I think he said goodbye to the old world and let the new one in. At eight o'clock in the morning in Frankfurt we turned our backs to the past and flew to America.

CALIFORNIA

We had a long flight ahead of us before we landed in Los Angeles. For hours, we could see the ocean and the bright sunshine above us. As we approached the land, we encountered turbulence and storms. The safety belts had to always be buckled. The plane took such dives that the passengers were shrieking of fear. It was frightening to see the lightning. I felt like the plane was standing in the fast-moving clouds. It looked like a crazy battle being fought below us as the plane was surrounded by lightning bolts on both sides.

At ten in the evening, we saw the city lights of Los Angeles. We got our immigration papers and working permits in the airport, which marked the beginning of our life in the free world.

We looked for the Tolstoy Foundation representative. It was past midnight when I saw the sign: IMRE FAMILY. The young man asked if we spoke English.

"No, Hungarian, Slovaks."

He looked at our papers. "You came from Slovakia; you must speak Russian."

"Yes, we speak Russian." Dezső's eyes lit up. "I'm Dezső."

"I'm Boris."

They hugged like friends. Arranging our affairs in America in Russian was unbelievable. In the socialist states, it was mandatory to learn the Russian language, but we never thought we would have the chance to use it.

We drove in the direction of LA. The city lights and hundreds of cars on the freeway amazed us. All five lanes of the 405 and 101 highways heading south and north were bumper to bumper.

Around three o'clock in the morning, we turned onto a dark street. Boris stopped the car in front of a motel. There were bullet holes in the walls, the windows had bars, and the neighborhood looked like a dumpster. I got out of the car, nearly stepping on a homeless man sleeping on the sidewalk, covered with blankets.

"Mom, look, we're in Hollywood!"

Indeed, on the mountain, not far away, I saw the HOLLYWOOD sign.

"Yes, this is Hollywood, too, but this part of town is completely run-down. The famous, shiny city of arts is north of us. Unfortunately, this is the only place where we can get accommodations for immigrants. Our budget is small, and we have to make the most of every penny, to be able to help as many families as possible."

The motel was a long, two story, rickety building. There was downstairs access to the rooms, straight from the street. Before we reached the metal staircase, a woman with trembling hands, with a half-smoked cigarette hanging out of her mouth, sat behind the barred window. Boris gave her our papers and got the room key. We struggled with our big suitcases on the narrow staircase. He stopped next to our room door, and he gave us the key and a card with the address to the office where we were expected at ten the next morning.

Dezső opened the door and turned the lights on. I stepped in; cockroaches ran on the bed and walls. Dezső got a towel and smacked the bugs. The boys were scooping them up from the dirty carpet using the laminated motel regulations sign and flushing them down the toilet. A terrible smell in the bathroom made me gag. I wasn't able to get the window open. Dezső removed a bunch of needles from the window track. After we finished cleaning, we washed up and lay down, still dressed. We were hungry, but we didn't have any food. Boris said there was a grocery store nearby, open day and night, but he warned us not to leave the room after dark.

"In this part of town, night time is dangerous to be out on the streets, especially for white people."

My family fell asleep in minutes, but not me. It seems unbelievable, when I look back on that night, how none of us panicked. We arrived in America and we planned that the next day we would manage our next step leaving this place.

I couldn't close my eyes; I constantly felt the cockroaches crawling all over me. I turned on the bedside lamp and covered it with a towel so I could keep watching them in the semi dark. I spent the night tiptoeing with the towel, killing cockroaches. At six in the morning, Dezső went to the store to get something for breakfast.

We were in front of the Tolstoy Foundation office before ten o'clock. The California sky was a gorgeous blue that could not be found anywhere else. The sunrays were dark yellow, just like gold. Walking amongst the palm trees, looking at the Hollywood sign far away, our surroundings shocked me. The big houses with broken windows, dried out trees, bushes, empty swimming pools, garbage on the street, and next to it homeless people laying everywhere was devastating.

A middle-aged man arrived. "I'm Sergej," he said. "I'll handle your case."

"Welcome in America. I will briefly tell you what the plan is for the next six months. The Tolstoy Foundation will cover the motel expenses and we will give you food stamps for every month. In the mornings, with other families, a school bus will take you to the "English is My Second Language" class. After six months, hopefully you will be able to communicate on a basic level. Then we will find work for you, so you can start living independently. Learning the language is the key to success."

"Mr. Sergej, before we move on, I would like to start work right now without going to school. I don't need any language abilities for locksmith or welding work."

"Oh, my friend, it's not that simple."

"I am very grateful to the Tolstoy Foundation for everything you did for us, but under no circumstances can we stay in this motel. Please call a couple machine shops or factories where I can work. This way I save you lots of money and we can live on our own."

"Mr. Imre, that is impossible. Our protocol is like I told you."

"Then, I have to find a job on my own. I am 44 years old; I don't have time to go to school for months. I want to work and learn the language same time."

"Then I give you one month of food stamps and wish you best of luck. If you manage your life on your own, I will close your file. Don't make any hasty decisions. It is very difficult to start a new life in America, especially without speaking English or having any connections."

We left. Csaba was holding my hand as he whispered, "Mom, let's go home, I don't like it here."

"Don't worry, everything will be fine."

Dezső, with Attila, looked in the phone book for machine related companies. Since we didn't know any city names in the area, we had no idea how far the places were. Dezső got frustrated.

"I don't know how to start the search. If I get into a taxi, one place is three hours away; the next is in a completely opposite direction. It is so sad that Sergej doesn't want to help me. Now let's go to the grocery store. I can't think on an empty stomach."

We passed a McDonald's restaurant. I was hungry for a cooked meal.

"Boys, who wants to eat some American food?"

They ran to the door. After the airplane dining and simple sandwiches, we were famished. The hamburgers were delicious with the crispy fries and big glasses of Coke.

In the grocery store, we got everything for our dinner and for the next day, breakfast. It was hard to shop because we didn't have a refrigerator. In the motel, I glanced at Attila's jeans as the boys turned on the TV. I remembered the German couple.

"Dezső, do you remember we have an address from the jeans shop. I put it somewhere, but where?"

"Honey, try to find it. That Hungarian guy could be our savior."

I looked in every pocket of my purse, in my wallet, but it wasn't there. In Germany, I bought a little book for addresses and business cards. I found it in there. Westlake Village was north of Hollywood, about a two hours' drive. The next day, Dezső called Ferenc, the owner, and made an appointment to meet him.

The next morning, we called a taxi and Dezső left with high hopes of finding a job. He didn't return for two days. For me, that seemed to be a good sign, and I thought that maybe he was already working in probation. We had lunch in McDonalds and sat in a little park. What a contrast between the beautiful, fast, shiny cars speeding on the road and homeless people covered in dirty cloths under the bushes.

Back in the motel, Attila sat next to me. At sixteen, he understood the severity of our situation.

"Mom, do you think we can make it in America?"

"Definitely. We knew we would have to face big challenges, but our strong will, knowledge, and experiences will make us successful believe me."

"I'll help you every way I can, even work after school. I don't want to stay here."

Csaba couldn't fall asleep.

"Mom, what happens if Dezső doesn't come back? What are we going to do?" Csaba's face was white. At the age of ten, I could imagine how he perceived all of these drastic changes after having a safe home for all his life. He curled up in my lap.

* * *

Saturday, after breakfast, we heard a knock on the door.

"I'm back!"

I could tell from Dezső's voice that he had good news.

"Hurry, tell me what happened," I said.

"The machine shop is in a nice industrial center in Westlake Village, which is an upscale town. When I got there, the shop door was open. I didn't see anybody or hear any machine noise. There was an old lathe, and a better looking milling and grinding machine. On a long bench were scissors and some surgical knives. A man soldered a pair of scissors with an interesting shape. I waited until he finished. It was just a couple of seconds because he angrily tossed it in the trashcan.

"Hello! My name is Imre Dezső. We spoke on the phone a couple hours ago."

"Hello! You were fast."

He hugged me vigorously it is a Hungarian custom.

"I came in a hurry. My family is in a dirty motel room in Hollywood. We have to get out from there."

"When did you come to America?"

"Two days ago."

He burst out in laughter. "Man, I almost starved to death for months when I came to America. I washed dishes, cleaned restaurants. Sometimes I slept under the bridge. Do you speak English?

"No."

"You are in a very difficult position."

"I'm a versatile professional, which I'm sure my employer will greatly appreciate."

"What can you do?"

"I have a machine design college diploma, three years of tool making apprentice course, a welding school. I can solder and learn the locksmith trade. I professionally operate lathe and milling machines and can design missing machine parts on my own innovations."

"I tip my hat to you if you can do all of that at a professional level," Ferenc said. "I repair medical tools. Every week I collect blunt knives, and scissors, and the following week, I return them to the hospital and pick up others. I could have more work if I have somebody who can do different, more complicated work."

He brought me the broken scissors he had just been working on.

"This pair of scissors broke at the joint; it is impossible to solder it. The doctor would pay good money when I can fix it because it is a custom-made, very expensive piece. He said if I can't fix it, just toss it in the garbage. Can you solder it?"

"Of course."

So, I soldered, grinded, and polished it in twenty minutes, then handed to him. It looked like new.

"Dezső, this is outstanding work. I can't even tell where it was broken. I give you a deal. I have a bunch of broken medical instruments in this closet that the hospitals wanted to throw away. If you can repair these, I will hire you."

Yesterday evening, I put all the repaired instruments on the table. They looked brand new. When Ferenc came in the morning, he was speechless. He hired me.

Then Ferenc said, "I have an old car behind the shop. Take it and bring your family. Be here by early afternoon so I can help you get an apartment near my shop. I'll be your guarantor because you don't have any record to check on you. Around here, the living is expensive. Unfortunately, because you don't have a car, you must stay in this area."

THE FIRST YEARS

In the afternoon, we arrived at Ferenc's office. He was happy to meet us.

"Good to see you all. I must tell you, your husband is a very lucky man to have found me. When I came to America, the first year was miserable. Many people come to this country thinking money grows on trees and the fences are from sausages."

I couldn't understand what the point of his story was. How he could compare himself to Dezső when he had no profession. Sharpening knives and scissors was his accomplishment after twenty years. I wanted to assure him that I never thought money grew on trees and he was the lucky one if Dezső would work for him.

"Do you have any money? The apartment monthly rent is $790 and you have to pay the first and last month now."

"Yes, we have."

"First, we will go to the bank and open an account for you; then, we'll go to rent the apartment. Monday, we'll register the kids for school. I'll take you for sightseeing to show you all the important spots you need to know. The grocery store, bank, doctor's office, and Kmart have everything you need which is close to the apartment. California's public transportation is not good. Everyone drives cars. It would be useful for you to soon buy a used car."

That afternoon, we were handed the keys to our first home in America. Yes, it was expensive, but living with middle class, working people and having our children go to good, safe schools made us feel good. Our place was empty, and we didn't know how long it would take us to get even the most basic things, but we had a home. I stood in the middle of the living room and said a little prayer.

"Thank you, Lord, for bringing us to this country. Please bless our home with health and happiness. Guide us on our journey; give us bravery and stamina to solve all challenges in front of us. Amen."

I laid the sleeping bags on the floor that we had thankfully brought with us from Europe. The kitchen had a refrigerator, stove, and oven. I had two pressure cookers I brought from Slovakia with me, and I knew that when we buy a few plates, bowls, and cups, our kitchen would be equipped for the start. We walked to the grocery store and bought everything we needed.

Our first dinner was hot dogs, standing in the kitchen. Later not having chairs, we stood on the balcony and watched the neighbors coming and going in an exotic park surrounding the apartment complex. Csaba sat on the bedroom floor and spread his Smurfs in the corner. He had over fifty of them by that time. Attila decided to go out and find the nearby Kmart store that Ferenc had mentioned.

Dezső hugged me.

"I know it's not going to be easy for some time, but we'll succeed. I have a good job."

In the morning, we had a good breakfast and Attila wanted to show us the Kmart.

"Dad, it is the best store I have ever seen. They have everything."

On the first street corner we reached, a large sign read GARAGE SALE. People were selecting all kinds of stuff. I saw a few pieces of furniture, too.

"Dezső, let's take a look."

The couple spoke German. Dezső asked if the furniture inside the garage was for sale. They showed us the table with six chairs, along with a sofa, armchair, and an old TV.

"We are moving back to Germany; that's why we're selling these old things."

Attila told them how we had just come from Germany and that our apartment was empty.

"If you want these pieces, we'll give you a reasonable price."

"How much?"

"Hundred dollars."

"For everything?"

"Yes. We Europeans should be cohesive. If you want, later we will take the furniture to your place with our truck."

I was amazed at how we had furnished our apartment after only being in America for one week.

At the Kmart, we got plates, bowls, and cups. All the way home, I hummed my favorite songs. I never thought that a bunch of used furniture would make me so happy.

We got home, and I started to cook our dinner with great excitement. I put together our favorite dish, chicken paprikas and my homemade noodles (nokedli). I thought I would invite the German couple for dinner. Having a meal together at the table that we just bought from them would be fun.

At five o'clock, they arrived. Elsa came into the kitchen, carrying a big box with tablecloths, plates, glasses, and a bottle of champagne. The boys arranged the furniture in the living room and the dining room, turned on the TV. It worked perfectly. The smell of the food quickly inundated the house. Elsa curiously peeked into the pot.

They stayed for dinner and liked my cooking. With the champagne, we toasted to a prosperous future. We had a wonderful evening talking about life experiences, continuously seeking success and happiness. Dezső shared his plans in such an optimistic way, I felt his unstoppable energy. That evening, we found our way back to that road which we had started walking twenty years prior. It wasn't a new beginning; rather, it was a way of moving forward.

On Monday, Dezső started work at seven in the morning. Ferenc came for us at nine, and we enrolled the kids in school. On the way home, I asked him what the job possibilities were for me in the city.

"There isn't much. Women like you in this neighborhood don't work. I don't want to offend you, but if you find a job, it would be in a fast-food restaurant where people like us don't work for minimum wage."

"I can't afford to be picky now. It would be better than nothing. We don't have anything right now; we are sleeping on the floor, so every penny counts."

"I know it's not easy, but it's humiliating to go work with inferior people when you are in your forties."

"Look, I don't speak the language, so I don't have much choice. First, we must learn English. Then, I can climb higher."

"I wish you the best of luck."

He wasn't thrilled with my philosophy. He wanted me to be despaired, to be someone who needed comforting. I couldn't quite put my finger on it, why I disliked him.

By the afternoon, the kids returned from school. For three months, they attended English language classes with other students from different countries. Both loved it and told me the American school is much better than back home.

"We don't have any homework, just to read loudly fifty words, fifty times. The teacher wants us to mark on a paper fifty lines, showing that we completed the task."

"It means that you must know them by heart."

"No, we just have to recognize the words."

Attila consented to Csaba's explanation. I told them how I wanted to learn twenty words every day.

"Mom, you need to learn sentences."

Attila copied thirty sentences from his notebook for me. Some sample sentences read: I don't speak English. I have family. I came from Slovakia. My name is, my husband's name is, my sons' names are, I am looking for job, show me what I need to do, etc. This way, learning English seemed easy. I wanted to speak English as soon as possible.

Dezső wasn't excited about school. He wanted to work long hours, earn money, and climb on top of his imaginary peak, from where he could provide everything for us. With his talent, technical knowledge, and handicraft, success was undeniable. He came home happy after his first work day.

"It smells great in here. I'm so hungry!"

It seemed we had a bigger appetite in America. Dezső had a second plate from his all-time favorite strapachka (Slovak dish), with lots of bacon on the top. True to his habit after dinner, he kissed my hand.

"Our Almighty blessed the hands which prepared our meal. Thank you, it was delicious."

With Dezső, I felt loved and respected all the time. As the years passed, he became earnest. He didn't joke as much as when we were young. I missed that side of him, as I still had the youthful, mischievous impulses in me, laughing at silly things, and making fun of our own condition. Yes, all of the difficulties we went through took a serious toll on both of us. But I wanted to stay youthful since we were starting a new life from the ground up. We were living in a free country with endless opportunities, so it was important that we stay energetic and optimistic to live long enough to enjoy it.

After dinner, the kids turned on the TV, telling us that watching TV is an essential part of learning English. We sat on the balcony, and I listened to my husband's work story.

"At lunchtime, Ferenc called me to his office," Dezső began. "I agreed on ten-hour workdays, including Saturdays, from seven to five. He hired me as an independent contractor. He won't pay taxes or health insurance for me. He provides the machines to work on, but I am not his employee. I'll be paid hourly $6.50 as my income to cover the rent and groceries, and maybe we can save a couple hundred dollars a month. I am happy."

"That means you have to pay taxes from your income. He's a very sneaky man. I am telling you that when we want to be successful and independent, we must speak English. Ferenc knows now you stay with him because you can't look for another job. He will never appreciate you so long as he has the assurance you will stay with him because you don't speak English."

"Marika, I disagree. He is an unqualified man without any profession. You saw his shop. For so many years, he didn't achieve much. If I boost his business, he'll be grateful to me. Now, he's conceited, which is understandable. He has helped us in many ways."

"So far you are right, but I'm talking about the future. Our goal is to open our own shop."

A week later, Attila and I started working at McDonalds. Dezső wasn't thrilled; we barely got to see each other. When we got home late at night, he was already in bed. In the mornings, we hugged before he ran to work. Making fries at the age of forty embittered me; back home I was a leader, managing many people, but my strong will to reach our goals gave me the energy and optimism.

One evening, Ferenc came by with a fourteen-year-old Buick. A businessman friend of his was selling it for one thousand dollars, in great condition. We bought it, and it became our first car in America.

Attila found out that in the close city of Thousand Oaks, there was a free evening school for immigrants called, "English is My Second Language". Classes met three times a week from six to nine in the evening. For my sake, Dezső arranged to work from six to five. This way, we were able to start school. Our classmates were all ages and of nineteen different nationalities. The teacher, a sixty-five-year-old Native American woman, was the kindest educator I've ever met. Her hair was black, in two side braids, with colorful ribbons across her forehead. Her clothes were just like in the movies. The majority of the class had been living in America for years, so they understood a lot, but couldn't speak fluent English. Dezső and I were like deaf mutes. We didn't understand, and we didn't speak. The first evening, the teacher called on me in front of the class. I flushed and nervously went to her.

"Do you speak English?"

"No, little understands."

"My name is Zena. What is your name?"

"Maria Imre."

"Repeat after me. My name is Maria Imre."

When I repeated, she praised me, and the class applauded. She had many simple questions and she corrected me so I would answer in full sentences. One evening, Zena called me out again. It was the day we learned prepositions. She put a pen on the table and told me to pick it up. I didn't understand. She held my hand and we picked up the pen together. Put it down, put it under the table, next to the table, above the table, and turn the light on. She dragged me to the light switch, said "come to me," drew me to herself, told me to go away, then pushed me away. We repeated these words so many times until I was able to do what she said.

I felt uncomfortable, but I wanted to learn so badly, I didn't care if the class made fun of me.

"Marika, with all your effort and struggle, I am learning much easier than you. You have a fantastic spirit. The class is having a good time laughing at you."

"I don't care. I need to be in contact with people. I must communicate, share my thoughts, and listen to them. That's what makes me feel I'm alive."

On Friday, I got home exhausted. I had to work from eight in the morning to five in the evening. Dezső was in a bad mood. I didn't ask questions. I just made dinner, and with my English book, I laid down in the bedroom. Soon, Dezső followed me.

"Honey, I'm not going to school anymore," he told me.

"You're joking."

"I'm not. I had a huge fight with Ferenc today. It's so much work that I can't keep up. He wants me to train workers to solder. He doesn't understand that my knowledge is not something that can be learned in a month, it is the result of twenty years of experience. If I teach, I can't work. If the apprentice botches the things, I'll have to work twice as much to fix things. From now on, I will work twelve hours a day."

"But learning the language is essential."

"I can't study if I'm tired."

"I don't want to fight with you."

"You are. Honey, I'm not a chatty person. You can be the spokesperson of our family, and I'll be the working class. I can earn lots of money with my professional work. Ferenc raised my wage."

I couldn't fall asleep. I was upset and disappointed with my husband for not understanding how important it was to know the language. It would be impossible to open our own machine shop without speaking English. He believed that he would come to learn English in time, from me and the co-workers.

On Saturday night, over dinner, Dezső casually mentioned he was going to work on Sunday, too.

On Sunday, I was off. Attila had to work, and Dezső left early morning. I thought with Csaba, we could go shopping at Kmart. He has been begging for a G.I. Joe action figure, which had become the most popular toy of the time. It was expensive for our budget, but I didn't care. I wanted to surprise him.

"Come with me to Kmart? We can stop in your favorite park, too."

"I'd like to watch a movie."

"Please, do it for me, just the two of us? It is going to be fun."

"Okay."

I did my shopping. I got pillows, some cleaning stuff, and Csaba's toy. I hid the large box under the pillows. He went browsing around the shop. We met at the register.

"Guess what I found! An amazing bicycle! It has a gear shift, too! I'll show to Dezső. At home I had a bike, and here I have nothing."

When I paid at the register, Csaba saw the G.I. Joe box. He hugged me.

"Mom, I love you so much. Oh, this is the best toy I have now."

He held the box tightly against his heart. "Let's go home; I don't want to go to the park."

"I need a little relaxation in the fresh air, and you need some exercise, too."

"Okay," he agreed.

I had my English book with me. At the park, Csaba often shouted, "Look how fast I can climb up this rope!"

A fat woman with a warm smile sat down next to me. She got a newspaper out of her bag and made some notes in it. Csaba came over.

"Can I go for a run around the park?"

"You can, as long as I can see you, and don't go between the trees. You saw on TV that there could be sick people who kidnap children."

"Okay!"

Csaba ran off. The woman then talked to me in very broken Hungarian.

LIFE CHANGING ENCOUNTER

L ittle Hungarian I speak. Mother, father Hungarian. You here live?" the woman said.

"Yes, I live nearby. I don't speak much English," I said, slipping into my native Hungarian to continue the conversation.

"See learning."

She pointed at my book. "Very good, must speak. When come America?"

"Six months ago," I said.

"What work?"

"My husband works in a machine shop, and I am working at McDonalds."

"McDonalds not good. Very not good. Small money."

"I know. I have no other option."

"You like clean houses?"

"Yes, but I don't speak English."

She patted me on the shoulder.

"I help. I work newspaper. I advertise you my phone number. I go houses with you and speak clients. Here live rich people, you make many money. You want it?"

"That would be nice."

"I'm Clara."

"Maria."

"Have phone?"

"No."

"Okay, give address?" I told her my address. "When find clients, I come," she said. Then she got up and pointed at her watch.

"Must go many work writing newspaper." She gave me a hug. "Food you have? I help."

"I have, thank you." I sat on the bench, watching her leave, until she turned the far corner. From behind, she looked like an angel. A big, unbuttoned cardigan dangled at her sides, just like wings. What happened seemed so unreal, I didn't even tell my family about Clara.

Two weeks went by without any news from Clara. On the third Sunday, I went to the park, thinking maybe I would find her sitting on the bench, but she wasn't there. On Thursday of the fourth week, I had just come home when Clara knocked on our door with bunch of flowers and a big, store-bought cake.

"Hello! I love cake, coffee with you," she said.

"Of course. Come, sit down."

I quickly made coffee. Clara put a stack of cards on the table with addresses and phone numbers.

"We lucky. Tomorrow eight house waiting afternoon we go." She looked around in the room. "You need lot money."

"Clara, thank you so much for your help. You are my guardian angel. How can I ever repay you?"

"You cook me Hungarian dinner." She laughed and pointed at herself. "Like good food."

Visiting the houses with Clara was an experience for me. The ladies were expecting us with great enthusiasm because European women were famous for their cleanliness. In six homes, older couples lived. Their houses weren't messy. Clara told them that I would work with my own cleaning products and asked for sixty dollars. Just the thought of it gave me hot flashes. I thought that it was a lot of money for cleaning, but to my surprise, everyone agreed to it. Two of the houses were smaller, but very messy, so Clara asked seventy-five dollars.

"America knows good business. Little money, bad job. Rich like to pay good work."

I could hardly wait for the evening to share my story with

my family. Until then, nobody knew about Clara. I knew Dezső wouldn't like the cleaning lady status. He would say that it was such a degrading job. But I didn't care. I felt my life changed that day. All my worries were gone. A great big gate opened before me. On Monday, I'd go through it and step into the world where, without Clara, I would never have had the chance to go. I wouldn't be looking for coins in the gutter. I'd be surrounded by people who could advise me, who could help me, who could maybe be friends with me. We had nobody to turn to in America, I was so happy being with people. Until now I didn't have a soul who I can talk with.

While I was cooking, my thoughts were racing. I thought about what it was that I wanted to achieve in America. I was, at that point, forty years old. I always worked very hard in the communist country, just to have a nice home, a loving family, and a peaceful retirement. Happiness and satisfaction gave me tremendous energy, and then everything fell to pieces before we had a chance to enjoy what we worked for. Coming to America, I planned to adopt a completely new life philosophy. I wanted to live for the moment; I wanted to enjoy life at forty rather than waiting till I was old to have everything. Now I'd have a decent income, and we could live a balanced life, working and having fun. I didn't want to follow my parents' example. They were always worried, fearing for the worst, and constantly saving their money. I know they had their reasons. They had lived through the war, then everything they had been taken from them in the time of nationalization. Now what we did twenty five years later maybe was reckless because we left everything we had worked for during twenty years all because we wanted to live in a free country.

Our years fly by and we often realize that we didn't live at all. I don't dream to be rich. Walking by the ocean, visiting national parks, traveling in America with our sons, laughing, and having time to read and fear nothing. Yes, that is and will be my goal.

I wondered how I could make a cleaning lady position sound like an accomplishment. I came up with, "Guys, a wonderful thing happened to me! I became a cleaning lady for rich people!"

I knew that wasn't good enough and that I must come up with some funny approach.

At dinner, everybody enjoyed the food.

"Guys, how was your day?"

Nobody had anything to say. Csaba mentioned the teacher likes him a lot, and how she is always talking to him.

"That's good. My day was very interesting. I met a lady, Clara, who helped me."

Dezső stopped eating. "What did she do?" he asked.

"She helped me out of the pit."

"What pit did you fall into?!"

"The pit of hopelessness. I was sitting in the park, submerged in my thoughts. Maybe she saw on my face I couldn't see a bright future for us. She sensed my worries and found me homes to clean, where rich people live, who need a trustworthy cleaning lady. Imagine – they gave me the keys to their homes. They trust me. I'm starting Monday!"

"You want to clean homes?"

"It's better than making fries for a couple bucks. These houses are not dirty. The owners are kind, intelligent, our age and older people. I believe soon I'll be friends with them. These are the kinds of people we need in our lives."

"I didn't bring you to America to clean other people's homes."

"Honey, I will make $390 weekly."

He let out a deep sigh and put his fork down. "Congratulations! Maybe I can go cleaning homes too since it is so profitable."

After dinner we went for a walk. Dezső held my hand. "I hope you are not upset with me," I said.

"No, I have my own problems. I am getting mentally tired doing the same work every day like a robot. I don't have to use my brain. Soon I'll go crazy. Somehow, we have to open our own machine shop specializing in prototype designing and manufacturing them. Maybe Clara can give us some advice."

"Good idea. When she comes for dinner, we can talk to her."

After a couple of days, I knew I had made a good decision. My clients respected me. The ladies had coffee with me and we had nice chats about my family. They even liked my broken English.

On Saturday morning, Clara came. "You with me go to four more houses."

"Clara, there aren't enough days in a week."

"Work Saturday. In America, work come, you work."

I got all four houses to clean. One of them was very close to our apartment. The lady, a woman named Teresa, had an allergy to dust. They were so lovable; I took the job, planning to work for them every afternoon for two hours before I got home.

"Clara, when can you come for dinner?"

"Next Sunday. Cook nokedli, chicken paprikash." She smacked her lips.

"Telephone you must, your clients can't communicate you. I can't call things tell you."

She gave me her phone number and address to call her before our Sunday dinner.

On Thursday, I got the phone installed and immediately called Clara. She didn't answer, and my Friday call was unsuccessful, too. Saturday afternoon, I went with Dezső to see her. Her car was in the parking lot. We knocked on her door, and the next-door neighbor told us Clara had passed away; her heart was ill. This news broke my heart.

* * *

On a hot morning, we went to buy beds. I put on white shorts, and a red, crisp linen blouse. I felt young and happy. It was a big day; finally, we would sleep in a bed. We arrived at the warehouse. The parking lot was full of cars. Far from the entrance, we were able to find an empty spot. I walked between the cars when I noticed Dezső far behind me. He took a photo of me.

"You look very pretty today; your legs are the most beautiful I have ever seen." He laughed, and his eyes were so blue, I had to kiss him.

"Today, as I was brushing my teeth, I looked in the mirror, and an aging, bitter man looked back at me. I could see you behind me getting dressed. You were moving so youthfully, and your face, after twenty some years, still radiated. You don't age; I don't know where you get this enormous energy." He hugged me gently in a way that reminded me of our student years.

We spent two hours trying to find the most comfortable bed. Dezső sat on a big, king-size bed.

"Which size do you like?" he asked.

"The queen."

"Why?"

"Because we could be closer, and it's cheaper." I replied.

"I love your honesty."

We told the salesman we were buying two single and one queen-size bed. They gave us a thirty percent discount and free shipping. We were thrilled.

In the Bed Bath and Beyond store, the selection of sheets was big. I got a beautiful, Egyptian cotton, flowered one. In the kitchen section, Dezső picked a robot with a meat grinder, along with a mixer and dough kneader for me. He rubbed his face against the sheets.

"I'm sure we will enjoy sleeping in these," he said, and looked at me with a serious face. "I have to tell you, lately I was upset with you. I felt you taking life irresponsibly. You don't worry, nothing pulls you down. This morning, I understood your optimism. Your strong belief in us makes that possible. You're right we shouldn't keep putting off living. Whatever we can afford today, let's enjoy it. I admire you; you truly love life and bravely look to the future. You give me strength in America, you who did not believe in it."

"The issue wasn't I believed or not in America," I responded. "I love the country where I was born and grew up. Now it is a blessing what I brought with me from there. My knowledge, all the experiences, the humbleness, strong surviving will in a hostile environment, comes from our former home. Because of that, here I am fearless. I concentrate on achieving my goals and being happy. Nobody wants to take that from me. I still miss the feeling of home, the town, my family, friends and the people we left behind. I hope one day when I walk into the store, they will know my name. When we find friends who we enjoy spending time with, then I can call this place my new home. Remember we didn't come here to get rich. We came for a peaceful, happy life, for freedom. Now we must learn how to live in it."

* * *

I was getting ready for Christmas. The boys were to have two weeks' vacation, and it was the last day of school. When I got home, I found Csaba crying on the sofa, surrounded by family photos. He put them back in the shoe box and ran into the bathroom.

"Csaba, come out. I want to talk with you."

"I don't want to talk."

"I want to talk to you!"

He opened the door. A broken spirited, sad boy stepped out.

"Tell me what's wrong."

"I don't want to stay here. I want to go home. I miss my grandma and my friends. We don't have anyone here."

"Don't say that! We have each other."

"That's not enough. Today in school, we talked about how we spend Christmas. Everybody has grandparents, cousins, whom they will visit. They buy each other presents, cook and bake together, just like we used to do back home. I miss that. I will never be happy here."

I tried to hug him, but he wouldn't let me.

"Today the teacher asked everybody what we do through the holidays. I told her we don't have any plans, we don't have anybody who we can visit, and nobody is coming to our home. My grandma wants to come, but the communist people in Slovakia don't let her."

"Where are you getting that?"

"Dezső said to you that it would be a miracle if the communists let her come visit us. My teacher cried when I told her how lonely we are here and how sad I am."

My eyes filled with tears. Someone knocked on the door. Four women carrying boxes greeted me and rushed to the table to put their heavy load down. I recognized Csaba's teacher. She introduced me to the ladies, Csaba's classmates mothers..

"We apologize for dropping by unannounced. I feel so much for Csaba; it is very hard on him to have your extended family so far from here. We'd like to help you to overcome this sad situation. Please, accept these presents that the parents of Csaba's classmates bought for your family. We wish you a merry Christmas. God bless you and help you find your place in this country. After the holy days, we'll find time get to know you and make some fun days together."

I was speechless. In my life, I had always been the one in the giving position. Now, for the first time, strangers came to me with gifts. I was touched deeply, and my voice trembled.

"Thank you from the bottom of my heart. I appreciate your thoughtfulness."

I felt overwhelming gratitude… yes, America is an exceptional nation. Csaba also got invitations to spend time on his friends' ranches after Christmas.

Dezső came home exhausted. He crashed on the sofa.

"You shouldn't work twelve hours a day," I told him.

"I am not tired, I am upset. Over the past weeks, I worked on a complicated innovation for a surgeon. He is looking for somebody who can design and make prototypes. Ferenc told him maybe his company can do it. The doctor gave him sketches of an interesting surgical tool for spine surgery. I was able come up with a brilliant idea. Today he took the instruments to the doctor, who was so excited about my innovation that he immediately ordered ten more, which he'll send to different hospitals, for testing."

"This is great news."

"Just wait. Ferenc suggested that I can make them on Sundays because weekdays, he has so much work for me and he made me such a humiliating offer that deeply offended me."

Dezső said that Ferenc had offered to give him one hundred dollars for ten pieces.

"I need at least six hours to fabricate one piece," he continued. "That means for sixty hours, I can make $100 for a complicated, special toolmaker work."

"'Dezső, you are working on my equipment," Ferenc told me. "I thought you would appreciate some side job." I told him he is out of his mind offering me one dollar and ninety cents per hour. This is professional work, not sharpening a knife. So, he said I have to understand that he can't charge a high price to the doctor the first time, and he wants to make money, too. The doctor has lots of innovations to make, which will bring lots of money in the future.

Dezső was not a fighter; he was a hard-working, honest, humble man. He waited until he got praised. That was how we were raised back home. Let people see your qualities; don't be self-important. This was an unwritten rule in our former country.

"I have other news too," he said to me. "Starting next week, my new boss is Ferenc's brother, Zoli, an arrogant thirty-year-old, who worked as a helper on construction sites. I overheard from the office how he coached Ferenc."

"You never show him his work is important. Believe me, he will make those prototypes, because for him, $100 is big money."

Ferenc told Zoli not to lecture him because Dezső is his golden egg layer hen, and he has to treat him in a way that ensures he pours all of his knowledge into what he's doing. Dezső heard Ferenc say to Zoli, "We'll grow big, because the innovations will bring in huge profit. This surgeon has many ideas. If Dezső can make them, we will be millionaires. I got seven thousand dollars for the first piece and I'll get fifteen thousand for the ten additional pieces he ordered. That's how I can afford to hire you. Don't teach me how to do business and how to handle Dezső."

"Now you know how much he needs you," I said. "You name the price; take charge of your destiny."

"You are right; finally, I'll be making more money than you."

"What do you mean?"

He blushed.

"I felt uncomfortable that you earn more than I do."

"So far, we never kept score how much we each earn. I remember once you told your mother that we share everything, our money, our bed..."

"Please stop."

"What changed between us since we got here?"

"I feel emasculated. I promised you that you will be the lady of the house in America and instead you are cleaning houses."

"Stop this nonsense! I want to be part of our life journey. I want to go hand in hand with you." Days later, Dezső came home with flowers.

"For ten prototypes, I asked $5,000, and I got it."

"Wow, congratulations!"

"You should have seen the pained look on Ferenc's face as he handed me the check."

* * *

During the holiday season, we rested. My clients gave me paid vacation time, and Ferenc closed the shop. Attila worked overtime all week. He was saving money for a car. Csaba spent his vacation at his friend's ranch. Every day, the two of us drove down to Zuma Beach. We were like honeymooners, laughing over silly things, chasing each other in the wet sand. We snuggled in the warm sand and watched the sunset. Our new year started with optimism and contentment.

In the spring, Ferenc's business bloomed rapidly. The quality repair jobs made the shop famous. Couriers delivered and picked up the instruments. Ferenc planned to move to a bigger shop.

"Dezső, I have big plans with you. I want you to do only innovations. The surgeon gave me sketches for new prototypes. In the evenings, you can think about it."

At lunchtime, Zoli came to Dezső.

"I have a brilliant idea. While you are repairing instruments, you can think of solutions for the new innovation. Once you have the idea, within a few minutes make a sketch, and based on that, I will make the technical drawing adding my own ideas to it, making it perfect. After that, you can fabricate the prototype based on my design."

Dezső laughed so loud that Ferenc came out of his office. "Tell me what's so funny; I could use a good laugh, too."

"Is your brother normal?"

"Dezső, how can you ask such a thing?"

"Do you guys have any idea how innovations and prototypes are developed?" They didn't understand the question. "I'll tell you," Dezső continued. "Engineers spend months sketching ideas and comparing their work. By their drawings, the toolmakers make a couple prototypes. Then the engineers try them, which one works the best, which one easiest to handle, which one is more aesthetically pleasing, what else can be improved, etc. This process could last months. Zoli wants me to come up with innovations while I'm working. A sane person would never think that is possible. Forgive me if I can't stop laughing."

"Dezső, he meant well. He wants to help you."

"He can't help me. My ideas are in my brain. I can make my invention without any sketches. I visualize them. I've been doing innovations for thirty years. It is insulting when someone who doesn't have any education wants to help me. He can do it on his own if he's so smart. He must know I'm the one who elevated this shop and made it famous. I am the only one producing everything here. If I stop working, there won't be anything to polish, buff, or package. Then you can bring the scissors and knives again for sharpening.

Ferenc's face turned red. Zoli shouted, "Kick him out immediately! Fire him!"

"Zoli, go into the office!" Ferenc yelled.

He wouldn't go. Ferenc took his arm and pulled him out of the shop. Dezső went into the locker room. Ferenc ran after him.

"Dezső, don't be silly; don't take him seriously. You are right. It's good that you got it off your chest. He was out of breath. Sweat ran on his forehead.

Dezső watched his trembling hand and thought what a coward Ferenc was.

"I'll ban Zoli from speaking to you."

From then on, Dezső set the price for every prototype he worked on. Ferenc always had comments when he wrote the check, but he paid it. The doctor was surprised that somebody could make his idea work better than he originally had in mind.

"The doctor is very happy with your work," Ferenc said. "He told me: 'That engineer of yours is a genius; I have lots of work for him.'" "You know Dezső, will be nice when you can work on these things faster, then we can make more money."

"Feri, do you know the Hungarian saying? A job is only worth something when it is done slowly, precisely as the stars moving in the sky? It takes time to come up with a unique, original solution which doesn't exist in this world."

* * *

My best client was named Teresa, the woman with the dust allergy. I cleaned her house for two hours every afternoon before I got home. Her health worsened; the allergy gave her a constant cough. The doctor recommended that they move to Palm Springs for a year, and that maybe the dry air would help her. They immediately made arrangements and rented a furnished apartment there.

"Maria, when I get better there, we'll move permanently."

She was an intelligent lady. We talked about life in Slovakia, about customs and how we lived there. She compared the advantages and disadvantages of both regimes since Teresa was a psychologist. She liked to analyze relationships between family members. Our family life impressed her.

One afternoon, I found Teresa in bed. She had lost her voice.

"Maria, we have to move, but we are worried leaving our house when nobody lives in it. What do you think? Can your family move here for one year? We are taking our personal things, but the furniture and everything else would stay here until we make the final decision."

"Teresa, we can't afford such a big house to rent."

"We thought that you could stay for free for watching over our belongings."

I wasn't sure if I understood the offer correctly.

"Maria, we love your family. You can save money. If we stay there, we'll sell this house. Perhaps you could buy it."

Two weeks later, we moved in and kept our furniture in the garage. I felt great living in an elegant, furnished home. In the evenings, I sat down to play piano. My fingers were stiff from all the hard work, but I still could play some concert pieces I learned by heart in music school. It had been thirty years since I used to daydream about my life as Dezső's wife, while playing Chopin's waltzes.

Attila graduated from the high school with outstanding grades. His teachers were amazed by the strength of his European education. He got the maximum score in math, geography, and biology, without ever studying the subjects in America. He spoke fluent English. We wanted him to continue studying.

"I want to work. My classmates are all earning money. I will gain some experience and then decide what I want to do. I need a car. In the Ford Company, I found a used Mustang for twelve thousand dollars I have seven. With five thousand in loans, if you be my guarantor, I can buy it. Today my friend is taking me to a job interview at Domino's Pizza; they are looking for a manager. I have a chance to get it, but must have a car. This place is ten miles from here."

The next afternoon, we went to buy the car. Attila's face was flush with joy as he waved from his car. What we didn't plan on was buying a little Escort for my cleaning business.

At this time, while we were living in a big house, I sent an invitation letter to my mom. I phoned her every Sunday morning, which was afternoon in Slovakia. We both made our coffees and talked. In the beginning, we often cried, as it was hard to be apart. When she got my letter, her hope to see us made her happy, but the communist leadership in the town rejected her application. She knew it wasn't an option for us to come home (we had been sentenced to a ten-year imprisonment for illegally leaving the country). If she couldn't come, she would never see us again. She spent her days in the cemetery, next to my dad, and in the church, praying.

"Mom, don't give up hope. In a couple months, I'll send you another invitation. We will try again and again until you can come."

A couple of months later, Attila found a new job in the Protection One Company, which provided 24-hour security for companies and private residences. Three months later, he became the night shift supervisor. His enjoyment of his job was amazing. Catching burglars, collaborating with the police, and protecting the defenseless had become the center of his life. I couldn't imagine where he got his passion for investigating and fighting for justice. He often worked during the day in his free time, watching traffic on the monitors around the houses they protected. He had an innate sense for detecting in the crowd those who were staking houses during the day, in preparation for their crimes at night.

Csaba made a lot of friends in high school. Our house was full of boys and girls, and what made me happy was how they enjoyed spending time in our home, rather than roaming the streets. Csaba often went on trips with his friends' families. Nature and animal loving were his hobbies. He came home with fascinating stories. They caught rattlesnakes for dinner and climbed mountains. His skinny, fragile body completely changed. He developed muscles, and his tanned face glowed with health.

The days and months flew by. Dezső and I worked relentlessly towards the goal of opening our own machine shop. Teresa called a couple of times. She felt better in the dry, desert air. It looked like they planned to sell the house.

Dezső worked long hours in the shop experimenting with his inventions. Ferenc made him redo the perfect prototypes a couple of times, with small changes that Zoli drew. All of them had the same principle of what Dezső had designed, but with a slightly different appearance. It made no sense to create worse versions, but Ferenc was the boss and paid for each additional version.

"Marika, I think the doctor first gets the imperfect instruments and gradually Ferenc gives him my first, perfect version. This way, the doctor pays three times for his orders. He can believe this is the process of the innovation."

Our sons grew up and developed their own circle of friends with whom they spent their free time. Dezső and I liked to walk on the beach. It was the best, relaxing time listening to the roar of the ocean and watching the breathtaking California sunset. We could trace the golden rays of light on the calm, slightly moving, massive body of water. When the sun went down, the ocean turned dark and morphed into thick, black oil. Other times, it raged and smashed with frightening force against the huge rocks. We climbed on top of a cliff and watched the round edge of the world. The big cargo ships disappeared, or turned up beyond the horizon.

Teresa called us to say that they had bought a house in Palm Springs.

"Maria, we ordered the moving company, but we can't come to Agoura. I have important doctors' appointments. Can you show the movers what to take? We will come next week to talk about what to do with the house."

Our home became empty. We brought our beds in, the table with the chairs, and the old sofa with the TV. The house echoed with emptiness. Teresa was amazed when she stepped inside.

"Mike, I didn't realize our house was so big! We had too much furniture in it. Mike, her husband, stood on the balcony. He loved the view of the Santa Monica Mountains. Then he sat down on our old armchair.

"Dezső, let's discuss the future of this house. If you want to buy it, we can give you a good deal. The house doesn't have a mortgage, so you can get the loan from us because I don't think the bank will give you a big loan, you don't have credit history. The value of the house is about 240-260 thousand dollars. We will give it to you for 250. I'm asking for a 25 thousand dollar down payment and the monthly installment will be $2,500 over fifteen years, with interest."

We were silent. Teresa looked at me and said, "I know, it's a lot. If you can't afford it…"

Mike intervened. "Dezső, do you have 25 thousand dollars?"

"We have, but $2,500 for fifteen years is scary for me. My wife works very hard physically. Her health is more important than the money. If I have constant work with innovations, I say yes."

Teresa whispered to Mike, prompting him to say, "Okay, I can lower the price to 240 thousand. This way, when you can't pay your mortgage, sell the house and make at least twenty thousand profit on it. You don't know the American way to do business. Here nobody buys a house for lifetime. After three years, you will easily make 30-40 thousand profit. Then, you buy another house. With all that cash in your hand, put 25 thousand in down payments and get the loan from the bank. Now with the 30-40 thousand profit, open your machine shop without borrowing any money on it. Are you with me?"

We were quiet.

"Dezső, as long as you're working for somebody, you'll be an average guy. By saving every penny and working yourself to death like you do, you can achieve what you left behind in Slovakia, but not more. To reach a higher level of living, you must have your own business. Opening a shop is hard; it takes time until you get known. It is possible that in the beginning it will bring less cash than what you earn now. That's why you need to have a fallback. I wish that your American dream comes true. You deserve it."

Dezső shook Mike's hand. "Thank you, Mike. I appreciate your advice."

We felt lucky with this opportunity not to pay rent, but instead invest money in our own home.

"Marika, it is a monumental thing to buy a house in California, especially for us. It's a big achievement, but I don't feel the same as I felt back home when we moved into our house we built. That was a different feeling. I guess as we get older, we are aware of all the obstacles that could come up, and that makes us cautious, even with happiness."

"The problem is we don't have time. We wasted twenty years of our life back home, our most beautiful years, full of energy and optimism. We created our wonderful family. Lived an extraordinary private life and built our foundation for old age. We lost that. Here we are forcing ourselves to get to the point where we bin, successful careers, wealth. Unfortunately, the result of twenty years of work cannot be reached in five years; it doesn't matter how hard we work. I feel like we are always behind and our strength is lessening."

On Sunday, I called my mom. The first thing she said was, "Marika, I got the visa! I'll be with you soon."

"Oh, Mom, that is the best news ever! I'll buy your flight ticket tomorrow. I'm so happy! I have big news, too. We bought the house we are living in! We are homeowners."

"Oh, that is great. I can't wait to be there! Marika, I'm sorry to say I have sad news. Someone assaulted Pali, Jónás Pali, on his way home from synagogue. The mailman found him dead on the sidewalk, early morning. He used to joke that a thief would not be very happy with him; he never carried more than 10 Korona."

I felt chills down my spine. A pure hearted, generous man, a best friend departed from my life. The Germans killed his family, he survived, and a lowlife came and killed him.

"Are you there?" my mother asked.

"Yes, Mom, I feel terrible. We loved him so much."

"I know. We talked about you every time we met. He worried about you and it made him upset when you left the country. He said, 'Marika won't be happy there. She loved our town, Losonc and Kassa." "He teared up, and we cried together on the street."

"May the Lord rest his soul."

* * *

It was Dezső's second month working on an innovation. He sat on the balcony, drawing, crumbling up papers, starting new sketches.

"Dezső it's late, I'm going to bed."

"Come, sit by my side, perhaps you inspire me. I have the solution, but I can't figure out how to fabricate it."

He showed me the sketch. It looked like a drawer.

"What's the problem?"

"This is a tiny vertebral implant, for spinal injury. It's a 15mm x 10mm x 3mm small box. This platinum box has a drawer which will be filled with the patient's bone marrow and ousted to the box. The surface is densely drilled with holes that make the implant easily heal together with the vertebras."

"Wow, it is so miniature. I can't even imagine how you start the process of making it."

"That's my problem! Tomorrow evening, I'll stay in the shop and try to figure it out. Don't wait for me with dinner."

The days went by, but creating this new prototype was difficult. Sunday morning at six, Dezső was already gone. I had no idea when he got up. I stayed longer in bed, feeling all of the hard work in my lower back and in my arms. I'd been cleaning two houses every day. Sunday came, and I tidied our home and did the laundry, but the night wasn't enough to recuperate.

I hated to have coffee by myself. Sundays were the only times that Dezső and I had quality time together. The coffee had just started to drip when I heard the garage door open and my husband stepped into the kitchen with a red rose bouquet. He kissed me and showed on the palm of his hand the little, shiny implant. He pulled out the drawer from it and then pushed it back. It looked amazing.

"How did you do it?" I asked.

He laughed, and said, "With these two hands."

He kissed them with theatrical gestures. The wholehearted happiness suited him.

"I woke up at four, after having a dream about the solution. I rushed to the shop. It is unbelievable how my mind works, like a computer. Even when I sleep, it's calculating."

We took our coffees to the balcony. He held his invention with joy and pride. No doubt, Dezső was blessed with a special gift to discover technical tasks. He loved his world with numbers, creativity, rules, and logic, where results can be verified.

That evening, I chilled a bottle of champagne. Sipping the cool drink, watching the sunset, talking about our long journey and how we got to where we were made us proud.

"Honey, I feel that I'll invent fantastic things. I'll meet someone who assigns the task to me, who has comprehensive ideas, but can't make them functional. I'll be the one to bring them to life."

He said this with such conviction, like he was seeing into the future.

Mom's Visit

The long-awaited day finally arrived. The four of us stood at the Los Angeles airport. We spotted Mom among the arriving passengers. Csaba ran to his beloved grandma. We were all crying, laughing, and hugging each other for a long time. I thanked God for bringing her to us. For so many years, I'd been feeling guilty for leaving her behind. She never held it against me and now followed me across the globe to be with me. Tears of joys were over my face as she kissed me from every side, again and again. Through my tears, I saw that strong, willful woman who brought me up in a very difficult, historical time after the war.

The long hours of traveling wore her out. She slept two days and nights. On Saturday morning, she stepped out of the bathroom, fully revitalized. Dezső remarked, "Mom, America made you look young!"

"Son, I was very tired, but now I feel great. I never thought I would travel the world at seventy-two. I missed you all so much, I had to do it."

"Enjoy your time with us. We love you."

Csaba was always by her side. Every morning, before school, he climbed into her bed, and they giggled together, recalling his childhood memories. Our life had changed. Mom cooked, baked, and cleaned for me. When I got home, I took her to stores or walked in the park. Evenings were fun chatting, remembering all of the family stories and going through old family photos. When Dezső was with us, he got talkative.

He told about how his father loved bean stew. His plate was once so full that the thick soup nearly overflowed. He walked into the dining room, slowly balancing the plate. Dezső and his brother were chasing each other around the table. When his brother almost caught him, he ran out of the room just as his dad was about to step in. They collided. His father nearly fell over, trying to keep his balance. The plate flew out of his hand and smacked him in the face. The stew dripped down his neck, and he looked like a scarecrow! He was cursing and shouting, "Come here right now!" But he couldn't see. He shared how his father was a very strict man; raising four boys wasn't easy. He punished them every time they did something bad. Dezső ran into the stable loft and hid in the hay. Late night, his mother persuaded him to come down. She promised him that his father would not spank him.

Csaba laughed and said, "He spanked you anyway, right?"

"He didn't, but I got a terrible punishment. I had to clean the stable alone for one week, which was horrible. When I see crap, I throw up."

Mom laughed, remembering the time when we brought Attila from the hospital, back home to our first apartment. Dezső threw up along the length of the corridor. Mom told the story to our sons, and that was the highlight of the evening.

In the bedroom later, Dezső shared a new story about Ferenc.

"Zoli made a sketch of my little implant, making it larger, with fewer holes on the surfaces. On the doctor's sketch was a note: 'the size must be exactly what I suggest and the walls must be densely drilled with holes.'"

Dezső told me how Ferenc handed him the sketch and said, "See Dezső, this is why it's good to have Zoli; he fixed your little mistakes."

He told me how he had asked Ferenc if he had the doctor's sketch since Zoli's design is what the doctor didn't want.

Ferenc said, "Don't argue with me, just get it done. I'll pay you."

"They are up to something," I said. "Why do they want to make a worse version of a perfect prototype?"

"Maybe one day we'll find out," said Dezső

The months spent with mom were unforgettable. On the weekends, we made trips to San Diego, San Francisco, Los Angeles, and Beverly Hills. We walked along the Walk of Fame, visited museums, along with Universal Studios and Disneyland. I never saw my mom so happy. Her attitude for life changed. From the old lady from a little town who spent her time in the church and the cemetery, now she acted like a modern, young woman. I got her stylish pants, T-shirts, and a bathing suit. The beach was her favorite place to be. With Csaba, she went into the ocean, sunbathed, and walked with me for miles in the sand. We took a boat trip to Alcatraz and cruised in the open ocean, under the Golden Gate Bridge. She even walked up to the giant trees in Sequoia Park. Her cheeks were glowing from the fresh air and excitement. These are my most beautiful memories of my mom.

The months went by at an astonishing speed. In the evenings, Mom crocheted a beautiful patterned doily for my dining room table.

"Mom, have you made a decision about staying with us?"

She put the lacework in her lap. "Yes, I did think about it. I would like to stay with you, but my heart is telling me to go home. I want to die there and rest next to your father. America is a beautiful place to visit, but I miss my home. I have my little group of friends who I get together for coffee. I like to sit in the cemetery next to your father's grave. I still miss him. I go to church for a prayer, where I remember our family events. That's where your father and I promised each other eternal love, where we baptized you. There are so many memories; all mean so much to me. You said your 'I do' in that church." Her eyes filled with tears. "I'm not going to ask you if you're happy here. I worry for you. You are a housekeeper. Do you remember the kind of jobs you had back home? Everybody looked up to you, now you are cleaning other people's dirt. What do you enjoy about this life?"

"The progress of how I am moving forward. I bought the airplane ticket for you. Back home, I never had that kind of money to fly to America. I work hard, and I am rewarded for it. Mom, look around. We have the most beautiful furniture from Italy. My husband just got a new town car. When we open our own machine shop, I will stop working. I'll help him with the paperwork. Can't you see we are happy?"

"No, you are lonely. Your husband works long hours. You came to America for freedom, but you don't have time to enjoy it."

"For a long time, we lived in a system where we didn't have our own will. We weren't allowed to make any decisions about our life. We had to follow the communist rules. We were like sheep, guided by the shepherd and dogs in that regime. We were not allowed to step out of the flock, because we got punished. Forty years living in oppression, our brains are wired to obey and execute orders. We had to praise those who stripped us of our rights. Now we are free, exposed to good and bad. Our age and life experience keeps us very cautious stepping forward. We must learn to think independently and not be scared to dream. Mom, it takes time to change our mindset."

* * *

Dezső came home very tired. Ferenc moved his shop to a much bigger, modern building. All the workers helped with the packing. In the new place, there were CNC machines for mass production jobs and they hired ten professional workers. Ferenc and Zoli were upbeat.

Ferenc said, "Dezső, we must work on several innovations, which are urgent. The doctor has a presentation in London on an exhibition about spinal surgeries where he wants to introduce the prototypes we made for him based on his ideas.

He'll pay top dollar for your work. Hurry up, and you can get rich with your great solutions. When he sells the prototypes, we can get a very big order for manufacturing them. That's why I bought the computer programmed CNC machines. We have a brilliant future ahead of us!"

* * *

Before Mom went back home, I drove to the beach. I stood with her, embraced in the wind, by the rippling ocean, with tears. We held hands, thinking we might never get to see each other again. We said goodbye at the airport and watched as the plane took off with my mother.

We missed Mom. On Sundays, Dezső and I sat quietly on the balcony. He worked on a new invention. All around the house, we had X-ray images, artificial vertebras, and complete backbones. He looked like a surgeon when he cut and drilled these bones with his inventions. I watched how deeply he submerged himself in his work. The world around him disappeared. I stood up.

He told me, "I'm sorry, honey, I don't pay attention to you, but I must push myself to come up with the ideas. The doctor is waiting for it. I love you very much."

He kissed me. He was a good kisser. Then, he lightly kissed both of my eyes, and then my cheeks, forehead, and when he reached my neck, he whispered, "You make me a very happy man. Soon I can make you the queen of the house."

That afternoon, Attila introduced us to his girlfriend, Anna, a quiet girl. Whatever I asked her, she answered yes or no. Attila later told us that her father was an alcoholic. I wasn't impressed. She didn't have a smile or an opinion; she just sat on the sofa like she wasn't even there.

Csaba grew into a good-humored, energetic young man ready to work in his father's machine shop when the time came.

On a rainy afternoon, Dezső brought me a big surprise. He

held a big envelope and made me sit down on the sofa. "Honey, it is almost ten years we are working endlessly in America, time to have some relaxation. I take you for a nice vacation to Hawaii." He said that like he was inviting me for a dinner. I was speechless, and he enjoyed my amazement. I hugged him and we sat quietly. For all those years, I never thought to have a real vacation. Dezső must have felt our energy was almost used up. To get away from everything and enjoy life was what we really deserved. We had ten wonderful days on the island which reminded us of our honeymoon thirty years before.

New Possibility

I had been experiencing more and more back pain. I knew I should find an easier job. One cold, rainy day, I got home.

"Hello everybody!"

Nobody answered. I started the fireplace, got the local newspaper, and sat down in front of the fire. The warmth felt nice. I opened the Acorn newspaper. Clara worked there as an editor. I watched the flames; I could see her smiling face. She played an important role in my life, took my hand, guided me, and within moments, vanished like a shooting star. As I flipped through the paper, an advertisement caught my eye, printed in thick letters: "English speaking women needed for house work Monday through Friday from 7am to 5pm (sometimes weekends), who can babysit, too. Leave a message and phone number. I'll get back to you shortly."

I called the number, but I only got the answering machine. Soon Attila came home.

"It's so nice and warm in here. The wind is cold; it's freezing. Anything good in the paper?" he asked.

"I found this ad. The person on the answering machine has an accent. I wonder what nationality he is."

"So? You have an accent, too."

"Can you listen to him?"

"I think he is maybe Polish or Yugoslavian. Call him; you don't have to take the job."

I called and said, "My name is Maria Imre." Then, I gave my phone number and said, "I'm calling about your ad. I am fifty year old woman, married, with two sons. I came from

Slovakia, but I am Hungarian. I don't speak perfect English. I live in Agoura. Bye."

Attila laughed. "Congratulations. You spoke well."

Within moments, the phone rang.

"Can I speak with Maria?"

"Speaking."

"I am glad you called. My parents brought me to America from Yugoslavia. My wife is Italian and my father, who lives with us, speaks a little Hungarian. I would like to meet you and your husband for a friendly talk because I am looking for a helper who is a family-oriented, loving person. Can we do it tonight? We need help as soon as possible. My wife is eight months pregnant."

"Could you tell me what kind of help you need?"

"We are looking for someone who could do housework, help in the kitchen, and watch the children when we are not home. We need a warm, intelligent woman who will be treated in our home like a family member. My wife, Rita, is a hardworking woman. After we meet, we will decide whether we can work together."

During dinner, I shared my plan with Dezső.

"Honey, do you think this position will be easier than what you're doing now?"

"I don't know. Being with the family, maybe in the beginning could be hard, at least until we are used to each other. If we meet and I don't feel like I can connect with them, then I won't even give it a try. Honey, I need human contact, children, love – I crave that."

Their house stood on a hillside, surrounded by palm trees, and was fully lit, visible from the highway. We took a private road up to an automated iron gate. The man, Batta, greeted us so friendly, like we were old friends. His father waited in the door with a big smile.

In Hungarian, he said, "Welcome!"

Batta said, "My dad had some years in Hungarian school, but that was sixty some years ago. He doesn't speak, but he understands a lot."

The house was tidy and clean. The huge crystal chandeliers, granite flooring, and eggshell color carpet in the living room indicated they had good taste. A staircase led upstairs. The walls were decorated with oil paintings and the room was lit with table lamps, inspired by the works of Italian sculptors. Batta's wife greeted us with a platter of homemade cookies. She couldn't have denied her Italian ancestry; her long, brown hair and beautiful eyes reminded me of actresses in Italian movies.

"Come, sit down. May I offer you a coffee?"

Dezső smiled. "I only drink coffee in the morning. I know Italians drink it day and night; that's why they are so beautiful."

Rita thanked him for the compliment.

"It's true; we do drink a lot of coffee. Some people say it's healthy, but I didn't hear anything about its effects on beauty."

We all had a good laugh.

"My wife makes a very good cappuccino, and she is an excellent Italian cook. I bet that Maria is an expert in Hungarian cooking."

I heard giggling coming from upstairs. Two little girls in pajamas sat there. Two others stood behind them. Batta caught the surprised look on my face.

"Children are blessings from God. I can say it's tradition in our families to have many of them."

"I told you girls that you are not allowed to come out of your rooms. Since you're here, come down and introduce yourselves to Maria and Dezső."

The youngest immediately sat in Batta's lap.

"My name is Daniela. I am two years old."

Then, "I'm Lara, I just turned four."

"My name is Elena, I'm six."

"I'm eight, and my name is Natalia."

Batta watched his daughters with fatherly pride. Then, he called up the stairs.

"Son, why don't you come down, too."

A blond boy came down. He said, "I am Marko. Soon, I'll be ten years old."

"Maria, do you think you can work for us?" Batta asked.

I looked at the very cute children. The little ones even had their mouths open, waiting for my answer. Taking care of children is a huge responsibility, not an easy task, but the atmosphere in this family was so loving and kind, I already felt connected with them.

"I can try it."

"I am glad. Kids, time to go to bed."

They all kissed their parents and said goodbye to us. My eyes met Rita's. She said, "I see that you are surprised. They are not always like this. Batta told them that if you see them misbehaving, you will get scared and won't come back. With this many children, we must have discipline."

Batta turned to Dezső. "How do you feel about your wife's decision?"

"My wife loves family more than anything. She is a good mother, also a hard worker. Now she cleans two houses every day. If she wants to work for you, I support her."

"I believe, in our house, the work will be easier and a friendlier surrounding."

"Batta, you are right but there is one thing I am worried about. Kids have accidents; they scrape their knees, cut their fingers..." I said.

"Maria, we know that. It is simply a part of growing up. We can't hold their hands all the time." Batta paused. "I'm thinking, after a one-month trial, when we feel comfortable with each other and you decide to stay, I'll register you at my company as Rita's assistant and pay you according to the law,

fifty percent for overtime and one hundred percent on holidays.
I'll give you a raise every year. How does that sound?"

"Very good. Thank you."

We said goodbye, and ten minutes later, we were home. I sat
down in front of the fireplace. Dezső brought some brandy. It
felt good after the exciting meeting.

"The family is very sympathetic to me. I already love them.
Now, tell me what's happening in the new machine shop."

"I got a desk. We arranged my corner in the shop with all
the machines I work on. Ferenc hired a secretary and a full-
time cleaner. That little shop I started to work in has grown
into a decent professional business. I am proud of what I was
capable of doing through seven years. I don't envy the success
of Ferenc's company, but it hurts my ego how they don't show
any appreciation towards me."

He looked up to the sky and sighed. "God help me! Bring
someone into my life that I can do business with. Now I have a
new innovation, a very unique implant. It looks like a barrel with
thread around. I screwed it between the artificial neck vertebra,
demonstrating the perfect size and setting. I gave it to Ferenc,
and he told me it is very interesting work and he and Zoli will
think about it and see what they can do to make it better."

I saw the anger boil in my husband's mind. His face got red.
These two individuals without any profession got so lucky and
couldn't praise him. They were evil.

"Later, Ferenc brought me a drawing. They changed the
beautifully rounded edges into sharp ones and made the thread
very shallow. I pointed out the thread must be deep to be tight
between the vertebra. Then, Ferenc raised his voice."

"'I am paying you do it!' he actually yelled at me."

"Unbelievable," I said.

"Maybe Ferenc is patenting some innovations on his name.
He's taking all the doctors and my sketches from me. Before,
he didn't. The first innovations I made, those drawings are

still in my drawer. Now I don't have anything to prove it's my work because what I make, they draw a changed version. When they use that for the patent registration, they can prove it's theirs."

"This is why we must find a lawyer."

"I can't risk my job. I am sure Ferenc will kick me out."

"We should advertise. I make innovations from ideas and manufacturing prototypes."

"Honey, I don't have a shop."

"Dezső, we can sell the house."

"That's out of the question. I don't want to risk our hard-earned money. We must wait."

"I disagree. America is not the place where you are waiting, hoping that someday something will happen. You have to know what you want and go for it. I would go ahead and open the shop. It is risky, but I believe in you, and most importantly, you know what you are capable of doing. Without risk, you will never open a shop. You must do it."

"I'll think about it."

Saturday morning, I had just ended a conversation with Mom when Dezső came home. I was surprised. He looked serious but same time he was excited just he didn't want to show it. I knew him so well and patiently waited for the story he will share.

"I have some interesting news. When I got to work, none of the workers were there. The cleaning man was washing the shop floor. Ferenc, Zoli, and the secretary, all dressed up, were sorting papers."

Ferenc said, "Dezső, we are not working today. I have a business meeting with a client who wants to see my shop if we have the capacity for the serial production work."

He got two broken prototypes out of the closet.

"I need these to show him how the development looks in early stages. Please roughly weld them; it will look better that way. When you finish it, exit through the back door. I don't want you to interrupt our meeting."

"A short time later, I heard a heated argument. A man spoke in a firm voice." I saw a slight smile on my husband's face.

"I am not satisfied with our collaboration anymore! I always explain the essence of my idea. I give you a rough sketch, too. At first, I used to get perfect prototypes. Now, one is worse than the next. I must meet your design engineer."

"I couldn't hear what Ferenc said. But a little later, I heard more."

"Well, if he doesn't work every day and doesn't speak English, then I'll come back when he's here, and you can interpret for me. Until I can speak with him, I am not ordering anymore innovations."

"I left very fast. Honey, I'll meet the doctor soon. Do not think I'm crazy, maybe I can work for him without having Ferenc as the middle man." Dezső hugged me, he was so happy, like he won the lottery.

"Do you think Ferenc will let you meet the doctor? If I was in his shoes, I wouldn't let the doctor even come close to you."

"Honey, what will they do when he refuses to give them any work? Now their business is set up on the doctor's ideas and my inventions." I hope you can meet him, I really do.

* * *

We spent the weekend at the beach and had lunch in a little Italian restaurant. Dezső's eyes were sparkling blue again. It's true; the eyes are the windows to the soul.

"I can't stop thinking about the doctor. I know big things are about to happen."

I caught him watching me.

"Marika, I admire you. I am trying to be like you. Today I found myself humming. Morning I wake up truly believing in miracles."

He looked through the open window and watched the ocean. I loved him, just the same as almost forty years before. I looked in the bright sunlight at Dezső's temple with all of the silver hair. We were getting old and that was unbelievable.

On Monday morning, I got to Rita's house, and the kids ran to me with great enthusiasm.

"Maria, today you will drive us to school. You must learn where our school is because you have to pick us up in the afternoon."

When I saw the ten seats Cadillac limo, my heart raced. How I going to drive such a long car? Rita sat next to me; she wanted to know how I drive. To my surprise, I did without any difficulties.

In Batta's house, I found myself a second home. We did things together. She took the kids to the school, and I cleaned up the kitchen. The kids' rooms were tidy. Batta did room inspections before bedtime. If it was a mess, they earned fewer points and weren't allowed to go swimming or watch TV.

"Maria, you are not here to clean after them. Please teach them. We have lots of work. You organize it to keep the house clean. I cook every day. Of course, we are going to have coffee time, lunch time. I'll show you my garden, the chickens and rabbits. I pick all the fresh vegetables there for our salad, make lot of pizzas, and we eat homemade bread. Do you know how to bake bread?"

"Yes."

"Batta is a very busy man. Our company builds and sells houses. He leaves early and comes home late. It will be you and me with the kids. Sometimes grandpa watches them outside on the swing set or the doll house."

* * *

Sunday morning, it rained. Dezső and I stayed in bed talking.

"I promised Ferenc I will fix two wheelchairs today."

"Please, stay home. I got two new videos. We could start the fire, mix some cocktails, and watch movies."

"Tempting offer, but..."

The phone rang in the kitchen. I put my robe on and ran to pick it up. Without any introductions, a stranger spoke to me.

"I got this phone number from the phone book. I'm looking for Imre Dezső."

"This is his number."

"May I speak with him?"

"One moment."

I went into the bedroom, but Dezső was in the bathroom. "Somebody wants to talk to you."

"Who?"

"I don't know."

"Ask for the number, and I'll call back."

I got back on the phone and said, "Hello. My husband is in the shower. May I ask who's calling?"

"Your husband doesn't know me. He has done a few innovations for me. I'd like to meet him."

I almost dropped the phone. "Please, give me your number; he can call you back in a few minutes."

"Where do you live?" the man asked.

"In Agoura."

"I can be there in an hour."

I gave the doctor our address. Dezső came to the kitchen.

"What happened? You look so nervous. Who called?"

"The doctor. He'll be here in an hour."

At first, we hugged. Then, Dezső laughed like a child.

"I knew it! I felt it! He found me!"

In less than an hour, a yellow Corvette pulled in front of our house. A tall, bony, dark-haired, athletic man in his forties stepped out of the car. He got his briefcase and a big plastic bag full of artificial vertebra, rib, and spine bones. We greeted him at the door and introduced ourselves.

"George Nolsen, nice to meet you."

He looked more like a businessman, not a doctor. We came to the living room; he looked around.

"You have a beautiful home. Maria, please take the vase and the fruit bowl from the dining room table. I need to spread all the bones and sketches to explain my next innovation idea."

I was shocked by his confident behavior.

"I have a question for you," he said directly to Dezső. "Would it be possible that you work exclusively, just for me?"

"Yes, when I can open a machine shop."

"I want you to do it right now. If you don't have enough money, I'll lend you twenty thousand dollars. I want you to immediately resign from the company you work for. I don't want to deal ever again with the owner."

"Dr. Nolsen, can I offer you coffee or refreshment?"

"No, thank you. I didn't come as a guest; this is a business meeting."

"Dr. Nolsen, thank you for the loan offer. I accept it, but I have to know how long our collaboration would be."

"For many years. I want to develop a series of medical tools which don't exist in the world. As a specialist spine surgeon, I know exactly the kind of instruments I need to be able to heal patients with spinal injuries. I need a technically talented person to make my visions into reality. Based on the work you have done for me in the first months, I must say, your unique ideas were amazing. I will pay you five thousand dollars a month."

"Dr. Nolsen, that's not enough. I make that money now without any expenses, rent, electricity, water bills. That alone exceeds over two thousand a month."

"Forgive me, I didn't realize that. Then, let's agree to eight thousand a month. After two months trial, I will pay you an extra thousand, and from that, you pay off your loan from me."

"That sounds good."

The meeting went on for three hours. A couple of times, Dezső interrupted the doctor's explanations, suggesting different solutions on the spot.

"See, that didn't occur to me. Very good idea." In the end,

he stood up. "Here is my business card. I'm in surgery all day tomorrow. I'll be in my office after five o'clock. Let's meet there and I'll write you a check. In about a month, I hope you can start working from your own shop for me. Until then, in your spare time, think about a solution for our first project what I just explained to you."

"I'll do that. May I ask how you found me?"

"My friend and I went spying around your workplace. We saw three workers having lunch behind the shop. My friend approached them. All I knew about you was that you are Hungarian. They immediately told him your name. I found you in the phone book. When you resign, don't tell them you will work for me. I pressed charges against them; they hate me."

It was nearly dinnertime and we hadn't had lunch yet. Dezső came inside imitating the doctor. "Maria, I didn't come here as a guest; this is a serious business meeting. Tell me, dear Maria, what do you think about my negotiating skills?"

"You did very well."

We had a good laugh. My stomach churned.

"I'm hungry too. Let's go to the Carl's Junior for a nice hamburger."

TURNING DREAMS INTO REALITY

Dezső told Ferenc he got a great offer for opening a joint machine shop.

"If I strike a deal, I'll start with my family business."

"Dezső, that's a very bad idea. You can see it took me thirty years to get where I am now. Are you not happy with your pay?"

"I could earn more for my work, but at this point doesn't matter. I want to become independent. I'm fifty-one years old; I want to be my own man. Creating a family business with my sons is my dream."

Dezső and Attila ordered the machines. They rented a shop. During this time, Dezső often woke up in the night and stood on the balcony.

"Is something wrong?" I asked one night.

"No. I just keep thinking how I can leave in a friendly way from my job. I am truly grateful to Ferenc for everything he has done for us. I boosted his business; I hope he is grateful for that."

The next morning, Ferenc welcomed Dezső with open arms.

"I signed a contract with a hospital; I can give you a big raise."

"Ferenc, I'm resigning effective Monday."

Zoli came out from the office. Ferenc's face turned red as he shouted at Dezső.

"What? You can't do that to me! I brought you out from the cockroach motel and treated you as a friend."

"What happened?" Zoli asked.

"He is quitting!"

"What? I always told you, he is an asshole! He has no gratitude. Kick him out immediately."

"Ferenc, I am grateful. I have done everything to help you make your business flourish. I don't think it is anything to be upset about. I want to open my own company, that's all."

"Get out!" Ferenc yelled.

* * *

My days with Rita and the kids were filled with joy. Every day I thanked God for giving me a second family where I was loved and I loved them all.

One day, I got home in the middle of an argument. "Hey guys, what's going on?"

"Ask your son," Dezső said.

"Mom, I'd like to move out. My girlfriend has nowhere to live. I mean, her parents don't want her living with them anymore. She is old enough to be on her own."

"You want to get married?"

"No."

"Attila, that's not our custom. Her parents let her live with a man?"

"Mom, things are different here. Some kids move out at sixteen."

"It's not about the age. It is about love."

"I love her. Her father is constantly drunk. She will be grateful…"

"Attila, gratitude is not a reason to live with a woman."

"I love her."

Dezső looked at his son, disheartened. "I don't like her at all," he told Attila.

"Dad, you're not the one who has to live with her."

"Attila, with your dad, we were dating over four years. We knew we were made for each other."

"When everything goes well, I'll marry her." Attila said this with frustration.

I got upset. "When it doesn't? You move on to the next one?"

"Our son made his decision. Remember, if you leave, don't ever come back!" Dezső shouted.

Attila left the room. That night, neither of us could sleep. I was angry with Dezső. I didn't come to America to lose our son because he fell in love. I knew I must talk with him. Dezső got up before five the next morning. I was awake. He came to me.

"Try to talk to our son. Maybe he will listen to you. We must stop him from ruining his life."

Before I went to work, I knocked on Attila's door. He wasn't home. I wondered if he'd come back. I called Rita.

"Would it be inconvenient if I don't come today?" I asked her.

"No, I'll be home all day. Is it anything I can help?"

"No, thank you."

I called Attila's workplace. It was his day off, but I was hoping he would be there. He wasn't. I washed my car just to kill time, and that's when he came home.

"Are you not working?"

"No, I need to talk to you."

I will never forget his sadness and hopeless impression on his face.

"Attila, I want you to be happy. I'm not forcing my opinion on you. I'm advising you. This girl is not a type who will be with you in better and worse."

"Mom, you don't know her. It's not her fault how she was raised. She looks up to our family, values the support, and loves how we live. Please, don't judge her."

"I'm not judging. When we met her, there was nothing about her that was lovable. She is not kind, she is quiet, and she never laughs."

"Mom, I want to make her happy. I know that no mother could love a son more than you love me. Please try to understand that what you like, I don't have to like. I have different tastes, different dreams. If you want me to give up my happiness, I'll do it for you," he said, tears streaming down his cheeks.

"I'll talk to your father. When you like her that much, follow your heart."

That evening, we barely talked at the dinner table. When we finished, Dezső turned to Csaba.

"Look what I got you!"

Csaba opened the box and jumped with joy. It was the newest Nintendo Mario Brothers video game.

"Come, I love to see the little character go on his adventures," said Dezső.

I sat down in the living room. I could hear father and son having a blast with Mario's unsuccessful trials. It irritated me that Dezső intentionally avoided being with me. I went to the room where they were playing.

"I can hear you guys having fun. Let me see what your favorite hero is up to."

"Mom, I already passed the first level. Now I'm on the second, but Mario keeps falling into the chasm."

"You need to practice the jump. Dezső, I'd like to talk with you. Come to the living room."

We walked into the other room, and he said, "I can see you are on your son's side."

"It's not about taking sides. I talked with him, and I don't want to lose him because he is in love with a girl. We can't tell him who to love or not love. Do you want to ruin his life? Our son loves us and he will stay home if we..."

"Then, it's settled."

"No, it isn't. I'm not going to blackmail him with my love. Remember, your mother was cruel to you and she lost you. She lived with anger; she died and never forgave you because you married me, a city girl. She knew we were happy, but never acknowledged that. I'm not letting you do the same to our son. Think about that. I love you, but please do not repeat your mother's mistake."

In thirty some years, this was the second time that I had ever confronted my husband. I was scared what would happen if he didn't support his son. I left the room and went to our bedroom, crawled into bed, pulled the duvet over my head, and cried. Dezső came after me.

"Please don't cry. I love our sons like you do; I want what's best for him. You scared me when you compared me to my mother. I am not cruel. I'll do peace with Attila, I promise."

In the morning, Lara, Natalia, and Daniela ran to me as I got out of my car.

"Maria, the baby is coming today!"

"Don't worry, it's not imminent yet. Batta went to an important meeting and he will be home in the afternoon," Rita said. "You take the kids to school; the little ones can stay with me."

When Batta got home, Rita was ready to go. She waved goodbye and left, holding on to her husband's arm. After five that afternoon, the phone rang. Batta called.

"It's a boy. A healthy, beautiful addition to our family. His name is Dario. Maria, please get the kids ready. I want to bring them to meet their brother."

Now I had the chance to relive my maternal feelings, cuddling and helping take care of Dario. From the start, he had a strong personality, and I loved his mischievous smile when he achieved what he wanted.

I rarely saw Attila during that time. When I got home, he had already left for work. On Saturday mornings, I went grocery shopping, and usually got home around lunchtime. Attila worked the night shift, and then he slept until noon. He looked tired when came into the kitchen.

"Would you like a nice sandwich? I got fresh bread, ham, salami, Swiss cheese, bell pepper, tomato."

"Salami will be great. Thank you, Mom."

I heard the garage door open. Dezső came in.

"Hey! Looks like I'm in time. Can I have a sandwich like that?"

He hugged me and sat at the table, across from Attila. They ate quietly. Dezső broke the silence.

"Nobody has asked me why I'm home so early."

"Why are you home so early?" Attila asked humorously.

"I can't get any work done. I must rest my brain." He laughed. "Nothing to be alarmed about. I want to relax and have some fun."

Attila looked at him. "Then, let's play bottom-slaps."

We burst out laughing. It was so long ago when the kids were little and kept dragging us to do something. Dezső used to say that.

"That was a long time ago, son. It's funny you remember it. What's going on with you?"

"I'm not moving."

He got up, ready to leave.

"Attila, sit down, let's talk," Dezső said.

"We already did."

"I know, but listen to me. I judged quickly, which isn't my style. I don't like your girlfriend and I thought that is enough reason to tell you not to love her. Your mom reminded me about my mother. She didn't like her either. It was very painful for us. She saw our happiness but never forgave me since I did not obey her. I don't want to follow her footsteps. Bring your girlfriend. There is plenty of room downstairs. Once upon a time, my father-in-law welcomed me to his home. He wanted to help me and your mom in the beginning of our life journey. We will do the same for you."

With this decision, Dezső proved he was a gentle, very loving, family man. We loved each other so much.

The next year carried on smoothly. Dezső and the doctor became friends. He had great appreciation for Dezső's work. Csaba became Dezső's apprentice.

Our family always loved animals. We got Csaba a six-week-old English shepherd dog named Khiana. That little puppy became part of our family.

Attila looked happy. I did my best to make Anna feel at home, but she remained in her own world. She never came upstairs for a chat; we only saw her at dinner. After one year, I asked her if she'd like us to meet her parents.

"No," was all she said.

"Aren't they curious to see where you live?"

"No."

It was beyond my comprehension.

My favorite holiday – Thanksgiving – was coming. All of us were invited to Batta's and Rita's festive feast. I got to meet all of their family members, at least 150 of them.

I held the Christmas celebration in our house. My home wasn't quite big enough for the large number of guests, but we made it work. The table in the kitchen, as well as the dining room and counters, were full of Hungarian foods. Everyone packed their plates. The older guests sat down, the kids sat on the stairs, and we, the middle-aged group, stood and socialized while we ate. My heart felt full of joy to entertain everybody who I loved like my family. The evening was unforgettable. Rita's father had the best time. He saw my Italian opera collection, and he insisted that we sing Figaro's aria. The Italian side of the family sang while he directed them with a wooden spoon. The whole neighborhood echoed from the singing. For as long as I live, I'll always be filled with gratitude for that time in my life.

Batta's family lived truly by the Bible. I was brought up in the Catholic faith, but we didn't go to church in the socialist country. It was prohibited. Our family secretly had a retired priest who was my dad's pastor from the past era, and he taught me about Christianity. My father said: you must have fate in our God. Wherever you are you can talk to God. I prayed every evening and felt God's love and protection for me. In Batta's house every Sunday, Batta, Rita, all the children, and Grandpa went to church. Sometimes, I joined them. I remember three-year-old Dario saying to me:

"Maria, come with me to church. If you don't, after we die, we can't meet in heaven."

I have so many precious, unforgettable memories from the time I was with them. Now they are all grown up and have children who are the same ages they were when I met them. It is so wonderful to watch all of the happy marriages and see Rita's and Batta's fifteen grandchildren. I enjoy visiting every time I have the chance.

Dezső's creativity skyrocketed. He lived his days with good humored, youthful energy. He and the doctor were in contact every day. Dezső's office looked like an operating room. The spine and all vertebrae and ribs laid on his desk filled with implants and surgical tools used for the surgery. It amused him to chisel, carve, and implant with the toll he just invented to hold different size and shape implants. This special tool has an adjustable part that makes sure when the doctor places the implant to the spine, he can't damage the nerves, because the stopper doesn't let the implant go deeper.

Dezső had no time to train Csaba, so Csaba started working for our friend, Miki, who did tile and granite work. Csaba always was creative and loved to work with his hands. He learned from his father how to be precise and do a detailed job. After a short time, Miki allowed him to cut the granite himself and do custom-made work independently.

On pleasant autumn evenings, we often sat on the balcony. I read a book, and Dezső flipped through papers, full of calculations. He had been so submerged in his work that he didn't even talk about it. I missed our evening conversations.

"Do you love me?" I asked one night.

He looked at me, astonished.

"You've never asked me this before. Can't you feel it?"

"I know you love me, but lately you haven't had time to show it. You can't step out of your world of inventions, but my world needs you, too."

"I'm sorry. In my defense, I am working on more and more difficult inventions, and time flies by so fast." He lifted my hand

and kissed it. "No one can love you more than I do. Words are not enough to express it." He held my hand with guilt.

"If I could, I would never leave your side, but I'm pushing myself so that the doctor can sell one of his inventions. He promised me I'll get the serial production. That's a more comfortable way of making money. Then, I can open our family business, where my sons can be my partners."

His calculations won him over again and I couldn't stop thinking about a conversation I had with Batta.

Batta had said, "Maria, is Dezső still working for a monthly wage for the doctor?"

"Yes."

"That's not fair to him. Dezső is entitled to a percentage of the inventions. He is the designer and the prototype maker. The doctor can't perform surgeries with his ideas. Dezső could also get a percentage of the sold pieces. He needs a contract made with the doctor and an attorney. You should start thinking about securing your retirement."

"Dezső believes the doctor gives him what is legitimate for his work. He trusts him 100%. When I try to suggest getting some information from a lawyer, he gets very irritated. Last time he told me, 'The doctor's appreciation for my work is enormous. He is the best surgeon and I am the best inventor, he told me that. We are friends. Friends do not cheat or lie. Believe me, I'll be generously rewarded.'"

As the sun was setting, it got chilly. I tried to put my thoughts of the conversation with Batta aside, and I put down my book.

"I'm cold, I'll get my sweater. Should I bring one for you?"

"No, but a nice drink would be good. Brandy?"

For a while, we sat quietly. Then Dezső started the conversation.

"I plan to talk with the doctor, but I don't know how to approach him. We are friends. I want to find the right way to ask him a couple of things."

"What do you mean?"

"Ask him to put my name on the patent papers or can I have some percentage when they get sold."

"Then, ask him."

"What if he gets offended?"

"I don't know. Whatever you think, do it. I would have no problem talking to him about your work contract. The kind of work you are doing, nobody does for a monthly wage."

"I told you many times, I'm not a child whose mommy has to come to settle things for him."

The next day, I cooked dinner, and Anna came into the kitchen. She stretched her hand out to me. A beautiful diamond engagement ring was shining on her finger.

"Congratulations!"

Dezső and Attila came in.

"I asked Anna to marry me, and she said yes," Attila said as he hugged her.

She turned to me.

"My mother would like to meet you. She wants to make arrangements for the wedding. She must tell you about the American wedding customs, probably you are not familiar with them."

THE WEDDING

A nna's mom was polite, but not friendly with me.

"Maria, I'll tell you what needs to be done in preparation for the wedding. The groom's parents pay for the bridal bouquet, the flower arrangements, the photographer, the wedding cake, and the limousine that takes the young couple to the wedding ceremony. The hall rental and the dinner expenses will be divided by the number of guests attending. We pay for the wedding dress, the priest, and the alcohol."

I was speechless. Anna's father turned to me. "You have different customs?"

"My parents paid for my wedding. My husband bought the wedding ring and the bridal bouquet. In Hungary, Slovakia, the bride's parents make the wedding. Of course, I will pay my share; you don't have to worry about that. I had the opportunity to attend weddings in America. Two flower arrangements on the side of the priest and a flower arch above the young couple cost seven thousand dollars. I can't afford that. At every wedding, the guests bought their own alcohol at the bar. A glass of champagne with dinner to toast the newlyweds was charged together with the food. We have a close family friend, Misi, a professional photographer who comes from Chicago. The photo album will be his gift for Attila and Anna."

The father again topped off our glasses.

"To tell you the truth, we can't afford to take on many expenses either."

"Then I suggest we don't spend money on useless things," I said.

"What do you mean, useless?"

"We should arrange the wedding according to our financial possibilities. It will be useful doing some research and then getting together again."

We agreed and said goodbye.

In the morning, the doctor called. He wanted to meet Dezső in a restaurant. We thought maybe he had some good news for him. When I came home, Dezső sat front of the fireplace.

"How was your meeting?"

"Nothing special. The doctor came from the courthouse; he sued Ferenc's company. They patented one of his inventions. He won the trial. He was happy about it. I took the opportunity to ask him if my name could be on the inventions. He got very mad."

"'Absolutely not!' he told me. 'These inventions are mine! I pay you even for that month when you didn't come up with any ideas. I'm giving you bonuses, too.'"

"I said to him, 'Doctor, I'm not greedy, but can't you give me a percentage, just one percent from the sold invention? I'm getting old...'"

"'No!' he said. 'I promised you, if I sell my inventions, you can be the manufacturer. You don't have to worry about ever being out of work!'"

"He got so angry, I was surprised," Dezső shared.

"What happened next?" I asked.

"He wants me to do a side job for a medical device factory. They can't solve a technical problem. He is sure I can do it. He gave me the blueprints and after that, we said goodbye."

"Now what?"

"Nothing. Everything stays the same. One day, I'll get the production."

Attila's wedding day arrived. It was in an exclusive garden with a waterfall. Anna walked on the long sidewalk with her father. She wore a beautiful, pearl-studded, long gown. She was beautiful. Attila waited for her, looking like his father many years ago. At dinnertime, we sat with Rita, Batta, and all of the children, having a good time. Anna's family and friends were loud, and the celebration got wild. Her father got drunk, wobbling from table to table. Finally, he collapsed. Nobody made a big deal of it.

Misi took many photos, capturing every step, from preparations for the wedding at home through all of the evening events. When we saw the guests getting drunk, we went home. I was sad. I always dreamed about a big family, but Anna's parents would never be close to us. That was obvious.

Then, we celebrated Dario's first birthday. Life had granted me a very special gift; I was there to witness Dario's first smile, first steps, and first words. I enjoyed his day-by-day development, which I didn't have with my own children. Attila was six-months-old when he started to be cared for in the factory nursery. Csaba was with my mom. Surrounded by all of these children, each different and special, was a wonderful experience.

LIFE IS UNPREDICTABLE

At dawn, we woke to a loud roar and crashing noise. Dezső jumped out of bed. The paintings were all popping off the walls. I ran into the living room. The dining cabinet doors were all slamming open and shut. The crystal glasses, vases, my Herendi porcelain collection, were all jumping up and down the shelves and ended up smashing on the floor. The house walls were cracking, the TV fell off of its stand. In the kitchen, the jars, spices, and plates were all on the floor, broken. We heard a loud, cracking sound. A two-inch crack formed in the middle of the living room floor. Through it, we saw downstairs. Attila shouted from outside: "Get out of the house, now!"

I grabbed Dezső's arm as the floor moved beneath us. On the street, families embraced, people wept, and lay on the ground. The earth quaked again. The elderly crawled on their knees. A house collapsed at the end of the street. Thick clouds of dust filled the air. Then, it was quiet. After a long period of silence, we got back to the house. My life size, ceramic, embracing couple bust had fallen on the granite slab in front of the fireplace, shattered into a million pieces. I got it from my husband on our fifth Christmas together. We shoveled all of the broken glasses into the trash. I can't describe the helplessness I felt. What were we going to do? We didn't have earthquake insurance. I got a splitting headache. Dezső sat down next to me.

"Dear, we are alive," he said.

For the first time in my life, I felt the loss had ruined me forever. I didn't have the strength to start all over again. I looked at Dezső. His eyes were closed, and tears ran down his face.

Late afternoon, the power came back. We saw on the TV all of the earthquake damage. Multilevel bridges had collapsed cars underneath with passengers inside. The entire area of Los Angeles was paralyzed. The news said: 1994, January 17, at 4:31am, a natural catastrophe hit California. The epicenter of the 6.8 earthquake on the Richter scale was in the Northridge area.

A week later, in Agoura, the grocery stores opened. Supplies arrived from north of us. The major damage was south. After three weeks, Attila got back to work. Dezső lost contact with the doctor. Batta came over to check the damages on our house.

"I don't want to sadden you, but fixing your house will be at least a hundred thousand dollars. The foundation split and slid unevenly. None of the windows open."

Dezső ran his hand through his hair. "What should we do?" he asked worriedly.

"I would sell, as it is. You won't be able to recover the money that you invested into it."

I was devastated. "I must speak to Teresa. They gave us the loan, and we have nine more years to pay. Mike is a construction engineer. Perhaps he can help."

I spent the night awake, taking inventory of my life. I worked very hard all my life. What I wanted was a loving family and a safe home. I wanted to raise my children the best I could, shelter them, and teach them about life. That is how I grew up. Gave them the home where all dreams, goals, and feelings are born. That is the place where we return to get energized, for hugs and advice. I wondered where will be our home. This house can collapse any minute and I can't do anything about it. I'm tired. *My body and soul want to rest but that is impossible. I was born to fight and stand up doesn't matter how difficult it is. I just need a little bit of time.* I was able to smile, and thought that God would help me to stand up.

Attila and Anna rented a small apartment, and they were safe. A month later, Dezső was able to drive on side roads to the doctor's office. His car was in the parking lot, but the building was closed. He picked a few pebbles and threw them at his office window. Moments later, the doctor opened the door. In his office, the floor and chairs were full of documents, catalogs, drawings. He pointed at his desk with many surgical instruments.

"My friend, we have a lot of work to do. I'm now working on an invention which will be a global success. Only you and I can make this idea reality. Do you see all those instruments? That is how many I need to perform a spine surgery. I want to make an invention where we make a basic piece to attach the entire set. This way, all these tools can be much smaller, fit in a suitcase, and be more efficient."

* * *

I wrote Teresa a letter about what had happened with the house. She called me and said that in two weeks they have a doctor's appointment in Agoura and will come to visit us.

In the meantime, I tried to enjoy life with Rita and the children. Often on our way home from school, we stopped at the Yum-Yum doughnut shop. We all sat around a table. Dario held his favorite powdered sugar covered doughnut filled with lemon jelly in his little hands. By the time he finished it, his happy face and shirt was covered with the white powder and the sticky jelly. He was so cute. The saleswoman came to us and praised the children for their remarkable behavior. She said: "You have beautiful children. They look just like you."

The kids giggled, but they didn't tell her that I wasn't their mother. When we got home, they ran to tell Rita what happened.

"So, you don't look like me?" Rita asked.

Daniela turned her big eyes at her mother. "Nobody said that to me."

"I think the lady had bad eyesight," I said. "She couldn't see I am old enough to be your grandmother."

We had a good laugh at this story. Then I got the news, we were going to be grandparents. Attila opened a bottle of champagne. Csaba patted him on the shoulder.

"I'm so happy for you. I'll be a very active uncle going to the playground, teaching how to ride a bicycle. We'll definitely have fun times."

* * *

Teresa and Mike arrived one afternoon. He went to look around the house. The always chatty Teresa was quiet for a while.

"Maria, we know the problem is tremendous and feel terrible that we didn't tell you about the earthquake insurance. We never had one. According to the map, this area doesn't fall under earthquake risk, which is why the bank doesn't require it either."

Mike and Dezső came back from inspecting all of the damage caused by the earthquake. He was serious when he talked to us.

"Fixing the house can cost over one hundred thousand. It cannot be sold as it is. Teresa, what can we do?"

"Mike, is the house safe to live in?"

"I'll call an expert to assess the situation, and then we will know for sure. I think it is. I thought the only way we can help you is to have you stay for a couple of years in the house for free. We would put it back on our name and you can save money to be able to have a down payment for another house. When you move out, we can fix this and sell it."

This was a generous offer. We thanked them. Unfortunately, the six years of loan payments were down the drain. It was a huge loss we suffered. I was so embittered, it scared me. We spent lots of time on the beach, even during the weekdays, just to get out of the house. Before long, Dezső came up with an idea.

"Marika, I'd like to move to the mountains, far from the city. What do you think?"

"Good idea. We can start looking around for what's

available. I hate to be in our house, so making trips around may give us some positive vibes."

Looking at houses in the mountains and by the ocean was fun, but the prices were much higher than in town. Every time we stopped at a gas station, I picked up real estate brochures, and at home, I searched for an inexpensive house, but no luck.

By this time, our grandchild's arrival was imminent, and I had been thinking about staying home and taking care of the baby. Rita's children were all in school, but when she needs me, I could always help her as a friend.

One morning, Rita was getting ready for a birthday lunch, drying her hair in the bathroom. I talked to her about Dario. His personality made us laugh. I watched her warm smile; after six pregnancies, she was a beautiful woman. Her towel slipped off of her shoulder. I bent down to pick it up; I felt a sharp pain in my lower back and couldn't straighten up. She canceled her lunch, and along with Batta, they drove me home and stayed with me for a while. After she picked up the kids from school, she came back to see me. The kids surrounded my bed. Dario hugged me as he whispered: "Please don't die, I love you."

The kids wanted to stay.

"Maria needs to rest now. Let's hurry home, I'll need your help with cooking, and later, we'll come back with dinner so Dezső, Csaba, and Maria can have food on the table."

"Maria, don't worry. I'll take care of you," Rita said.

She took care of my family for two weeks. The selfless care and love I received will never be forgotten. I talked with them about my plan to take care of my grandchild. They understood, and I stayed home but our friendship remained the same.

Past midnight, in 19th November 2001 I held my beautiful, brown haired granddaughter. She was so beautiful, I cried tears of joy. Dezső kissed her forehead and said, "Welcome to our loving family, little Nicole."

* * *

Two years went by, but we weren't able to find a house out of the city. I took care of Nicole from morning to evening. Attila and Anna had dinner every day with us, and then returned to their apartment.

The doctor was satisfied with the development of the new instrument. Dezső mentioned to him that he would like to get small serial production jobs which are usually ordered for presentations and hospital trials. He wanted to teach Csaba how to read blueprints and operate the machines.

"See, I completely forgot about that! I'll write you a letter of recommendation and give you a few addresses where to send it. I am sure you will have no trouble finding work for your son."

Taking care of Nicole made me feel young again. I sewed her cute dresses and matching hair bows. She always looked like a little doll. Her personality amazed us. She loved books and stories; we drew pictures and watched all of the Disney movies. In a funny way, I said she was exactly like me, her grandma.

New Beginning

One cold evening, I started the fire with the old real estate brochures. An advertisement caught my eye. It was surrounded with exclamation signs: !!! TOLLHOUSE 20 ACRE RANCH!!! For sale, 140 thousand dollars. Bank owned property, negotiable!!! I looked up the place on the map. It was three hours away, north of us, at the foothills of the Sierra Mountains. The house looked nice in the photo, and the picture of the view was breathtaking.

Dezső got very excited when he saw the ad. It had been posted three months prior; maybe the ranch was already sold.

"Honey, call them. When it is available, go with Csaba and check it out. I can't go with you; I'll be with the doctor, testing our new device."

A man picked up the phone and spent a few minutes looking for the house. Meanwhile, he reassured me, if it is sold, he can find a similar one.

"I found it! The interior of the house is in bad shape; the carpet has to be removed. Dogs and cats lived in the house locked up for days. I am telling you because I don't want you to be disappointed when you drive from far."

"I will come to see it tomorrow."

"Okay. I'll be in the office from nine to five."

In the morning, Csaba and I met Peter, the real estate agent.

After a one-hour drive through beautiful mountains and valleys, we reached a pebble side road and stopped in front of a ranch gate like those seen in Wild West cowboy movies. Peter had a hard time unlocking the rusty padlock that was hanging on a heavy chain. Opening the gate was problematic, too, because of the tall, spiky thistle. With Csaba, they managed to trample it down. The road split into two behind a wide, shallow creek. A curvy mountain road on the right side led us through the forest up to the house. As I got out of the car, I found myself in a magical place. On either side, as well as behind the house, sky-high mountains were guarding the house on the lower hill. In front of us, as far as the eye could see, a lineup of mountain chains gave us a breathtaking view. We struggled to make our way to the front door through the tall vegetation. When Peter opened the door, a strong, stuffy smell came out.

"Wait, I'll open the back doors and windows so the draft helps move the smell out."

My jaw dropped when we went inside. Clouds were painted on the dark blue ceilings, trees and deer on the brown walls. Dried cat poop hung off of the top of the curtains and the carpet looked like a dog toilet. The kitchen cabinet doors were broken; piles of cups and open dog cans were in the sink. There is nothing I can write about the bathrooms; perhaps it was impossible to clean them. The agent told us the owner was a pilot, flying between Los Angeles, Paris, and London. His wife left him; he'd been living in the house with three cats and two dogs. He used to have big parties. One morning, he went to work drunk. He was about to take off, but someone reported him for drinking all night in the bar. From the airplane, they took him straight to prison. The police eventually came and took the animals to the shelter. Nobody paid the loan, so the house became the bank's property.

Csaba took a quick look around the 20-acre land so he could report back to his father.

"Are you going to buy it?" Peter asked.

"I need to think about it. The house condition is much worse than I expected. There is no washer and dryer in the laundry room, and the kitchen doesn't have a stove. All of these things should be part of the house. If the bank drops the price at least twenty thousand, then maybe I will buy it."

"Let's go back to the office and talk to the bank representatives."

In the bank, an older woman greeted us. "I hear that you like the Tollhouse property," she said.

"I do, but it is not worth more than 120 thousand dollars."

"Unfortunately, I cannot let it go for that."

"The house is in very bad shape."

"I know, if it is in good shape, it would be worth 250 thousand. The land is beautiful and there is a small house down in the valley, rented out for 300 dollars a month. Did you see it?"

"Yes, it is in very bad shape, too. I don't know how somebody can live in it."

The lady looked at me through her funny looking, red-white striped glasses.

"I can try to talk with my boss. He has the final word."

A strict, very skinny man came over to us. "You can have the house for 130 thousand," he said.

"Thank you. I have to think about it. I'll call you."

I walked to the door.

"Perhaps we can make a deal," the man added.

"I said 120 thousand and I'll give you fifteen thousand as a deposit right now."

"Alright," he agreed.

I wrote the check and called my husband.

"Tell me the good news," Dezső said.

"I just bought you a twenty-acre ranch with a house."

"Oh, thank you dear, what a lovely present."

He laughed, sending me kisses through the phone.

On Sunday, we were all at the gate of the ranch, waiting for Peter. Attila, Dezső, and Csaba walked up the hill on foot.

Inside of the house, Anna said, "Awful. This place needs a lot of work."

"When you don't have money for a perfect house, you have to fix one. In a couple of months, you'll see."

"I would love to live in nature, too, but Attila's plans are tying us to Los Angeles."

"What plans?"

"He didn't tell you?"

"No."

"He wants to become a police officer. We are waiting for the response on his application. If they hire him, he will be able to attend the Police Academy for free."

"Are you happy with his decision?"

"If this is what he wants."

"Aren't you afraid that your daughter will become an orphan?"

"We believe that our fate is decided. You could get hit by a car; you don't need to be a police officer to die. You mustn't think like that."

"When Dezső finds out, he'll go crazy. At home, every spineless loser was a police officer."

"You are in America now. It is a privilege to be a police officer."

The men arrived.

"Honey, this place is beautiful, I am so happy you found it!"

Buying the ranch, having big plans with it, gave us energy for starting a new life again.

The following week, we, along with Csaba, started remodeling our new home.

Anna found a daycare for Nicole, but she cried and her personality changed. Dezső was upset about it.

"The best thing would be if you guys came up to the hills. I might start the serial production very soon and we can all live comfortably off that. Attila, I thought you could go to a computer programming school, and that way you can do the programs for our CNC machines."

"If your plan becomes reality, I'll help you with everything."

"That sounds like you don't believe…"

"Dad, I don't trust the doctor. I don't think you know how valuable the things are which you are making, and he gives you a monthly pay that is ridiculous. You could be a world-famous inventor. I don't think you need a production job. What you need is a fair contract that includes all your rights. You should be resting on the ranch; you worked so hard all your life."

"The doctor is a correct man. When we finish this last invention, he'll give me everything I deserve! I hate lawyers; I'm not going to sue my friend. We are like partners."

Dezső asked for two weeks' vacation. We worked on the house day and night. The creative spirit had returned to us. Our plans were filled with daring ideas. We wanted to buy cows, sheep, and chickens, plant fruit trees, and build a big vegetable garden. I could visualize my flower garden which I knew I must have around the house.

Attila and Anna surprised us with a visit. Nicole was so happy to see me. Anna came to help me bring some sandwiches and coffee outside under the umbrella. She whispered to me, "The LAPD rejected Attila's application."

"I am sorry to hear that."

I felt relief. God had listened to my prayers and the best part was how Dezső never found out his son's plan. We took the food out. Nicole sat on my lap. Attila watched her.

"Since you left, she doesn't sleep well and cries when Anna takes her to the nursery."

Anna got upset. "They say when I leave; she plays nicely and behaves very well."

"Of course, they say that. They don't want to lose a client."

"Move to Fresno. The Protection One has office there too. I would like to have Nicole with me; she would have a wonderful childhood on the ranch."

"We'll think about it."

* * *

Dezső's design process took longer than expected. The doctor again wanted to solve another invention, which was not his own. He promised to help a medical instrument manufacturing company in Tennessee. Both of them flew there. Dezső spent three weeks redesigning that surgical tool with success. The factory management offered my husband a job as chief of their innovation department, but his dream was to be independent. He liked his job with the doctor. The only thing that worried him was what he was going to do when the doctor didn't need him anymore.

We made our house ready to move in. After the first night on the ranch, we woke up to the sound of birds chirping. The view, the mountains, all had a fantastic effect on us. It felt like we are at a holiday resort on a vacation. Walking down to the gate and back to the house on the meandering forest road took our breath away. Dezső stopped. The creek flowed on the cliff side among the trees and the sunrays filtered through the tree leaves, rendering it enchanting.

"Pinch me so I know I'm not dreaming. I am so happy here!" He said, happily.

Dezső worked from home and went for a few days to the shop. A specially designed suitcase was ready to place the whole set of spine surgery instruments in it. Every piece of the set had a premade spot. I looked at these shiny instruments made with professionalism and craftsmanship at the highest level.

"Honey, you can be proud of yourself. It is amazing what you are capable of doing."

"I am proud of it and most importantly the doctor love it. Hopefully four-five months I can finish the set."

A couple of days later, Attila came again. He got a large suitcase out of the trunk. He laughed when he hugged me.

"Mom, we brought you your granddaughter for boarding. I can't watch her suffer in that nursery. We will leave her here when it's okay. In the future, we'll spend the weekends with you guys. What do you think?"

"I'm happy to have her with me."

From that time, my life got more meaning as I took care of my granddaughter. We sat on the floor, flipping through storybooks or playing with toys. On our walks, she loved all of the animals, especially our neighbor's horses. She noticed the deer and wild boars grazing beyond the fences and imitated the sounds of kittens, dogs, goats, roosters, and cows. In the evenings, we sat outside. With her grandpa, Nicole watched the shooting stars and the flashing lights of the airplanes. Csaba took her in our forest, showing her the birds, and she picked wild flowers for me. Csaba made her a swing between the trees. I could hear her laughter all the way up at the house.

Now we walked on the peaceful life path. I patiently waited for Dezső as he finish his largest invention set. We talked a lot about the serial production. Then, we would be able to move the shop to Fresno.

"My friend, when we finish this masterpiece, I'll immediately sell it," the doctor said. "Then, you get the production."

Dezső believed him. He was driven by his passion for invention. He focused on the doctor's ideas and wanted to do the best solutions. I worried for him. He was losing connection with the family, with the life around him.

Attila and Anna announced they were expecting another baby. I got excited and ran to Dezső's office, but he was in the middle of something. He just said, "Honey, that's great."

I walked a lot on our land and sat on a big rock from where I was able to see most of our ranch. The place became truly beautiful. The little trees and bushes were all growing nicely. Over one hundred rose bushes were blooming around the house and 130 different fruit trees started to have fruit on them. The Colorado blue spruce pine seedlings grow over one meter tall. They were Dezső's favorite, but he didn't even take notice of them. I went inside, just as Dezső walked out of his office.

"Can you come with me to see the roses? They are so beautiful."

"Darling, you are an amazing gardener." He looked at his watch, then said, "I have to call the doctor."

A couple of weeks later, Dezső took a week off. He wasn't able to concentrate. He told the doctor, "I must turn off my computer in my head. I can't sleep. I need some personal time. I don't remember when I last laughed nor had a good time with my wife."

In the evenings, we had dinner outside, and long conversations. For the first time, we really enjoyed our beautiful place.

After Nicole fell asleep, I joined him in the office, quietly knitting or reading.

"It's nice that you are with me. I thought we might tell Attila to move in with us until they find a house around here to buy. This is not good for Nicole not having her parents around."

I sat in his lap and laid my head on his shoulder. He was such a brave, good family man.

A month later, Attila moved in. Anna worked from home for the insurance company, and Attila's company relocated him to Fresno.

The ranch life with animals, orchard, vegetable garden, and flowers was not an easy one. Early in the mornings, I made myself a big cup of coffee and walked down the hill to feed my cows, sheep, and chickens. Khiana, our sheep dog, hated the ranch. Her paws were used to soft carpets and asphalt. Sasha, our ranch guard Rottweiler, was playfully running back and forth. The little kitten, Nosy, followed behind. We also had two geese. One morning I found them in the chicken coop and they stayed and walked with us down the hill. When I finished tossing the hay, we all came back to the house.

The neighbors thought my ranch was a magical place. All of my animals were extremely friendly. My trees and plants grew healthy and the flower garden bloomed from early spring to late fall. I took care of everything the best I could. I spent hours watching the calves running around in the pasture, and when they got hungry, always found their grazing mother. The number of lambs increased as well. The baby ram's mother died when he was born. Nicole and Csaba fed him with a baby bottle. We called him Big Boots because his feet were covered with black, curly hair. The chickens were the last stop on my rounds. Twice a day, I collected the eggs and I'd often feed them out of my palm. I loved to work in my vegetable and flower gardens.

Csaba and Nicole, with a slice of buttered, home-baked bread, would snack on the fresh tomatoes, radishes, and spring onions. My neighbors came strawberry picking because I ran out of ideas for what to do with them. I made jam, dried some, ate them, I even took some for the chickens. It is amazing how my hard work turned the ranch into a picture-perfect place that I called my sweet home.

For three years, we saved money for a big swimming pool, a garden terrace with a built-in grill, and a table with eight chairs. This became our family's favorite relaxing and dining spot. I asked Dezső not to work after dinners; then, he could spend the evenings with us. We watched the Sierra Mountain range until late nights. The snow-covered peaks gleamed in the moonshine. Sometimes an owl hooted nearby or a coyote howled in the distance. These nights were romantic. In the summertime, we didn't go to the house; we just lay on the lawn and watched the shooting stars. Our passionate kisses and long embraces transported us back to our youth, even though we were over fifty.

Sometimes I brought up the doctor, but Dezső got defensive.

"Honey, I'm worried for Csaba, he works on the ranch, like a journeyman," I said. "What will he become if you don't get the production orders?"

"The doctor gave me his word. I will pass my knowledge to Csaba, don't worry. I always think about him. He'll be a great partner for me. Attila is smart, but he is a security guard. That makes me sad."

"He is providing safety to hundreds of families. What's

important is that he enjoys doing it. You enjoy your work and that makes you happy. I had many different jobs and I loved them all. Everything in life is the point of view. Now I enjoy the hard work on our land. The grass had to be mowed because of the fire hazard. The smell of freshly mowed grass is heavenly. I get up at 4 in the morning; I learn how to weed whack. For me, this is exciting, and I love to see our place neat. This is the first time I feel this is my real home in America. I am FREE. The chief of the post office, Celine, the lovely French lady, the owner of the feed store, the saleswomen in the little grocery store, the nursery owner, they all call me by my name. The neighbors, the postal worker, the guy who comes to read the electricity meter, all enjoy chatting with me. We sit down for coffee and cake. I don't do sophisticated one-of-a-kind work, never did in my life, but I was and am happy. People respect me because I'm a positive person; I have kind words and a helpful nature. I was always that way; nothing changes me. Attila is happy with what he does; please don't make him do what he doesn't like."

My husband looked very tired. "Soon everything will be settled," he said.

Some days I was alone on the ranch. Csaba got remodeling jobs in LA, and Dezső stayed in the shop for three, four days. I came up with ideas to have fun. I organized chicken plucking get-togethers. I never laughed so much as when I watched my neighbors help me pluck chicken feathers. The foul smell and the look of the bloody chickens was something they found disgusting, but in the evenings, they enjoyed the chicken soup with homemade angel hair pasta, paprikash with nokedli, and fresh cucumber salad. These dinners were unforgettable. The men spoke about technical things, ranch machineries, and Dezső always ended up making some spare parts for old tractors or farm machines. I became famous for my homemade pasta from fresh eggs. Six of my lady friends came to me to learn how to make pasta from scratch. We used at least 50 eggs. Everyone brought a tablecloth for spreading the pasta to dry. That evening, we had a good dinner. When they left late at night, they walked down on the hill waving to me and saying they would see me soon.

I'll never forget my friends from Tollhouse. Gail, Eddy, Sandy, Ed, Kitty, Elaine, Don, Tommy and his parent, Dolores, and Mike; we all had a special relationship.

My friends admired my five-year-old granddaughter, Nicole. She was a big helper to me. She copied what I did, plucking the chickens, kneading the pasta dough. She loved the animals and helped me to take care of them. Every afternoon, the neighbor's horses waited next to the fence where Nicole fed them with carrots. With her little hands, she planted seedling with me in the vegetable garden. Sometimes she fell on the gravel road, but she never cried.

"Don't worry, Grandma, I am a ranch girl."

When tools or the fence got broken, she said, "Csaba comes and he'll 'ficked.'"

These are some of my precious memories raising my little Nicole.

Once, when I was cooking, a conversation between Attila and Anna caught my attention. He said, "The Fresno Police Department rejected my application. Out of thirty applicants, only ten got in."

"You could work safely and earn good money in your father's company," I heard Anna say.

"Don't be ridiculous. I already told you that I would go crazy if I had to work on a machine or programing the CNC. Besides, I don't think my dad will ever get the production jobs. Csaba isn't waiting for it either, he always works in Agoura. I decided to pay the expenses for the Police Academy myself. I'll get a loan to fund my studies. After I finish it, I can get a job at any station."

On my lonely walks, I dreaded the future. We were all getting tired not knowing what might happen the near future.

Dezső didn't share his thoughts anymore.

Morning he left to LA meet the doctor. He came home in the evening. The dogs ran towards the gate, and to my surprise, my husband beamed with joy. He picked me up and carried me to the house.

"Please sit down," he said. "I'll show you something that perhaps no other person got from their employer."

With a theatrical movement, he placed a letter in front of me (This is the original letter written by the doctor. My husband's official name in Slovak was Dezider which, in Hungarian, is Dezső. When the doctor made the work contract with him, he saw his name on the green card, that is why he called him Dezider.) It read:

September 28, 1998

Dear Sirs:

I am the chairman of the board, product designer, and past owner of this Inc., a 15-year-old California corporation specializing in the development of all together new medical devices and technologies. I have known Dezider Imre for seven years, and during that time have worked very closely with him on many projects.

Mr. Imre is quite simply the most talented machinist I have ever encountered, and I have worked with many over the years.

Mr. Imre's services have included extensive prototype development work and low-level production.

Beyond Mr. Imre's great skill as a machinist, he has often provided the kind of input which would normally only be expected from an engineer. Mr. Imre has repeatedly proven his ability to correctly proportion and dimension the component parts of the devices which have been designed so as to have the required strength to work repeatedly and reliably over time, and yet to remain as simple and elegant in design and manufacture as practical. This, and his ability to execute the physical embodiments of the device designs with an eye to their eventual manufacture, has proven very valuable to my company.

Mr. Imre has also provided valuable service to my company in the reading, editing, and drafting of technical blueprints. My company has cooperative agreements with some of the largest medical device manufacturers in the world and has worked with such companies as Johnson & Johnson Professional Group, Sofamor Danek Group, Zinuner, Inc., and many others. I have repeatedly witnessed where in readying my company designed products for manufacture, the engineers of these companies have sent to me prints which Mr. Imre reviewed and was able to identify improper dimensions or tolerances, or to suggest an improved way of achieving the same end, prior to the actual manufacture of the product. When such occasions would arise, Mr. Imre would contact the engineers and address the matter with respect for the individuals, courtesy, and great professionalism so that they would be receptive to his suggestions which generally would be accepted and then proven to be right when manifested in the final product.

Mr. Imre also demonstrates remarkable qualities of imagination and creativity. He is an artist. I have yet to show any company a device which Mr. Imre has made that was not met with "oohs and aahs" and "how did he do that, look at this."

Having known and worked closely with Mr. Imre for all these years, I would also speak to his character. Mr. Imre is intensely honest, extremely hardworking, and a personal pleasure to work with.

When I was a medical student, a professor advised me

that if I should ever need to write a recommendation for someone, that I should include at least one reservation so that the person reading that recommendation would recognize its honesty. However, I find myself at a loss in that regard as I cannot find any reservation in regard to Mr. Imre.

If my wholehearted and unreserved support for Mr. Imre and his talents requires further explanation; or should you have any questions in regard to this matter, please feel free to contact me.

* * *

By the time I read the last sentences, which were followed by his signature and his phone number, I could barely see the page through my tears. I looked up at Dezső. He was savoring the moment, waiting for my reaction, radiating with pride, but I just looked at him. I don't know what happened to me, I felt such hatred towards the doctor in that moment that I was about to rip the letter to pieces. I wanted to jolt Dezső out of his fantasy world. I tried to control myself, but I couldn't.

"Honey, what do you think?" he asked me.

He got his handkerchief out of his pocket and dried my tears while kissing my forehead.

"What do I think? Congratulations. I'm happy the doctor noticed your qualities that I've been admiring in you for over thirty-five years. I didn't need to come to America for a doctor to tell me who you are. Do you know what I understand from this letter? That he is sending you away with wonderful, flattering words. This way he doesn't have to do it in a drastic way because he is a great psychologist who has you all figured out. He knows that compliments and praises are enough to send you to the moon."

My words paralyzed Dezső. He looked at me, perplexed. I folded the letter and stood up.

"I put this letter in my wallet and tomorrow I'll go shopping with it. Let's see how much the doctor's words are worth."

Dezső's eyes filled with tears. He stroked my shoulder and went to his study.

A voice inside me shouted, "You are mean! You destroyed everything that kept him going and stuck a knife into his heart!" I ran outside. I felt like I was suffocating. The rain was pouring. Within minutes, I got soaked through with ice cold water. I turned around. Dezső stood in the window; his pale face frightened me. I ran to his study.

"Please, forgive me. Believe me, it's not you whom I want to hurt. It sounds silly, but I said those things because I love you. I can't stand any longer how the doctor selfishly exploits you and you don't see it! You think everyone is like you. You want to prove yourself. Yes, you are honest. You are doing everything in your power to serve the glory of a selfish man."

Dezső stood still like a statue. I didn't know what to do. I was cold. My hands were shaking. I wanted to hug him. No, no. I kneeled before him and suddenly had a flashback of the time when he kneeled front of me, begging me to go to America, America, America. I heard it echoing in my ear.

"No, I'm not going anywhere," was what I had told him then.

Now I was the one kneeling before him. This time he'll be the one to say, no I can't forgive you.

I held my hands in prayer and bowed my head, but Dezső lifted me off of the floor.

"Don't! Please don't ever humiliate yourself in front of me. I always look up to you and love you for as long as I live. Your hands are ice cold. Go change into something warm and we'll talk after."

I quickly threw on a warm sweater and ran back to him. He poured us two brandies.

"This will warm you up and loosen our tension." He lifted his glass. "To our love and that you may always love me!"

"I do love you. That's why I want to protect you from a

great disillusion."

"I'm starting to sense the doctor is taking me for a naïve fool, but I still have hope. I am ashamed to beg for crumbs. He wrote in his letter that my knowledge and character are unique. He considers me his friend and I want to believe that he is a man of his word. Marika, you never measured happiness in money."

"Dezső, it's not the money that I'm fighting for. I am offended because he is not giving you what you deserve. For years, I've been waiting for him to rightfully give you your share from the inventions. Not money, make your name known. There must be a law for it and he knows that. You will be fifty-six soon; serial production is not the right step in your career. Not after everything you've done for him! He is selling the inventions for millions of dollars! He is famous and you who made that happen, you are nameless. Think about it. Just a small percentage from each invention would secure our retirement and make your son's life easier. He is a greedy man; he gave you a letter of recommendation."

"Is there anything you need you don't have?"

"I have everything, but what if I say no? What do you do then? Go and steal, rob? You can't work harder than you do. What I was dreaming of, one day the world will know who you are, what you did, they know what the doctor wrote about you. That is wort more then money!"

He refilled our glasses.

"Dezső, take me to one of your meetings, I'll explain to the doctor in a very professional way what you deserve. Years ago, you signed a work agreement, which doesn't mention inventions and prototype fabrication. That contract sounds as if he hired a locksmith."

"I told you, I'll take care of everything."

* * *

At dinner, Nicole sat in Dezső's lap. "Grandpa, do you want to play with me?" she asked.

Dezső got up.

"Dad, stay a moment," Attila said. "I have a plan I'd like to share with you. I decided not to buy a house for now. We'll move to Fresno."

"Why?"

"I want to be a police officer."

"You are out of your mind!"

"I feel that law enforcement…"

"I don't care what you feel."

"Dad, this is my mission in life. This is what I want to do. I love America. I want to protect people from crime."

"I knew that you didn't want to work with me."

"I'll help you in everything – organizing, putting in orders, invoicing, whatever you need. But please understand, I have no inclination towards machine work."

"Only spineless people are police officers."

"That was in the communist country. Have you ever read about the FBI?"

"I am not interested. I didn't bring you to America so that you can get killed by a criminal. Attila, that would drive me mad. Please don't do it."

I watched Attila's face. I knew we couldn't stop him. He had made his decision. Csaba got up.

"One thing is sure, you can't live hating your job."

The following week, Dezső worked day and night. I don't even know when he got any sleep. I served his lunch in his study.

"Forgive me, I don't have time to talk. If I lose my train of thought, I'll have to start from scratch. I have solutions at night, but when morning comes, I don't remember them. My brain is slowing down. I want to surprise the doctor next week. If he likes my last creation, I'll make the prototype within a week and then we are done. After that, I need to rest."

Csaba came home after three weeks remodeling a house in

Agoura. He had been studying the history of Native Indian tribes. On hikes, he collected eagle and hawk feathers. He said, "Mom, maybe I have Indian blood in my veins. My spiritual thoughts are similar to theirs. This is why I came to America, to be able to live on this land. I'd like to create Indian spiritual masks. They had a fantastic artistic sense. They believed in an untouchable, otherworldly spiritual force. I also believe in the strength that comes from the mask elements: eagle feathers, bear skulls, claws, wolf skin. Their dance starts with slow movements and gets faster, more dynamic as the spirits inhabit them."

When Csaba showed us the first mask he made, we were shocked. He created a beautiful piece of art using hundreds of bird feathers and an animal skull. The eyes were cut out of peacock feathers, the deep green color created a strong mystical impact when I looked in the eye of this mask which represented peace, serenity, and eternity.

In the afternoon, my brother called.

"Mom had a stroke. It's small, but in her age, a big one could follow, which could be fatal. She's always talking about you. If you want to see her alive, come home now."

"I'm coming."

I ran to Dezső's office.

"Mom had a stroke. I want to see her. Come with me."

"You know that I will never go back to that country. You and Csaba get on a plane. I hope you will be in time."

I realized how lucky we were. In 1989, during Reagan's presidency, the Berlin Wall came down. In the year 2000, which it was at the time, we were free to travel in the socialist country.

When we stepped in Mom's room, there are no words to describe that moment, when her face lit up with that familiar smile.

"My dear Marika! I knew you would come. I've been waiting for you. Csaba, come, let me hug you both."

In a couple of days, she wanted to walk with me, and she

started to eat again and was constantly smiling. For three weeks, we had a very special time together. I manicured her nails, cut her hair, and styled it. Her happiness touched my heart.

Dezső called to say that our second granddaughter, Michelle, had been born.

"Honey, when are you coming home? I miss you a lot."

"Next week we'll be home."

Every afternoon, Mom lay down and I held her hand until she fell asleep. That afternoon, she was restless.

"When are you leaving?"

"In a few days, we need to return to America. The neighbors are taking care of the ranch. But if Csaba stays at home, then I will come back."

She had a weary smile.

"I'll be waiting for you. Please open the nightstand drawer. There's a paper bag that's yours."

I found lots of twenty-dollar bills in it.

"Mom, where did you get these?"

"You sent them over the years, and I saved them for you. You worked very hard for that money."

My eyes got teary. Her whole life she was always a helping, giving mom.

At night, she squeezed my hand. She couldn't fall asleep.

"Mom, you make me sad. We'll talk a lot on the phone, and I'll be back soon."

On the last night before we left, she sat in the bed, again not wanting to sleep.

"Do you think, this is the night I die? Your father was sitting by my side and I heard my mother's voice, too. They are waiting for me."

How we managed not to cry, I don't know. The last moments together and our last glimpses at each other made a deep scar on my soul.

A week later, Mom died. Her love, which had a magical

power that stretched across the ocean, is still terribly missed.

Dezső lost a lot of weight while we were away. He listened to my stories in silence. He didn't have anything to share.

Anna spent all of her time taking care of Nicole and Michelle. My newborn granddaughter was an energetic, beautiful baby. Whenever she saw her grandfather, she nearly flew into his arms.

Dezső changed a lot. I overheard him having heated arguments with the doctor.

A couple of days later at dinner, he announced the final drawing was done, and the next morning, he would be off to LA.

For breakfast, I set the table on the terrace. My husband came out freshly shaved, wearing a sport shirt and jeans. He looked very handsome and turned his eyes to the sky.

"Look at how amazingly blue the sky is today! Even the snowy peaks sparkle in bluish color. I haven't noticed it lately. Dear, today is a memorable day. I believe I'll return with good news."

He ate his sandwich, finished up his coffee, hugged me, and gave me a mischievous smile as he started the engine.

"I'll be home by dinner. Be ready for a great celebration!"

I thought about what I needed to do while he was gone for the day. The grass around the pool needed mowing, but somehow, I wasn't in the mood to do anything. I fed the animals and walked around. I heard the big water tank pump running empty. It took a long time to let the air out. It was hot. I made lemonade and sat by the pool. I planned to relax and later cook dinner. I fell asleep and woke up when a car come at a fast speed up the hill, making a huge dust cloud.

It was Dezső. He got out of the car and looked at me with a never before seen, grim expression on his face, and ran to the house. I followed him.

"What happened?"

"Nothing, I'll be right with you!"

I went to the kitchen with chills on my back, thinking

something very bad must have happened. I peeled potato, then went to the bedroom. Dezső was in the bathroom.

"Dezső, what are you doing?"

There was no answer. I opened the door. He laid on the floor. I shook him. His hands were ice cold.

"Dezső, can you hear me?"

He didn't respond. I put a pillow under his head and covered him. I heard Attila and Csaba come home.

"Guys, come! Something is wrong with your dad. He fell in the shower."

They put him on the bed.

"Mom, call the ambulance, right away! He had a stroke or heart attack."

"You don't need to call anyone," Dezső spoke up. "I have a pounding headache. Leave me alone. I'll get dressed and be right with you." The boys left, but I stayed with him.

"What happened? Stop torturing me."

"Calm down, nothing tragic happened. I can be angry sometimes, too. Go and get dinner ready. I'm hungry."

A bit later, he came to the kitchen. We all waited for him.

"I got angry. That's all." His lips were trembling.

"All my life I watched your mother handle life's obstacles. I didn't have to deal with them. I was busy with my work, concentrating on my dreams and making money. Now I realize how sensitive I am when somebody deceives me." He took a long pause, then said, "I went to see the doctor with our remarkable line of invention which we are finally finishing. I walked the corridor, and I could hear his voice through the open office door. I didn't want to interrupt the meeting, so I sat down next to his door. The doctor was purchasing an airplane."

"'How much is this one?' I heard him say. Then the other person responded, "Fourteen million." "Okay, I hope after all the luxury features I want to put in, the price be around twenty million.'"

"Then, the phone rang, and I heard, 'Yes, my attorney has

sent the contract, it is eighteen million. You want to do the production? I understand. Okay, no problem I'll tell my lawyer to exclude it from the contract. I don't have time now. Talk to my attorney.'"

"He slammed the phone down, irritated. As I sat there, an immense helplessness came over me. I still have the sense of servitude from socialism in me. I was afraid of the doctor. I didn't want to seem expectant in his eyes. I waited. Somehow, I believed he would surprise me with a contract worthy of my accomplishments. I wanted to show all of you, prove how the doctor would highly reward me for my excellent work. After what I heard, I couldn't bear to sit down with him, so I rushed out of the building, got in the car, and the next thing I knew, I was here. I have a splitting headache. I'll take a walk. I need fresh air."

After a couple of steps, he collapsed. His laugh was scary as he said, "I failed."

His face turned pale, and he was barely breathing.

"We must take him to the hospital right now!" I yelled.

Attila drove down the mountain at a frightening speed.

"Dezső, be strong! Together, we can start again. Don't let this man ruin our family," Csaba said.

Attila stopped front of the ER. A few moments later, two nurses came with a stretcher. By the time they got him out of the car, he was unresponsive.

We waited two hours, when finally, the doctor came to us.

"Your husband didn't have a stroke or a heart attack. We couldn't find the source of his condition. Did anything unusual happen to him in the past days?"

Attila told a short story about what happened.

"I see. That anxiety can trigger such trauma. Tomorrow we'll run a few more tests."

"Can I stay with him?" I asked.

"I don't recommend it. In cases like this, it is preferable

to limit the patient's exposure to emotional factors. We gave him strong sedatives. He kept climbing out of bed, wanted to go home. It is interesting, he wanted to talk to his wife, but he couldn't remember your name. He doesn't know where he lives or where he is. It is possible that there's been some brain hemorrhage that we are unable to see now. In the morning, we'll inject contrast material to be able to see exactly what is happening."

DESTINY

The next day, we walked to the doctor's office with fear.

The doctor said, "We found a cancerous tumor the size of a pinhead in your husband's left side of the brain, behind his ear. Unfortunately, it cannot be removed. It is the shape of a needle; just the pinhead is on the surface. Yesterday his brain got swollen, maybe from nervousness and a hot shower. That is why he collapsed. This is an aggressive type of cancer. Luckily we caught it at an early stage; maybe we can eradicate it with radiation."

"Does my husband know that?"

"Yes, I told him. We are required by law to first inform the patient and have him decide with whom I can share the diagnosis."

"How has this news affected him?"

"Your husband is a very intelligent man. He is approaching his treatment with tremendous optimism. I already contacted one of the top cancer treatment centers and arranged his treatment. You have an appointment with the best doctor there at three o'clock this afternoon. There's no time for contemplation. We must act fast."

Dezső sat on the bed with his head down when we stepped in the room.

"Dezső, you are strong. You will recover!" Csaba hugged him.

Attila sat down by his side. "Dad, we have to think positive. I know you can beat this disease. You never been sick, we will be doing everything possible to help you and support you. "

Dezső was very pale, but he smiled at me.

"I told the doctor, I'll undergo any treatment, as long as it takes. I must live. Marika, come here. My soul aches, I brought you here, into this country, far from your beloved ones. I can't leave you. I'll fight to my last breath to be with you."

We hugged. He pushed me away slightly to look me in the eye. "Don't worry. I must relax. I squandered my strength. I never thought that my career would end like this."

"Your career is not ending. Our care and love will help you recover."

Later that day, we anxiously stepped into the cancer treatment center. A soft-spoken doctor named David came to us. Over the next hour, he talked to my husband.

"Dezső, I thank you for your trust, sharing your deepest thoughts with me. In my career, I have never met such a disciplined and calmed patient as you. Living in stress for a long time is the source of many diseases. Now you have to relax and ease your tension. Take long walks, sleep a lot. You need to eat healthy, freshly cooked meals to build up your immune system."

"David, my wife is the best chef."

"That's great. I'll see you in three days, at eight in the morning. By then, your protective mask will be ready for the radiation. In four weeks, we'll take new images of your brain. I hope we won't find the tumor."

At home, Dezső looked relaxed and was feeling well. He spent his days pampering our four-month-old granddaughter and helping me feed the animals. He never stepped into his office, but he called his doctor friend.

"I have a cancerous tumor in my brain, but could be back in four months."

"My friend, I have connections at UCLA – cancer researchers. I can arrange..."

"Thank you, Doctor, but I don't need help. The doctor who's taking care of me is a specialist."

"Okay. Get well very soon. We have to finish our big set."

A week after the radiation, Dezső wasn't feeling well. At

night, he used all of his strength to hold my hand. My fingers went to sleep. I slowly pulled my hand away.

"What happened?" he asked.

"My hand fell asleep."

"Sorry. I came closer to you. I'm scared."

"What are you scared of?"

"I am dreaming all the time that I am standing on a cliff. I'm dizzy and fall down. It is a horrifying feeling free falling to the dark depths. It is good holding your hand."

There was one more week till we'd know the radiation result. During breakfast, Attila told us about an interesting article he found online. A Hungarian doctor in Budapest was experimenting with cancer curing, deuterium depleted water. Cancerous dogs had recovered from it. We thought we could ask Misi's dad to send us some from Budapest. Even healthy people were drinking the weak version, as a preventative measure. It was meant to alkalize the body and create an unfavorable environment for cancer.

"Dezső, what do you think?" I asked him.

"Marika, I leave it up to you."

In the afternoon, David called and said, "Maria, I have bad news. Before you come in, I wanted to check with you. Do you want me to tell your husband the result? He believes in the treatment so much that the bad news can crush him."

I couldn't speak.

"Maria, are you there?"

"Yes, what's the result?"

"We didn't succeed; the tumor is multiplying. I counted over thirty now. We can try chemotherapy; it may slow the process."

"There is no chance for recovery?"

"As a doctor, I have to say there isn't, but as humans, we never know. I have seen miracles in my career. We are all in God`s hands. We must keep our faith until the end."

"Please don't tell Dezső the result. Let`s give chemotherapy a try."

I shared the bad news with my sons.

They said, "What now? We can't let him die! Mom, let's order that deuterium depleted water. I'll print out the article to show to doctor David because Gábor Somlyai doctor achieved great results with it in Hungary."

The doctor told Dezső, since we were not completely out of the woods, he recommended a round of chemo. Dezső immediately accepted his advice. A nurse took us to the room where at least fifty patients sat with tubes in their arms and chests. Dezső rolled up his sleeve without emotion.

By the time I got back to the doctor's office, Attila and David were talking about the effects of the deuterium depleted water.

"I can't recommend any treatment other than the one approved by the Health Department. People talk about many natural remedies. From what I know, the water can't harm him."

Dezső got better from the chemo. One day he said, "I think this treatment is good for me."

Our best friend, Pipo Misi, made immediate arrangements and his father sent the water to us. I talked with Doctor Somlyai on the phone. He recommended stopping the chemo and relying only on the water, but Dezső wanted to continue with the treatment. After four treatments and constantly drinking the water, he didn't experience a headache or nausea. His memory around that time made me wonder, because sometimes he remembered things, but sometimes he didn't.

"Honey, I wanted to count my fingers, but I don't remember the numbers. What day is today?"

"Tuesday."

"You must be joking. There is no such day. Today is Saturday. I didn't go to work. Yes, it's Saturday. I don't remember when I have to take the prototype to the doctor."

Dezső's memory was clearly declining swiftly, and he knew it.

"Something is very wrong with me. I forget simple things. What happens when I lose my mind?"

"Dezső, that is a side effect of the chemo. Try to relax," I told him.

When he talked to David, it was hard to see how patient, but hopeless, he was.

"Doctor, don't you think it's strange that I want to say something and I forget the words? The next day, I remember, but I look around and don't know where I am. My mind used to be so sharp. I remembered the license plate of our first car in Slovakia. Now I don't know what year I was born. I want to be strong, but I am scared."

"Try not to worry; that is not good for your brain."

"Doctor, I'll do everything as you tell me; you have to understand, I must get better. My wife needs me."

His whole body shuddered as he sobbed uncontrollably. The doctor had tears in his eyes.

"Take this pill; you are tired from the chemo."

On the way home, Dezső kept falling asleep. Then, he reached for my hand.

"Marika, I saw your mom. She said I'll get better."

At night, in his sleep, he often talked.

"Call my friend immediately. He didn't pay me. Honey, what do you do when I die?"

His condition worsened. He lost his sense of balance. I held his hand, and from that day on, I helped him dress. I brought the wheelchair, but he didn't want to use it.

"I can walk with your help. I want to use my legs to stay in shape."

In the living room, Attila played with Michelle. Dezső sat down on the sofa.

"Everybody, listen to me. I have something important to tell you. Attila, soon I will lose my mind."

"Dad..."

"Let me speak. All my life, you guys have been my everything. All I ever wanted for my family was to be happy and I dreamed you could be proud of me. I wanted to secure a peaceful future for all of us. We came to America for freedom and happiness. Attila, I want you to follow your dreams. Be a police officer. We'll pay for your academy, uniform, and everything else you need. I wish you all the success in the world. Be happy, and I'll be happy for you."

Attila hugged him.

"Thank you, Dad. I love you very much."

Dezső smiled, but there was no light in his eyes. I stroked him.

"I need to rest now," he said. He went to the bedroom with uncertain steps, holding on to the wall.

"Mom, we should close the machine shop," Attila said. "There is no point paying all that money for it."

"Attila, I can't give up hope. Your father could get better."

In the morning, Dezső watched himself in the mirror.

"Marika, can you buy me a sports hat? I don't want you looking at my bald head. I look repulsive. Only my big nose is sticking out of my face. I don't want you to remember me like this."

"Please, stop this nonsense. Your hair will grow back soon. I love you, with or without hair."

He squeezed my hand so hard, it hurt. His entire body convulsed. He bit his tongue, and blood streamed out of his mouth. I shouted for Attila. By the time he got to the room, Dezső was convulsing on the floor, and moments later, his body went stiff. I put a wet towel on his forehead.

"Marika, where are you? I don't have much strength left."

I called doctor Somlyai in Budapest and he said, "Often patients feel worse and hit rock bottom before they get better."

After eight chemotherapy treatments, we waited for the MRI results. David immediately called us. He couldn't believe his eyes. The images indicated only six small tumors left from over thirty.

"I found the perfect dosage of the chemo. What a success! We'll start chemo again. Dezső's immune system is incredibly strong. He is on the way to recovery."

When Dezső found out the good news, his memory started to come back. He sat in the kitchen watching me cook dinner, and we talked about our past.

I called again doctor Somlyai and told him the good news. He was convinced that the tumors went away because of the water.

"Stop the chemo; it's poison that destroys his organs."

It was mid-November when we woke up to a beautiful, sunny morning. I set the table on the patio when the phone rang. It was Dezső's friend, the doctor.

"I'd like to inquire about Dezső's condition. I spoke to his physician and he gave me some good news. I have a favor to ask of him. An American medical instrument manufacturer stole several of my innovations. Since I'm the sole proprietor of these instruments, the only way to prove they are mine is for Dezső to testify for me. He is the only one who could tell them he made all my inventions in his shop."

"I don't think he can help you. His memory is very foggy."

"Can I speak with him?"

"Yes."

I was curious about Dezső's reaction as I told him, "Your doctor friend wants to talk to you."

His eyes lit up. "He remembers me?" Then, after I handed him the phone, he said, "Hey, Doctor, how are you?"

I watched Dezső's face in astonishment. He listened to the doctor with interest and talked to him like he was perfectly healthy.

"You know, Doctor, there are many things I can't remember, but if I can help, you can always count on me."

The doctor talked for a long time. At the end, Dezső laughed. "I will do my best. I promise you doctor. Please discuss the details with my wife. I might forget them."

Dezső handed me the phone and said, "The doctor needs

me. He wants me to meet him and his lawyers. Please write down the address and time."

The doctor told me we have to meet him Thursday morning, at 10 am, in the Marriott hotel in Fresno. The hearing would be in the conference room. "I would appreciate if you prepare Dezső, to avoid any confusion. He must know when and where he was born, where he lives, how long he worked for me, and where his machine shop is. I told him repeatedly that this hearing is crucial. Please remind him that so he must focus. Thank you. See you on Thursday."

Dezső's excitement surprised me. The light returned to his eyes, and he spoke with clarity.

"I'm the only one who can help my friend."

"Do you want to?" I asked.

"He's my only friend in America."

"Do you know what kind of help he's asking for?"

"Yes, I have to recognize instruments – the ones I made."

"Dezső, they will ask you many questions, like when you were born."

"March 8th, 1943 in Rimaszombat."

I kissed him.

He said, "Honey, write down all the important information, especially when I started working for my friend, where we lived in Agoura, where my shop is. I don't remember these things, but I have three days to memorize them. You can quiz me later. The doctor said he'll be grateful if I help him."

He kissed me while his blue eyes sparkled. I thought it unbelievable how the doctor's call brought him back to life.

On Thursday morning, Dezső woke up tired. He could barely keep his balance on the way to the bathroom.

"I'm nervous; I don't want to disappoint my friend. My steps are unsteady and I'm dizzy. Do you think it would be a problem if you take me to the meeting in the wheelchair? I don't have to worry about looking sick."

"Good idea. You can focus better."

In the car, he was tense. He turned the heat on. His hands were ice-cold.

"We should turn around if you're not feeling well."

"I have to do this. I must go through with this to secure our future. The doctor will be grateful to me."

The doctor waited in front of the hotel. I'm not sure he even said hello, just quickly opened the car door and helped move Dezső into the wheelchair. He raced through the long corridor and walked to the conference room where cameras and lots of lawyers waited to start the hearing. After the oath, a man elicited Dezső's information in an unpleasant, irritating voice. Dezső was calm. He spoke slowly and I could tell he focused on his words. I expected they would move on, but the ridiculous voice asked the same questions again in a different order. Dezső's date of birth, the address of the shop, and the date on which he started working with the doctor. He answered all of the questions again, but when he was asked the third time how many years he had known the doctor, he stayed quiet. Silence filled the room. The doctor stood up, but Dezső motioned him to sit down.

"I would like to point out I am ill, but as of yet, not mentally inept. Please don't ask me questions that I answered once. I don't come here to lie; I'm not a criminal who you need to catch in the act. One other important thing: due to my illness, my energy is limited, so it would be preferable to get to the point of why we are here. I believe that would be more relevant to the case than my address."

My heart jumped with joy. Dezső's old logic had returned. The squeaky voiced lawyer turned red and gave the floor to the group of experts who represented the company. There were six serving trolleys filled with numerous medical instruments, all looking much alike.

"Mr. Imre, please look at these medical devices and choose the ones you made."

He thoroughly looked at all of the pieces on the first and second table, but not one was his work. The tension between the two parties was felt in the air. On the third tray, there were different shapes and sizes of spinal implants, similar to the ones Dezső made. He placed nine pieces over the empty trolley table. On the fourth and fifth tray were spine surgery tools and retractors. He found five pieces he made.

Soon after, they called a one-hour recess. The lawyers wrote up every single piece and photographed them from every possible angle. The doctor came over to us.

"Congratulations, my friend. Your brain is sharp as a knife. We have many years of collaboration ahead of us."

"Doctor, I can help you. I despise cheating. I can't allow a company to steal what is yours."

"My friend, you are an exceptional person."

When we got back, the factory lawyers and engineers were still looking at the pieces Dezső picked out. One of them approached him and placed two identical looking instruments in his hand.

"How can you tell that you made these?"

Dezső spent a long time analyzing the two instruments. He looked over at the table where he had placed the items he chose.

"This is a tricky question, because I didn't make the instrument in my right hand, so it's not possible that I put it on that table. There are thirteen instruments, and I have selected a total of fourteen. This piece here in my right hand wasn't on that table. It's not my work." They looked at Dezső, astonished. The technical expert of the factory addressed the next question.

"Mr. Imre, how can you prove that you made these instruments when all look alike?"

One of the doctor's lawyers rushed to Dezső with a glass of water. He was crying. He took a sip of water and dried his eyes.

"Forgive me, I'm overcome with emotion. I know I can't answer a question with a question, but I will do it anyhow. How can a mother know her children out of hundreds of children? These here," he said, while pointing at the table, "are my children. I gave birth to them. What you see here is part of my life."

I rushed out of the room, wondering to myself how I could ever carry on without him.

At the end, the doctor escorted Dezső to the car, showering him with praise. He shook his hand and patted him on the shoulder.

"My friend, you won this trial for me, and I am unspeakably grateful to you. Thank you for your help."

"Doctor, I would like to ask you for a favor."

"Tell me."

"You know how much I love airplanes."

"Yes, the model you made me as a gift is on my desk. Everybody admires it. Nobody has ever seen such a handmade, detailed model from so many pieces."

"I designed every part of it, scaling down with precision the original dimensions of a plane."

The doctor extended his arm for a handshake.

"I haven't told you my request," Dezső continued.

"Oh, tell me."

"I would like you to show me California from the air from your airplane. I would enjoy the flight."

"How do you know I have a plane?"

Dezső smiled. "Perhaps it's a product of my diseased mind?"

"I did buy a plane. Anyway, as soon as you feel better, I'll come for you and show you California from above. I must rush now. I'll be in touch."

I helped Dezső get into the car.

"I'm very tired. Today was my last attempt to secure our future. Please give me a sedative; I'm afraid I'm going to pass out."

He closed his eyes and immediately fell asleep. I drove out of the city. I felt there was nothing left ahead, and I was tired, too. I stubbornly believed that together, Dezső and I could conquer it all. I believed that the day would come when a correct, honest man would notice him and share success equally with him. But business doesn't have heart; money dominates the mind and personality. I knew then from the doctor's behavior that Dezső would remain an unknown, nameless man behind millions of dollars.

We all spent the evening in cozy togetherness. Our six-month-old granddaughter, Michelle, always wanted to sit in her grandpa's lap. She was amused by Dezső's pretend sneezes.

"Dezső, you are just like you were when I was a little boy. I remember, you made us laugh. It´s good to remember the past. We had a nice life." Csaba talked to his father with teary eyes.

Attila enrolled in the Police Academy. He enjoyed the night drills and won first place for target shooting. He studied a lot; he knew the articles of law by heart.

"I always said you are smart. You could have a great career with your brain," Dezső told Attila.

"Dad, I have a career that makes me happy."

TURNING POINT

Christmas was around the corner. Dezső's condition didn't worsen. He ate well, didn't lose weight, and most importantly, he was talkative again. He mentioned his shop and made plans to return to work in the New Year. He helped me decorate the Christmas tree, remarkably for the first time in his life, and we wrapped the gifts together. He noticed me watching him.

"Honey, I feel better, really. I'm still a little unsteady, but my memory is coming back. Come here, let me hug you. You're my forever love."

After the hearing, he never talked about the doctor. He paid attention every time the phone rang and asked who it was. I felt he was waiting for his friend to call.

On Holy Night, to our big surprise, he came out from the bedroom dressed in a suit and tie. He hugged us all, and he had a wide smile on his face. We wished each other a Merry Christmas. He got Michelle out of her walker and he asked me to take a picture of them in front of the Christmas tree. He wanted a family photo and one with just the two of us.

We sat down to the beautifully set table. Dezső's happiness highlighted our evening. Batta and Rita's family called us. Dezső spoke with them, too.

"We come to visit you and have a nice party for my recovery, like in the good old days. It's been a tough year, but now I'm full of energy!"

I sat by the fireplace, observing the carefree interactions, and thanked the Lord for my husband's recovery.

The next morning, Dezső and I stayed in bed for a long time.

"Honey, I woke up three times during the night, and every time, I returned to an interesting dream. I stood on a mountaintop. On my left side, there was a big, loud waterfall. I couldn't hear what you shouted at me. You stood in the valley below. I didn't know how to get to you. I finally heard your voice saying, "Jump, don't be afraid! I will catch you. I'm waiting for you."

"I jumped. I wasn't scared because you waited with open arms. In free fall, with high speed, I came to you and you caught me. We lay on the beautiful green grass. I woke up during the best part!"

He had a good laugh and kissed me. Nicole knocked on the door.

"Grandma, Grandpa, breakfast time, we're waiting for you."

"We'll be right there!"

"Dad and I already fed all the animals; I collected the eggs from the nests," she said.

I put my robe on and went to the kitchen.

"You are a true ranch girl. Thank you for doing my job," I told her.

Dezső's self-confidence was unbelievable. When he came to breakfast, he said, "I want to make the doctor another plane model, my favorite aircraft, the Boeing 787. I will surprise him with my gift when I return to work. We must make a trip to the hobby store; I need a bunch of things for the plane."

He worked on the model with exceptional enthusiasm. First, he sketched the miniature parts. He knew how to calculate again. He used a small saw to cut the plane wings out of plexiglass and cropped little color strips for the American flag. He patiently polished the pieces. I enjoyed watching him.

"Marika, next week we need to go to the shop. I'll make the body of the plane on the lathe machine and the windows on the milling machine. Then, only the many hours of handmade work will be left."

On New Year's Eve, I woke up early. Our neighbors came over to celebrate with us. Dezső personally invited them.

I greeted my cows with a smile and gave them more food than usual. The blue sky, the sparkling rays of sunlight, the trees, all turned my world into a beautiful, happy place.

"Thank you, Lord, for Dezső's recovery!" I shouted into the forest, on my way back to the house.

I got a few smoked sausages out of the pantry and put the sauerkraut into a bowl. We couldn't start the New Year without traditional Hungarian soup called korhelyleves.

While I was preparing it, I heard a great thud coming from the bedroom. I ran. Attila and Csaba were already in the corridor. Dezső lay unconscious on the floor. He must have lost his balance and grabbed the curtains. The holder hit him and left a big, bleeding wound on his forehead.

"Mom, quick, call the ambulance!"

Csaba kneeled by his father, but Dezső didn't move. The ambulance arrived. I went with Dezső. Attila and Csaba followed us in our car.

"Help me, I'm plummeting. Marika, save me!"

He gasped for air. He squeezed my hand with superhuman strength. His voice was distorted from pain as he shouted, "It's too late, you can't save me! I'm falling into a bottomless darkness!"

His words faded as he added, "It's all because of freefalling... nobody can reach for me, nobody. I'm sorry, I'm soorryyyyy!"

He stopped squeezing my hand. It looked like he had died.

After hours of waiting, a doctor came to us.

"Your husband's kidneys must have been failing for days now. Has he been taking any medication?"

"He has cancer; he's been doing chemo for months."

"I see. Many patients have similar problems."

"How can you help him?"

"Unfortunately, we can't. His brain is swelling. We're giving him morphine. I don't think he will regain consciousness."

"I want to see him," I said.

An older nurse said, "He's on the fourth floor. I'll call upstairs and tell them to let you in for a few minutes."

The sight in Dezső's room horrified me to my bones. They had tied his arms and legs to the bed. His body was convulsing. I kept kissing his forehead and talking to him, but he didn't respond.

I looked out the window. I felt frustration and anger as I clutched my hand in a fist. I was on the brink of insanity, and I fell to my knees.

"God, why, why did you do this to him?! There is no justice on earth; I know that, but you, who see everything, why are you punishing him? What did he do to deserve to die this way? Is this your love?! Then I don't need it!"

Attila scooped me off the floor. Csaba left the room.

"Mom, don't say that. Let's go home. Nicole and Michelle are waiting for you; they need you."

The next day, in the afternoon, we went back to the hospital. We only stayed in Dezső's room for a few minutes. It was unbearable to watch his pain and agony. They couldn't give him more morphine without killing him. I didn't sleep all night. In the early morning, I thought I heard Dezső's voice calling for me.

"Marika, where are you?"

I quickly got dressed and drove to the hospital. Dezső wasn't tied up anymore. He slept peacefully. I took his hand.

"Dear, can you hear me?" I asked. He blinked. I kissed his forehead and he barely, but noticeably, squeezed my hand. He sighed, and then he died on 3rd January 2001. I couldn't cry. I was grateful his suffering ended. Then, the doctor came in the room.

"He's likely to leave us today."

"He already did."

The next day, I called Dezső's friend, the doctor, and informed him about his death.

I said, "On January 26, at two o'clock in the afternoon, we'll have a memorial for my husband with my family, friends, and acquaintances. After we say goodbye to him, we'll have a meal together where we'll share stories of unforgettable experiences with Dezső. I will send you the information by post."

"My condolences and thank you for the invitation. We lost a valuable, exceptionally talented, good man in Dezső. I would like to ask you for a favor. When you close the machine shop, please send me all of the sketches and half made pieces of medical devices that he worked on."

Silence. Then, I said, "All the best." I listened until I heard he had hung up the phone.

I don't remember how the weeks passed following Dezső's death. I spent my time outside from dusk to dark, roaming the forests alone. I could feel the cold January wind in my bones, but I wanted to be alone. I did not want my sons to see my pain. Sometimes I heard Dezső's laughter, or I felt the squeeze of his hand.

Rita and Batta organized Dezső's memorial. Their family and friends prepared all the food and desserts. The doctor and nurses who treated Dezső, the mailman, people from the little stores in Tollhouse, Csaba's friends, every young and old member of our neighboring ranches came, holding their cowboy hats in hand as they paid their last respects to my husband.

We placed his ashes in a stainless-steel urn, with an embossed sailboat on it. He loved the ocean; he would spend hours watching the sailboats, which he considered to be the symbol of freedom. His portrait with the urn, surrounded by flowers, we displayed next to the pool. By two o'clock, all of the chairs on the lawn were filled with guests, and many of them stood around.

At two-thirty, Batta came to me. "We shouldn't wait any longer," he said.

"Who are we waiting for?" I asked.

"I thought the doctor would come."

"I don't think he ever wanted to meet us."

Batta shared a wonderful speech about Dezső's life. Some of his words from that day were:

"He was a terrific head of his family, a husband, father, and grandfather. Many didn't even take notice of him because he hated the spotlight. He never flaunted his talent. He was a very smart man. Numerous medical instrument innovations and inventions are a testament to his work. Dezső's honesty, hard work, and pure heart should be an example to all of us."

Batta went on to say how Dezső had once told him, "Batta, I am an incredibly lucky man. I was blessed with a wonderful woman who is my partner, my friend, my love. She stands by me in good and bad."

"Dezső's life was hard," Batta continued. "He was born during the Second World War. He had memories of the years of nationalization, when the communists took his family's ranch, and when his father died. At thirteen, he'd reap the fields with his three brothers before going to school, so his family would have food on the table. At fourteen, he became a tool locksmith apprentice. At sixteen, the factory successfully used his innovations and referred him for further education in the Industrial School in Kassa, where he met his wife, Marika. He unloaded train cars in the night to be able to take his sweetheart out for coffee or a movie and also send his mother money. After two years of military service, he took a job at the machine factory in Losonc, and he got married. The factory management quickly took notice of his professional knowledge and he became production manager of the military unit. In socialism, the political beliefs outweighed knowledge, so, throughout the years, he was in constant conflict with the Communist Party leaders. He endured many humiliations and it was a miracle that he eventually escaped with his family to America.

His departure from our world brings heartache to all of us who had a chance to know him. We have to accept our Lord's will and believe that there will come a day when we'll all be reunited with our loved ones. I ask the Lord to bless Dezső's family and everybody who is present here. On Earth, we must continue living in the spirit of faith, hope, and love. Those who believe in our Lord Savior will have eternal life."

Many of the guests told stories about Dezső and every kind word they said felt like a balm for my soul.

Attila graduated from the Police Academy, but he couldn't find a job in Fresno. He got hired at a police station in a nice town called Visalia, over a one-hour drive from us. It was out of the question for him to commute to work in snow and fog. We found Attila a house which he was able to buy.

Csaba worked constantly in Agoura, remodeling homes. All week I was alone, and on the weekends, my family spent time with me. Attila suggested that we sell the ranch.

"Mom, taking care of this ranch at your age is very hard. Csaba sleeps in half-ready buildings in a sleeping bag, living on sandwiches to earn money to keep the ranch. You won't be able to do this for long."

I didn't know what to do. I spent hours sitting in Dezső's chair on the patio with Khiana and Sasha, our dogs. My neighbors' visits became a burden. I closed the gate so nobody could bother me. I locked the whole world out of my life.

"Mom, it's been over a year since Dad died. Visalia is a quiet little town. You and Csaba could move and our family will be together again. Nicole and Michelle miss you."

"Please, give me time to find myself," I told him. "What I would really like is to go home..."

"This is your home. You have us here, your sons and grandchildren. I don't understand how you can even think of something like that."

"You're right, but be patient with me."

One afternoon, I was ready to walk to the mailbox, but I couldn't find Khiana. Sasha barked on the patio. I found Khiana dead under Dezső's chair. Losing her added to my depression. I knew I had to have a way to find purpose in my life, just one more time. I didn't know how to do it. Ever since Dezső died, I'd been angry with God, turning away from him. One late afternoon, I finished feeding the cows and struggled to walk up the mountain on the muddy road. I stopped and looked up at the sky.

I said, "Help me, God! You are the only one who can help me! Please forgive me. I'd like to find my place here before I enter into your world. All my life you were with me, giving me strength, hope, and a loving heart. I don't want to keep stumbling in the dark. Please, come back into my life."

Spring came. I got very busy on the ranch, so I didn't have much time to think about myself. I pared my fruit trees and rose bushes. One morning, Cali, my favorite cow, went into heat and broke the fence. She went to visit the neighbor's bull. Sandy, one of my neighbors, called and made me laugh.

"Cali's on the wrong side of the fence, but don't worry; we let her in with her husband. Ed and I are walking over to fix your fence. Can we come up for a coffee after? Also, Tommy called. He loaded his truck with hay; he saw you running low. Just open the gate, and he'll stop by this afternoon."

Over two years after Dezső died, I still felt him by my side. On sleepless nights, I could hear his steps and him saying good night. Sitting on the patio in the moonlight, Dezső's face smiled at me from the pool water. I often spoke to him.

One day, there was a big storm. In the evening, the moon came out. I walked outside, looking at the damages the strong winds caused. I couldn't see the pool water from all the fallen leaves.

"You know, Dezső, I don't care if the filter gets clogged, I'm not going to clean the pool. I'm exhausted. I can't go on living like this. I will always love you, but you're not here with me. I speak to you, but you don't answer. I want to return to the

286

real life. I have to, for our sons and granddaughters. I can't be with your spirit in these mountains. I made peace with God. I asked Him to forgive me and watch over us, our sons, and our grandchildren. One day, we'll meet again, but until then, I want to live my life."

A dark cloud covered the moon and the strong wind nearly swept the leaves out of the pool. As I stood there, a big bolt of lightning illuminated the valley. On the mountain side, on the road leading down to the gate, I saw Dezső heading out from the ranch. A moment later, it was pitch dark and the rain started pouring. I stood and waited for the next lightning. Perhaps I could see him one last time. Maybe he would turn around and wave at me, but there was no more lightning. I ran to the house. I smiled, thinking how Dezső had left the ranch. He went to his world and gave me the signal to do the same.

* * *

I'm watching the sunset from my comfortable armchair. I put our framed wedding photo back on the table. Time flies! Dezső's been gone for twenty years. After all these years finally I kept my promise to him and wrote the memoir about us.

EPILOGUE

We sold the ranch. I helped raise my granddaughters. Now, they are beautiful young ladies. I wrote the story about their grandfather to make his memory eternal. Life is full of successes, surprises, moments of joy, disappointment, struggles, and failures. We experienced all of the depths and heights on the road of life with strength and joy.

After Dezső's funeral, we never spoke to his doctor friend, and he never contacted us. He had won the trial. In the history of America, no other company has ever paid over one-billion-dollar compensation. The doctor got paid and the man who made that possible stayed nameless but he will always be remembered in our family.

Wedding 1967

Maria's graduation picture 1966

Dezső's graduation picture 1965

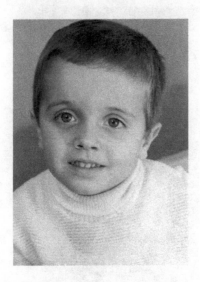

Attila 5 years old

Maria Graduation ceremony

Maria's father

Maria's mother

Dezső's graduation ceremony

Maria's parents' home where she grew up

Attila's first morning in America

Dezső, Maria, Csaba's first picture first morning in America

Our home in building (unfortunately all the other
pictures got lost when we came to America

Hawaii Dezso and Maria

Our home we built in Vidina

Dezso's mother and brothers with us

On the bullet train way to Frankfurt for the
interview to the American Embassy

Csaba's first day in the school showing to the
class Slovakia the country he came from

Dezso and Attila in front of our first home,
the apartment in Westlake Village

Maria as a little girl with her mom and grandma

Maria's mom leaving LA back to Slovakia

Dezso in his shop

Christmas in Maria's house with Dario

In Voja's and Rita's house with all the children

Nicole

Our family

Dezső's memorial

Dezső's ashes

Dezső's last Christmas

Family Christmas before Dezső passed away

Csaba and Michelle

Csaba

Dezső and Maria

Dezső

Nicole and Michelle

View on the ranch Tollhouse

Flowers around the house

Winter on the ranch with Csaba's rock formations

Kassa (Kosice) Maria on the 45th
reunion in front of the industrial school

Maria's graduation picture with her classmates and professors

Happy grandma (Maria) with the newborn Nicole

Michelle's first steps on the ranch with grandma (Maria)

Leaving Munich to Frankfurt

Last family picture in Europe on the
bullet train way to Frankfurt

Frankfurt airport waiting for our flight
to the USA (Maria, Csaba)

HUNGARY DIVIDED

Hungary was part of the dual monarchy of the Austria-Hungarian Empire. A multination state which was the major power in Europe next to Russia. The Austria-Hungarian Empire was held responsible for the start of WWI and after the conclusion of the war, Hungary was decimated as penance for their role in war. The Treaty of Trianon signed in 1920 stripped Hungary of land and people. Hungary lost half its population with over three million Hungarians stranded outside of the newly established borders of Czechoslovakia, the Kingdom of Serbs, Croats and Slovenes. The whole of eastern Hungary and Transylvania were awarded to Romania. Even now, over a hundred years later, the Treaty of Trianon holds a bitterness to patriotic Hungarians. Every ethnic state hates the other. This continues today, especially against Hungarians in Slovak republic (Felvidék) and Romania (Székely-föld) that openly oppress and discriminate against Hungarians.

ABOUT THE AUTHOR

I was born 1947, in the small town of Losonc in the former country of Czechoslovakia. During the nationalization of private property in 1952 my parents lost everything, our family had a hard time surviving. Because of my Hungarian nationality and having capitalist parents I experienced oppression from a young age. Coming from a loving, hard working family I learned to appreciate life itself and never give up on my dreams. I studied engineering in Kassa at the Magyar Tannyelvű Gépészeti Ipariskola, from 1962 to 1966, where I met my future husband. My family escaped from the communist regime and migrated to the United States as political refugees in 1985. Our long time dream came true, starting a new life in a free country at the age of 40. I currently live with my family in California.